ZFS

FRANCISCO DE QUEVEDO, LOVE POET

Francisco de Quevedo, Love Poet

D. GARETH WALTERS

THE CATHOLIC UNIVERSITY OF AMERICA PRESS
WASHINGTON, D.C.

CARDIFF
UNIVERSITY OF WALES PRESS
1985

Library of Congress Cataloging in Publication Data

Walters, D. Gareth
  Francisco de Quevedo, love poet.

  Bibliography: p.
  Includes indexes.
  1. Quevedo, Francisco de, 1580-1645—Poetic works.
2. Love in literature. I. Title.
PQ6424.Z5W34   1985   861′.3   85-11674
ISBN 0 8132 0623 5

British Library Cataloguing in Publication Data

Walters, D. Gareth
Francisco de Quevedo: love poet.
1. Quevedo, Francisco de — Poetic Works
I. Title
861′.3 PQ6424.Z5

ISBN 0 7083 0899 6

Typeset in Wales by Afal
Printed in Wales by D. Brown & Sons Ltd., Bridgend, Mid Glamorgan

For Christine, Leonora and Hywel

Contents

Preface

The subject of this study was described by the great Argentinian writer, Borges, as not so much a man as a literature in himself. This statement, meant as an accurate designation and not as a conventional dust-jacket eulogy, is all the more remarkable because Borges arrived at this view of Quevedo with a less than total appreciation of his output, for in the same article he writes dismissively of the love poetry. Only since the 1950s has this part of Quevedo's work been seriously considered. The reasons for this belated recognition of Quevedo's amatory production are many and it does not fall within the scope of this preface to explore them fully. There can be no doubt, however, that the immense popularity of Quevedo's satirical and burlesque prose works has had an adverse effect on the reception of a markedly different aspect of his literary output. The neglect suffered by the love poetry can be partly ascribed to an unwillingness to accept an alternative voice to the satirist and the buffoon: somehow, Quevedo, the love poet, is an impostor, a mask that disguises the true self.

Borges saw Quevedo as the supreme artist — the great wordsmith — of Spanish literature, a figure to keep company with the likes of Dante, Shakespeare, Goethe and Joyce. Despite this, however, it cannot be said that the Spaniard's work has attracted the same attention and acclaim outside a narrow circle of academics. Furthermore, he has not enjoyed the renown and affection that some of his Spanish contemporaries and near contemporaries — Cervantes, Lope de Vega, Calderón — have attained. His eclipse at the expense of these writers is especially marked in this country. An age more responsive than the present one to a heady blend of the scurrilous and the sententious had delighted in the wit and cynicism of Quevedo's prose works. Eager as we are now to understand the message, we fail to heed the tone in which it is imparted: we underestimate the sheer verve of the medium. The error is not that we take Quevedo too seriously but that we *only* take him seriously. Allied to this vein of writing is the image of an unsympathetic and caustic figure that has arisen partly on account of the work, partly on account of a flawed and incomplete biographical understanding. Thus Quevedo is found wanting in such qualities as warmth, humanity and compassion — qualities that allegedly distinguish a work like *Don Quixote.* Whether valid or not, such an appraisal, fostered by certain histories of literature, perhaps had the unfortunate effect of dissuading would-be readers and students from sampling another facet of Quevedo's work. At worst, the judgement amounts to a dilemma: the essential Quevedo is unattractive, but any deviation from this ascribed image is bogus.

Even within the love poetry itself, there has been a pronounced tendency to selectivity. This has gone beyond legitimate qualitative considerations — gauging a poem's success — and has resulted in the consignment to oblivion of a large part of the amatory output. A dangerous consequence of this could be to regard the well-known as characteristic, and the neglected as untypical or even aberrant. But when we come to define a poet's ethos — which is my principal aim in this study — then it behoves us to look at the whole of that area of his output that involves this ethos. It would be invidious to claim that one poem is more representative of a writer's experience than another, for such an assessment often relates more to the critic's preference or taste rather than to the writer's commitment. Such preconceptions will, at best, cause our view to be limited; at worst, they will mislead us. I do not believe it to be an exaggeration to claim that this is the basis on which Quevedo's love poetry has been too often examined. Even with the revival of interest in his verse, there are still large areas of his amatory production that have warranted no more than a passing glance, whereas a dozen, at most, of the poet's 'characteristic' poems have sent out a hypnotic summons. What has surprised me, though, during this exploration of the nether regions of the love poetry is that while one may not find as much pure gold here as in those compositions already treasured by posterity, neither is there much by way of dross. In particular, the reader may well be impressed by the variety and inventiveness of some of Quevedo's rarely-studied longer amatory poems, notably the *canciones* and the *romances.* If this book does nothing more than to give greater prominence to such forgotten works then it will not have been in vain.

For the benefit of readers who have little or no Spanish, I supply a translation of quotations and critical observations. It goes without saying that in translating Quevedo's verse into English prose much is lost. I would only hope that the translator's standard lament might be offset by the hope that the reader who relies on the translations may yet glimpse something of the overwhelming impact of Quevedo's thoughts and emotions. In three cases I felt justified in amending the punctuation of the text as it appears in the Blecua edition in order to convey more clearly what seemed to me the obvious sense of the original.

Julián Olivares's recent study, *The Love Poetry of Francisco de Quevedo,* appeared when my manuscript had been completed and submitted to the publisher. I have taken as much account of this study as was possible in the circumstances, and this is reflected in a number of footnote references. Though our approaches differ, it is pleasing to note that on some key issues (e.g., the reaction to the courtly ideal) we reach broadly similar conclusions.

Anyone who has worked in the area of Quevedo's poetry in the last twenty years will realize how great a debt is owed to José Manuel Blecua for his editorial labours. For my own part, I have also been encouraged by his friendly and supportive letters over the years. I am grateful also to my colleague, Nicholas G. Round, who supplied me with one particularly fertile idea; to Dr. T.D. Crawford of University College, Cardiff, who provided me with invaluable assistance in preparing a computer-produced concordance of Quevedo's sonnets as part of the preparation for my doctoral thesis, and which suggested profitable lines of inquiry; to the British Academy for a grant enabling me to study at the Biblioteca Nacional, Madrid in April 1981; and to Mr. John Rhys of the University of Wales Press for his helpful and sensible suggestions as to how to convert a manuscript into a book. My greatest debt is to Professor José María Aguirre of University College, Cardiff, who supervised my thesis on Quevedo and who thus witnessed my first rash excursions into the subject with patience and good humour, and whose example and constructive criticism always encouraged me into better ways. Neither he nor any of the above-named are responsible for the infelicities of idea or expression that I have incurred in this study.

Glasgow, December 1983.

Introduction

Francisco Gómez de Quevedo y Villegas was born in Madrid on 17 September, 1580. His parents were from the area near Santander known as La Montaña;[1] his father, Pedro Gómez, who died in 1586, was secretary to one of Philip II's wives, Doña Ana, to whom the poet's mother was a lady-in-waiting. Quevedo was brought up at court but of his childhood little is known. He was educated in a Jesuit school, the Colegio Imperial of Madrid, and his affection for the Jesuits remained with him all his life.[2] In 1596 he entered the University of Alcalá de Henares. These were eventful years, to judge by the vivid account of student pranks in the *Buscón (The Swindler)*.[3] In the first years of the seventeenth century Quevedo studied at Valladolid where the court was in residence from 1601 to 1605.

Spain was enjoying a period of peace if not prosperity and the court of Philip III offered a complete contrast to the austerity of his predecessor's. It was, above all, a pleasure-seeking court, festive and brilliant, but Quevedo remained, according to Mérimée, a 'spectateur intelligent mais désintéressé'.[4] His perspicacity as an observer helped to make him a satirist of considerable stature, although, while still in his twenties, other facets of his complex intellectual personality were being revealed. He exchanged letters with the distinguished Belgian humanist, Joos Lips, better known by his Latin name, Justus Lipsius,[5] and, inspired perhaps by this friendship, turned his attention to translating and writing commentaries on the works of the Stoics. From 1609 Quevedo was involved in a dispute concerning his estate at Torre de Juan Abad near Villanueva de los Infantes. He had inherited from his mother the ownership of the village situated at the foot of the Sierra Morena. The dispute, which dragged on for many years, revolved around the vexed subject of the payment of rents,[6] though the estate did at least offer Quevedo a retreat and refuge on many occasions:

> en este dulce retiro . . .
> Aquí me sobran los días
> y los años fugitivos
> parece que en estas tierras
> entretienen el camino.[7]

in this pleasant retreat . . . Here I have an abundance of time, and it seems that in these lands the fleeing years detain the path.

It was a place that allowed him the opportunity to study and to write:

> Retirado en la paz de estos desiertos,
> con pocos, pero doctos libros juntos,
> vivo en conversación con los difuntos
> y escucho con mis ojos a los muertos.
> Si no siempre entendidos, siempre abiertos,
> o enmiendan, o fecundan mis asuntos . . . (no.131)

Secluded in the peace of this wilderness, together with few, but wise books, I live in conversation with the deceased and listen with my eyes to the dead. If these books are not always understood, they are always open, and they emend or fertilize my studies . . .

In 1613 Quevedo left Spain to begin a distinguished, ultimately stormy, career in the service of Pedro Girón, Duke of Osuna, who was Viceroy in Sicily and later Naples.[8] This brought Quevedo into the fray of Spanish political life: as Osuna's adviser and envoy, he exploited the corruption of high officials in the Duke's interests by a shrewd distribution of bribes.[9] With Osuna's fall from power in 1620, Quevedo suffered imprisonment and internal exile, though with the accession of Philip IV in 1621 his fortunes were restored. He found favour with the new king and his powerful *privado*, the Conde-Duque de Olivares, whom he cultivated and flattered.[10] In 1632 Quevedo was granted the honorary post of royal secretary, though within a few years he was to become an embittered critic of the king and Olivares. In 1634 he married Doña Esperanza de Mendoza, a noblewoman who had been a widow for some twenty years but within months the couple had separated. This was not Quevedo's only serious emotional relationship, however. A decade earlier a report on morals had referred to his long liaison with a woman named Ledesma by whom he had several children. Apart from these involvements, little, if anything, is known about Quevedo's relationships with women.[11]

In the late 1630s Quevedo's despair and indignation at the conduct of government and of Olivares in particular became intense and his attacks more pointed. In December 1639 Quevedo was arrested, probably for treason, and imprisoned in harsh conditions in the monastery of San Marcos in León for four years.[12] He was released, in poor health, in 1643 after Olivares had fallen from power. He died in Villanueva de los Infantes on 8 September, 1645.[13]

Cervantes' oft-quoted description of Lope de Vega as 'monstruo de naturaleza' ('a monster of nature') could with equal justification be applied to Quevedo. If Lope's is the more voluminous, Quevedo's is the more heterogeneous output. It reflects an astonishingly wide range of interests: religious, philosophical, polemical, satirical, moral, amatory and burlesque. The mood and tone is immensely varied. The author of idealized love poetry is also the creator of a harrowing picaresque novel; the writer of the noble treatise, *Política de Dios, gobierno de Cristo (Politics of God, Government of Christ)* (1626), is the instigator of obscene invectives against Góngora. Understandably perhaps, it was the burlesque and irreverent Quevedo that long attracted the greatest attention: the European diffusion of the *Buscón* (1626) and the *Sueños (Visions)* (1627) testify to this. Furthermore, Quevedo has acquired a certain notoriety in the popular imagination as the butt of ribald jokes and anecdotes, mainly apocryphal.[14]

Quevedo is still considered primarily a satirist. His *Sueños*, a series of prose fantasies, are valued as a reactionary's diagnosis of the moral and social malaise of early seventeenth-century Spain. The last of his works in this form, *La hora de todos y la fortuna con seso (The Hour of All Men and Fortune with Wisdom)* (1635), is the most overtly political of the satires. It develops into a scathing examination of domestic and foreign policy under Olivares prior to the catastrophes of the 1640s and in one section, 'La isla de los monopantos' ('The Island of the Monopantos'), there is a clear attack on the *privado*.[15] Until recently it was maintained that Quevedo's final imprisonment was the direct consequence of a poem criticizing Philip IV and Olivares which had been placed beneath the king's napkin at his breakfast table. The event and, almost certainly, the poem are apocryphal;[16] but the venom of Quevedo's satire and his reputation as a fearless adversary contributed to the durability of the legend. Works such as the *Buscón* and the *Sueños* contain a strongly personal element in addition to the stock topics of satire. There is, for instance, the ridiculing of the pedantic fencing-master, Luis Pacheco de Narváez, deriving from a quarrel concerning a treatise Narváez had written on the art of fencing.[17] The upshot was that the two men took up swords; Quevedo removed Narváez's hat, earning as a consequence his lifelong enmity. Narváez has been dubiously immortalized in a number of Quevedo's works, but years later he was to collaborate with two other enemies of Quevedo, Pérez de Montalbán and P. Diego Niseno, in a vitriolic attack on the writer's life and works, the *Tribunal de la justa venganza (Tribunal of the Just Revenge)* (Valencia, 1635).

As with his prose satires, Quevedo's burlesque and satirical verse dates from all periods of his creative life: a span of at least forty years, from the poems written before he was twenty-three and published in Pedro Espinosa's anthology, *Flores de poetas ilustres de España* (1603), to the jocular ballads composed during his final imprisonment. Satirical and burlesque verse comprises the largest part of Quevedo's poetic work, but such is the sheer volume of output that other genres such as the moral and amatory are by no means insignificant in number.

Like many of his contemporaries and predecessors, Quevedo did not publish his verse, though a large number of his poems, particularly the burlesque compositions, circulated in manuscripts and chap-books.[18] In the last year of his life he revealed a belated interest in the publication of his poetry,[19] but the first edition, entrusted to his friend, José González de Salas, did not appear until 1648.[20] The idea had been to publish the poetry according to subject matter in sections corresponding to the Nine Muses. The 1648 edition contained only six sections and González de Salas was still preparing the remaining three *Musas* when he died in 1651. The papers passed to Quevedo's nephew, Pedro Aldrete, who published the complementary edition, *Las tres Musas últimas castellanas (The Three Last Castilian Muses)* in 1670. Aldrete's scholarship was inferior to that of González de Salas and the 1670 edition is variable in quality, containing as it does both poems that González de Salas had prepared and others which were clearly apocryphal.[21]

Questions of attribution have beset editors of Quevedo's poetry down to the present century. Astrana Marín's edition, [22] while providing a number of hitherto unknown poems, is replete with apocryphal compositions, a feature aggravated by a tendency, repeated by the editor in other studies on Quevedo,[23] to give speculation the status of documented fact. Blecua's editions[24] constitute a substantial improvement, especially in the most deficient areas of Astrana Marín's editing, by his discovery of a large number of false attributions and his painstaking listing of sources.[25]

In his most recent edition, Blecua attributes to Quevedo a total of 220 love poems; the majority of these are sonnets, of which sixty-five are addressed to Lisi. Until recently Quevedo's love poetry has attracted neither the popularity nor the acclaim of his satirical work. Even sympathetic *quevedistas* like Mérimée[26] and Borges[27] have been generally dismissive of the amatory verse, and Otis H. Green has compiled a long list of critics who have undervalued this part of Quevedo's output.[28] In a way, the discovery of Quevedo as love poet is as striking an event as the revaluation of Góngora. Dámaso Alonso, perhaps the critic more than anyone responsible for the rehabilitation of Góngora, also made a significant contribution to the awakening of interest in the love poetry of Quevedo with a sensitive essay, first published in 1950.[29] This study, pioneering as it was, perhaps set the trend for a line of Quevedo criticism which valued his love poetry for its stylistic originality and which correspondingly considered the themes and subject matter as conventional and unexceptional. Such is the character of one of the more recent and best studies on the love poetry by J.M. Pozuelo Yvancos.[30] The more thematically orientated approach has in any case been rather hamstrung by the appearance within a few years of each other of Green's monograph, mentioned above, and a study by Amédée Mas[31] which expressed views diametrically opposed to those of Green. This debate has not been fruitfully developed; indeed, in his recently published anthology of Quevedo's poetry, James O. Crosby suggests that 'hoy en día no tenemos ninguna definición ni de su estilo ni de la temática de su poesía' ('at present we have no definition either of the style or of the themes of his poetry').[32] In short, with the exception of Mas, the consensus of critical opinion on Quevedo's love poetry implies that it should be assessed in terms of stylistic, linguistic and expressive richness or novelty because its ethos makes for an unexceptional, even classic, example of late Renaissance amatory verse, within the courtly-Petrarchist tradition.

For Green, Quevedo's love poetry is witness to the survival into the seventeenth century of a particular concept of love and woman which he considers to be courtly and which, he claims (pp.3-9), is a refutation of those critics who were of the opinion that love had by this time been 'emptied of its ideal content' (p.3) and that the woman had been toppled off her pedestal. This polemical attitude is revealed in Green's rather selective approach, whereby Quevedo's love poetry is seen as a medieval outgrowth. The method of thematic analysis is one that faithfully matches the one he had previously employed in his approach to the work of the *cancionero* poets.[33]

According to Pozuelo Yvancos, Quevedo's love poetry is the result of an attempt to assert some kind of linguistic or stylistic individuality in a field where the scope for such an aim is extremely limited. He sees the love poetry as explicable in terms of a dialectic between a 'norma lingüístico-estética' and a 'manipulación lingüística personal' (p.14), and contends that this 'noción de desautomatización' is not only 'explicativa de la literariedad quevediana', but also 'un fenómeno universal en la manifestación poética, que es la desautomatización de una serie de normas lingüísticas, estéticas y tópicos culturales que actúan como realidad contextual en la que el fenómeno poético se inserta' ('a universal phenomenon in poetic expression, which is the act of breaking loose from a series of linguistic and aesthetic norms and conventions of culture which function as the contextual reality into which the poetic phenomenon is inserted') (p.16). For Pozuelo Yvancos, then, Quevedo's love poetry serves to confirm a theory of poetic creativity. But the consequence of his whole approach is that, in terms of an understanding of love and in the presentation of an individual emotional experience, Quevedo seems no different to, say, Garcilaso, Herrera or Góngora. Hence the medium is everything, or, as Celina S. de Cortázar puts it plainly: 'lo indiscutiblemente quevedesco no es lo que dice, sino la forma en que lo dice' ('What is indisputably characteristic of Quevedo is not what he says, but the manner in which he says it'.)[34]

There is no gainsaying this expressive vigour though, as Close has clearly demonstrated, the case for Quevedo's originality and more specifically his modernity in this respect has been overstated, particularly by Dámaso Alonso.[35] On the other hand, the significance of the message has been both understated and misunderstood — misunderstood largely because its distinctiveness has been overlooked. There has been a readiness not only to take Quevedo's amatory poetic ethos for granted but also to relegate the amatory experience to a number of merely linguistic or stylistic effects.

It is my contention, however, that the 'desgarrón afectivo' ('emotional disruption'), to use Dámaso Alonso's much quoted label, is not confined to lexical innovation or to an intensification of the commonplace, but is indicative of something more significant and radical. The façade comprising the courtly-Petrarchist-Neoplatonist synthesis is formidable, as is to be expected in a poet writing at a time of confluence of varied but complementary traditions; but it is not immune to the irruption of ideas and the expression of emotions that can be shown to differ from those of poets operating in the same historico-literary context. Many of Quevedo's poems do not comply with our expectations of what should and should not figure in that context; there is much that is unconventional, even allowing for the fact that the reality of love is based on non-fulfilment and that a number of the appurtenances of Quevedo's 'system' are normal rather than exceptional. His distinctiveness can be seen in the following ways: (i) in the definition or understanding of the nature of his passion; (ii) in his reaction to the failure of his aspirations; and (iii) in his approach to, and description of, the object that arouses these aspirations. These features, which are my concern for the first three chapters of this study, are not mere decoration or variation. They represent something fundamental: far more than the icing on the cake, they are its very ingredients.

1 J.M. Salaverría discusses Quevedo's origins in some detail in his introduction to Quevedo, *Obras satíricas y festivas* (Madrid, 1965), 7-11.

2 See Ignacio Elizalde, 'Quevedo, San Ignacio de Loyola y los Jesuitas', *Letras de Deusto*, X, no.20 (1980), 91-106.

3 In Chapter V. See *El Buscón*, ed. Américo Castro (Madrid, 1967), 58-68. Although the *Buscón* is a pseudo-biography, it is certain that Quevedo's personal experiences contributed to various details in the novel, as for example the confrontation between Pablos and the pedantic sword-fencer in Chapter VIII. For a study of the roles of author and protagonist see Edwin Williamson, 'The Conflict between Author and Protagonist in Quevedo's *Buscón*', *Journal of Hispanic Philology*, II (1977-8), 45-60.

4. *Essai sur la vie et les oeuvres de Francisco de Quevedo* (Paris, 1886), 12.

5 The correspondence between Quevedo and Lipsius is to be found in L. Astrana Marín, *Epistolario completo de D. Francisco de Quevedo-Villegas* (Madrid, 1946), 1-9; see also pp.509-24 for an account of the relationship between Quevedo and Lipsius.

6 The dispute is examined by A. González Palencia, 'Quevedo, pleitista y enamorado', in *Del "Lazarillo" a Quevedo* (Madrid, 1946), 257-426.

7. See *Obras completas I. Poesía original*, ed.) J.M. Blecua (2nd ed.' (Barcelona, 1968), no. 771. Poem numbers also refer to *Obra poética*, ed. J.M. Blecua, 4 vols. (Madrid, 1969-81). Quotations are taken from the former edition.

8 Pedro de Alcántara Téllez Girón y Guzmán, the third Duke of Osuna, distinguished himself in the war in Flanders. In 1610 he was appointed Viceroy of Sicily. For an account of Quevedo's career under Osuna, see C. Pérez Bustamante, 'Quevedo, diplomático', *Revista de Estudios Políticos*, XIII (1945), 159-83; and 'La supuesta traición del duque de Osuna', *Revista de la Universidad de Madrid*, I (1940), 61-74.

9 Quevedo provides a vivid account of his success in this regard in letters written to Osuna in 1615-16. See *Epistolario*, pp.23-40.

10 In the play, *Cómo ha de ser el privado*, written around 1627-8, there is exaggerated praise of Olivares. See Raimundo Lida, *Letras hispánicas* (Mexico City, 1958), 150-5.

11 Ramón Gómez de la Serna dedicates a chapter of his study on Quevedo to an examination of his relationships with women: *Quevedo* (2nd ed.) (Madrid, 1962), 182-95. But, as I shall suggest in the course of this study, this is an area of much speculation and fancy, and Gómez de la Serna is as guilty as any in this respect.

12 For the reasons behind Quevedo's imprisonment, see J.H. Elliot, 'Nueva luz sobre la prisión de Quevedo y Adam de la Parra', *Boletín de la Real Academia de la Historia*, CLXIX (1972), 171-82.

13 For a fuller account of Quevedo's life, see J.M. Blecua, *Poesía original*, ix-lx; and Donald W. Bleznick, *Quevedo* (New York, 1972), 30-40.

14 See Juan Goytisolo, 'Quevedo: la obsesión excremental', in *Disidencias* (Barcelona, 1977), 117-18; and Francisco Ayala, 'Hacia una semblanza de Quevedo', *La Torre*, LVII (1967), 93-4.

15 This section was originally conceived as a work in its own right, but eventually incorporated into *La hora de todos* around 1644. Olivares is alluded to as Pragas Chincollos, an anagram of his own name, Gaspar Conchillos.

16 See J.M. Blecua, 'Un ejemplo de dificultades: el *Memorial Católica, Sacra, Real Majestad'*, *Nueva Revista de Filología Hispánica*, VIII (1954), 156-73.

17 A work that bears an appropriately grandiose title: *Cien conclusiones o formas de saber la verdadera destreza fundada en sciencia y diez y ocho contradicciones a las de la común* (Madrid, 1608).

18 See E.M. Wilson, 'Quevedo for the Masses', *Atlante*, III, no.4 (1955), 151-66.

19 In a letter to Francisco de Oviedo, dated 22 January 1645, Quevedo writes: 'a pesar de mi poca salud, doy fin a la *Vida de Marco Bruto*, sin olvidarme de mis *Obras en verso* en que también se va trabajando'. *Epistolario*, p.482.

20 *El Parnaso español, monte en dos cumbres dividido, con las nueve Musas castellanas . . .* (Madrid, 1648).

21 See J.O. Crosby, 'La huella de González de Salas en la poesía de Quevedo editada por Pedro Aldrete', *Homenaje a don A. Rodriguez-Moñino* (Madrid, 1966), I, 111-23.

22 *Obras completas: obras en verso* (Madrid, 1932 and ss).

23 Notably in his biography, *La vida turbulenta de Quevedo* (Madrid, 1945).

24 *Obras completas I. Poesía original* (Barcelona, 1963); 2nd ed. (Barcelona, 1968); 3rd ed. (Barcelona, 1971); and *Obra poética*.

25 J.O. Crosby draws attention to what he considers shortcomings in Blecua's editions: 'Has Quevedo's Poetry Been Edited? A Review-Article', *Hispanic Review*, XLI (1973), 627-38.

26 Op. cit., 393-9.

27 "Considerados como documentos de una pasión, los poemas eróticos de Quevedo son insatisfactorios", *Otras inquisiciones* (Buenos Aires, 1960), 60; rpt. in *Francisco de Quevedo*, ed. Gonzalo Sobejano (Madrid, 1978), 26.

28 *Courtly Love in Quevedo* (Boulder, Colorado, 1952), 5-6.

29 'El desgarrón afectivo en la poesía de Quevedo', in *Poesía española* (Madrid, 1950), 531-618; my references are drawn from the 5th ed. (Madrid, 1971), 495-580.

30 *El lenguaje poético de la lírica amorosa de Quevedo* (Murcia, 1979).

31 *La caricature de la femme, du mariage et de l'amour dans l'oeuvre de Quevedo* (Paris, 1957).

32 *Poesía varia* (Madrid, 1981), 521.

33 'Courtly Love in the Spanish *Cancioneros*', *Publications of the Modern Language Association of America*, LXIV (1949), 247-301; rpt. in *The Literary Mind of Medieval and Renaissance Spain* (Lexington, 1970), 40-92. Future references are to the latter.

34 *La poesía de Quevedo* (Buenos Aires, 1968), 12.

35 'Petrarchism and the Cancioneros in Quevedo's Love-Poetry: The Problem of Discrimination', *Modern Language Review*, LXXIV (1979), 836-55.

CHAPTER I

The Nature of Love : Desire

It has been claimed quite commonly that the love poetry of Quevedo is based on the idea of renunciation of desire and that the emotions he describes are, variously, chaste, spiritual or platonic; the author of an American doctoral thesis has even referred to the lover in the poems to Lisi as asexual.[1] According to Otis H. Green, there was a hierarchy in Quevedo's love poetry as in his personal amorous experiences from *amor ferino* to a love of chaste detachment and that only the latter had meaning for him.[2] Courtly love — which Green defines as 'chaste eloignment' — is not 'un tema más'('one more theme') but a central theme of the love poetry. These assertions and Green's endeavours to justify them are open to question, however. In the first instance, we know little of Quevedo's personal experiences, certainly not enough to be able to speak of different kinds of relationships. Secondly, Green quotes extensively from Quevedo's prose works and letters to support points regarding the love poetry. Again, even if we accept the validity of courtly love as a system which later poets recognized, a reference to courtly love as a 'theme' in seventeenth-century poetry must cause some misgivings.

Dámaso Alonso, though without reference to any governing ethos, has also seen renunciation as a ubiquitous idea in Quevedo's amatory verse: 'Por cualquiera parte, en la poesía erótica de Quevedo, encontramos la misma filosofía de amor. No sólo no aspira a poseer; llegará a defender que el amor no debe buscar la posesión'('Everywhere in Quevedo's love poetry we find the same philosophy of love. Not only does he not aspire after possession, he will go so far as to maintain that love should not seek possession.').[3]

Manuel Durán develops this idea by relating it speculatively to Quevedo's psychological make-up. Incapable of the self-abandonment necessary for a successful relationship with women, Quevedo discovered a safeguard or a refuge in courtly love.[4] The fact that the woman was unattainable was thus an advantage to him, in that it freed him from the necessity to come to terms with someone who posed a threat to his independence and self-sufficiency. Durán may have intuitively come upon a truth about Quevedo's character, though it cannot be tested, but he again refers to courtly love, as did Green, as if it were a clearly defined system that had renunciation as its central, if not exclusive, tenet — a hazardous assertion in view of the variety of approach discernible for example in the work of the fifteenth-century *cancionero* poets, who best represent the Spanish contribution to courtly love poetry.[5]

Though Pozuelo Yvancos differs from Green in establishing the principal source or basis of Quevedo's approach to love, he too stresses the idea of renunciation.[6] He suggests that this is founded on the Neoplatonism of León Hebreo, Bembo, Ficino and Castiglione, and quotes instances of lexical parallels between their work and a handful of sonnets by Quevedo. On this limited basis, he claims that the semantic macrocontext of the love poetry is Neoplatonic (p.59) and that 'muchos (sic) son por ejemplo los poemas en que Quevedo trata el tópico de la renuncia al cuerpo'('Many (sic) are, for example, the poems in which Quevedo deals with the topic of physical renunciation.') (p.60). These same poems had been used by Green as proof of Quevedo's affiliation to the courtly love ethos. Although Green is aware of the common ground that exists between the two systems, he argues for the primacy of the courtly love system.[7] Amédée Mas has suggested, nonetheless, that the chapter could be rewritten with only the slightest amendments to make the opposite point: 'On pourrait récrire ce chapitre, sans presque rien y changer, pour établir que les plus courtois des poèmes de Quevedo sont envahis par les thèmes platoniques'.[8] Alone among the principal commentators of Quevedo's poetry, Mas is sceptical about the notion of renunciation as a dominant factor. Of Green's view that the true Quevedo is the 'penitente' who rejects 'the attractions of the myth of courtly love with its cult of suffering and passion for their own sakes' (p.79), he observes pithily: 'En somme, le seul amour authentique, pour Quevedo, c'est l'amour qui renonce à la possession. Mais le seul Quevedo authentique, c'est celui qui, par esprit de pénitence, renonce à tout amour, même à l'amour qui se renonce. En vérité, c'est beaucoup renoncer, et acheter bien cher l'authenticité!' (pp.306-7). Mas also points to the inappropriateness of the term 'theme' in connection with courtly love (p.303). He emphasizes the absence in Quevedo of themes that have been considered to epitomize courtly love, principally the idea of love as an ennobling force. To affirm, however, that 'l'amour courtois proprement dit, Quevedo l'ignore' (p.306) is too extreme a view, as there are in Quevedo's poetry topics which can be clearly related to earlier poetry, whether we choose to label it courtly or not, and which need to be understood in that context, e.g., secrecy, absence, the lover's unworthiness, reason versus desire, the *galardón*, and an awareness of the stages of love (sight, touch, consummation). What Mas is right to query is the affirmation that these topics constitute a system and form the central theme of the love poetry. Quevedo is a courtly love poet in the same way that he is a Petrarchist. One may debate, as Close has done, whether it is the

Petrarchist or courtly influence that is the more significant,[9] but in the final analysis, his work is, like that of poets of every generation, necessarily dependent on the efforts of his predecessors.[10]

I start with those sonnets that have been quoted by Pozuelo Yvancos as proof of the Neoplatonic basis of Quevedo's amatory verse. They are the explicitly theoretical of his observations regarding love and desire. The lexical reminiscences of Neoplatonists such as Ficino, Bembo, Castiglione and León Hebreo have been clearly documented by both Pozuelo Yvancos (pp.59-94) and Green (pp.24-31). But some reservations can be expressed concerning their conclusions. In the first instance, the number of poems that have such a clear Neoplatonic association are not many, as I have already suggested. There are, at most, eleven such poems among a field of 220. Beyond this bare statistic, however, are two further and more important considerations. Firstly, Neoplatonic terminology and derivative ideas and images are not as conspicuous in the poetry of Quevedo as in the work of his contemporaries and immediate predecessors. Such terms include allusions to the heavenly or celestial, particularly with regard to the beauty of the beloved. These figure prominently in the poetry of Herrera and, to a lesser extent, Francisco de la Torre. Another feature is the concept of height and ascent and the reference in this connection to the myth of Icarus, as is quite commonly found in the poetry of Villamediana. These traces or reminiscences of Neoplatonism are not numerous in Quevedo's verse — a matter of nine or ten poems at a maximum.

Secondly, Pozuelo Yvancos has paid insufficient attention to the theoretical Neoplatonic sonnets as *poems* as opposed to 'ideas wrapped in form', to quote from Rene Wellek and Austin Warren's *Theory of Literature* (3rd ed., Harmondsworth, 1963) whose chapter 'Literature and Ideas' makes salutary reading in this connection. Close's criticism of Otis Green's approach is applicable also to Pozuelo Yvancos' analysis of Quevedo's Neoplatonic sonnets when she speaks of a need to distinguish between a 'poetic ethos' and an 'ethical system'.[11] Pozuelo Yvancos omits to mention studies on two key sonnets which have been available for some time and which point very clearly to the necessary distinction between theory and the symbiosis of idea and experience. What emerges from a consideration of these two sonnets is a conflicting voice or register which forms part of the *experience* of the poem and which questions, even challenges, the *idea* expressed in it.

One sonnet expounds a commonplace of Neoplatonic theory — the contrast of physical desire and spiritual love:

Mandóme, ¡ay Fabio!, que la amase Flora,
y que no la quisiese; y mi cuidado,
obediente y confuso y mancillado,
sin desearla, su belleza adora.
    Lo que el humano afecto siente y llora,
goza el entendimiento, amartelado
del espíritu eterno, encarcelado
en el claustro mortal que le atesora.
    Amar es conocer virtud ardiente;
querer es voluntad interesada,
grosera y descortés caducamente.
    El cuerpo es tierra, y lo será, y fue nada;
de Dios procede a eternidad la mente:
eterno amante soy de eterna amada. (no.331)

Flora commanded me, ah Fabio!, to love her and not to desire her; and my passion, obedient and confused and blemished, without desiring her, adores her beauty. What human emotions experience and bemoan, the understanding enjoys, wooed by the eternal spirit and imprisoned in the mortal cloister that treasures it. To love is to know an ardent virtue; to desire is an act of will that is selfish, gross, fleeting and coarse. The body is earth, and shall be so, and was nothing; from God the mind proceeds to eternity: I am the eternal lover of the eternal beloved.

But as Arthur Terry has shown, it is far more than a statement on the superiority of the spiritual over the physical, though Dámaso Alonso,[12] Mas (p.313) and Pozuelo Yvancos see it as a straightforward exposition of a theory about the poet's passion. The last-named refers to the importance of the poem as being one of the few in which 'Quevedo se enfrenta al amor de un modo teórico, objectivo e intenta explicar, observándola desde fuera, a la luz de la tradición neoplatónica, el sentido de su pasión'('Quevedo approaches love in a theoretic, objective fashion, and attempts to explain the significance of his passion by observing it from outside, in the light of the Neoplatonic tradition.') (p.67). Green recognizes that the sonnet 'expresses an effort, but only an effort, to rise from *lo deleytable* to *lo honesto*' (p.27), but the full significance of the poem is best understood by Terry. There is 'a real and very deep anguish. The "¡ay Fabio!" of the first line sets the tone for the rest. The speaker's love obeys but is "confused" and "stained"; in theory, the superior love of the understanding transcends the suffering of "el humano afecto", yet his whole experience tends to deny this'.[13] Furthermore, the proclamation in the tercets of the eternity of spiritual love is expressed in a flat and matter-of-fact tone, not improbably deliberate, that is consistent with the impression received from the opening of the sonnet that the poet's heart is not in the exposition of the doctrine. One need only compare the statement of eternal love here with the impassioned assertions of love surviving death in some of the sonnets to Lisi to appreciate this difference.[14] Terry suggests that the implied comment of the poet on the theory he has been expounding is 'How absurd, and what a torment!' (p.xxvii).

As a point of comparison, the kind of unambiguous exposition of this fundamental Neoplatonic dichotomy that Pozuelo Yvancos suggests as the interpretation of the above sonnet is better illustrated by the following sonnet by Lupercio Leonardo de Argensola:

> No es lo mismo el amor que el apetito,
> que en diferente parte se aposenta:
> la virtud al primero lo alimenta,
> al segundo, aliméntalo el delito.
>
> El Cielo elige amor por su distrito,
> donde toma del alma larga cuenta;
> el otro con el cuerpo se contenta,
> viviendo en Flegetonte y en Coccito.
>
> El uno siempre aumenta, el otro apoca
> su casa principal y patrimonio;
> de aquél es la sed cuerda, de éste loca.
>
> Y al fin, cuando de sí da testimonio
> sale amor por los ojos y la boca;
> el otro sale a guisa de demonio.[15]

Love is not the same as appetite, for it resides in a different place: virtue nourishes the former, the latter is nourished by an offence. Heaven chooses love for its district, where it has a long acquaintance with the soul; appetite is happy with the body, living in Phlegethon and Cocytus. Love always increases, just as appetite diminishes its first home and inheritance; the former's thirst is wise, the latter's, mad. And, ultimately, when it gives evidence of itself, love emerges from eyes and mouth; appetite comes out in the guise of a devil.

Here there are no doubts or misgivings; there is none of the questioning or torment of the Quevedo sonnet.

Another sonnet to Flora, that immediately follows the one just considered in the first edition of Quevedo's poetry, is considered by Pozuelo Yvancos (pp.92-3) as explicable in terms of the Neoplatonic cosmology centred on Love and moved by it:

> Alma es del mundo Amor; Amor es mente
> que vuelve en alta espléndida jornada
> del sol infatigable luz sagrada,
> y en varios cercos todo el coro ardiente;
>
> espíritu fecundo y vehemente
> con varonil virtud, siempre inflamada,
> que en universal máquina mezclada
> paterna actividad obra clemente.
>
> Este, pues, burlador de los reparos,
> que, atrevidos, se oponen a sus jaras,

artífice inmortal de afectos raros,
igualmente nos honra, si reparas;
pues si hace trono de tus ojos claros,
Flora, en mi pecho tiene templo y aras. (no.332)

Love is the soul of the world; Love is the mind that returns in a lofty, splendid journey the sacred light of the unextinguishable sun, and in diverse circles the whole glowing choir; it is a fertile and vehement spirit with manly virtues, always aflame, which mingled in the structure of the universe, mercifully performs its paternal functions. So this mocker of defences which, daringly, oppose his darts, the immortal creator of rare emotions, equally honours us, if you would care to note; since if he makes a throne of your bright eyes, Flora, in my breast he has a temple and altars.

In a perspicacious analysis of this sonnet, Alan K.G. Paterson discovers a secondary and contrasting significance in the presence of a veiled but irreverent eroticism.[16] He sees the sonnet as providing an instance of how 'a line of thought, or argument, leads us into the heart of an *agudeza*' (p.132). The quatrains expound an orthodox view of Neoplatonism to which Paterson addresses himself by reference principally to Ficino. But in the tercets there is a dramatic change from a divine to a frivolous physical love. An awareness of this secondary level leads to the realization that the second quatrain is ambiguous, particularly as regards the double meaning of phrases like 'espíritu fecundo', 'varonil virtud' and 'paterna actividad' (p.139). The 'Neoplatonic idol' is toppled. Paterson's conclusions corroborate my previous observation on the need to approach these poems as poems and not snippets of philosophy in a metrical form. The point that arises from the sonnet, according to Paterson, is that 'the experience of Amor, expressed intellectually or erotically, is one and indivisible' (p.140). Further: 'if we respond to this reconciliation, nothing can be further from the mind than the Neoplatonic view that activities of the body and soul are sharply distinguished in order to exalt the latter' (p.140). Hence, whereas in the preceding sonnet the Neoplatonic doctrine was grudgingly acceded to, here it would seem to be refuted.

Even Dámaso Alonso, a principal advocate, as we have seen, of the spiritual aspirations of Quevedo's love poetry, suggests that the following sonnet might not be the true voice of Quevedo, in that it consists of a piece of advice offered to a friend and that the poet would not necessarily believe in it:[17]

Quien no teme alcanzar lo que desea
da priesa a su tristeza y a su hartura:
la pretensión ilustra la hermosura,
cuanto la ingrata posesión la afea.
  Por halagüeña dilación rodea
el que se dificulta su ventura,

> pues es grosero el gozo y mal segura
> la que en la posesión gloria se emplea.
> Muéstrate siempre, Fabio, agradecido
> a la buena intención de los desdenes,
> y nunca te verás arrepentido.
> Peor pierde los gustos y los bienes
> el desprecio que sigue a lo adquirido,
> que el imposible en adquirir, que tienes. (no.335)

He who does not fear to attain what he desires hastens his sadness and satiety; his striving dignifies beauty as much as bitter possession makes it ugly. He who obstructs his own happiness has a detour of gratifying delay since pleasure is coarse and the glory to be had from possession is unsure. Always show yourself, Fabio, grateful for the good intent of her disdain and you will never have cause for repentance. The contempt that follows acquisition drives away pleasures and happiness more certainly than the impossibility of attainment which you possess.

There is no disguising the fact, however, that here is a clear expression of the view that the gratification of desire is base (ll.4 and 7). But it is only part of the story. To the phrase 'pues es grosero el gozo' is added a rider: 'y mal segura/la que en la posesión gloria se emplea'. There is regret that the pleasure of sexual fulfilment is short-lived. Furthermore, the opening of the sonnet has described how the attainment of the goal brings with it an immediate sadness and a feeling of satiety. This is not a moral observation, however: it is more in the nature of *omne animal triste* disenchantment after striving.

This fear of the loss of pleasure and an attendant sense of insecurity is present too in the madrigal beginning 'El día que me aborreces' (no.410). It is a contrived and rather flippant piece, as are all Quevedo's compositions in this form, but it is worth quoting because the closing lines offer a parallel with the sonnet:

> El día que me aborreces, ese día
> tengo tanta alegría,
> como pesar padezco cuando me amas
> y tu dueño me llamas.
> Porque cuando indignada me aborreces,
> en tu mudable condición me ofreces
> señas de luego amarme con extremo;
> y cuanto más me amas, Laura, temo
> de tus mudanzas, como firme amante,
> que me has de aborrecer en otro instante.
> Ansí que, por mejor, eligir quiero
> la esperanza del gusto venidero,
> aunque esté desdeñado,
> que el engañoso estado
> de posesión tan bella
> sujeto al torpe miedo de perdella.

> On the day that you hate me, on that day I shall experience as much joy as I
> suffer grief when you love me and call me your master. Because when, in your
> indignation, you hate me, such is your fickle state that you suggest to me signs
> of extreme love later; and the more you love me, Laura, the more I am afraid
> of your mutability, as your constant lover, that you will hate me again an
> instant later. Thus of the two, better to choose the hope of the pleasure to
> come, even though I be scorned, than the deceptive state of such beauteous
> possession where I am subjected to the squalid fear of losing it.

The madrigal reveals none of the ambivalence of the sonnet; the poet is not
influenced even slightly by moral considerations. Fulfilment in itself is
desirable ('bella'); it is again the awareness that it is a momentary
satisfaction that deters the poet. Better to anticipate than to achieve the
consummation of desire. The idea of the transience of sexual pleasure
combines with the description of the fickleness of the *amada* to create an
impression of love as a mutable, indeed continually deceptive, condition.
Amédée Mas succeeds, I believe, in defining the mood that is at the heart of
both these poems that speak of the undesirability of fulfilment, though it is
the sonnet that he specifically has in mind, notwithstanding its moral
gestures:

> C'est que la nature impose la tristesse, comme le dit crûment un adage latin,
> après l'accomplissement du désir, et la mort de l'amour ne serait pas loin de sa
> *consommation* (l'ambivalence du mot est lourde de sens) si des dieux
> propices ne veillaient sur lui. Ces dieux, ce sont les hommes qui les ont créés.
> Car l'amour "veut profonde, profonde éternité". Eterniser ses ivresses, rêve
> éternel des hommes, rêve de Paradis. Hélas! c'est à l'instant même où il vient
> de dispenser l'ivresse que l'amour commence à périr! Amour platonique et
> amour courtois font partie de l'immense effort des hommes pour donner
> chance de durée à cet amour qui va tout droit, si on le laisse aller, se consumer
> à sa propre flamme. (p.312)

It is thus clear then that not only are Neoplatonic ideas and notions of
spiritual love uncommon in Quevedo's love poetry but that on several
occasions his treatment of them and reactions towards them are far more
than mere enunciations of doctrine. We have the impression of one who is
questioning and challenging precepts that do not altogether conform to his
own experience and understanding of love.

If one poem more than others gives the lie to the view of Quevedo's love
poetry as principally motivated by a spiritual rather than a physical
aspiration then it is surely a sonnet to Lisi, based on a hypothesis deriving
from the topic of the lover's need to preserve silence and secrecy. The poet
muses longingly on the delights that would accrue to him if only his eyelids
were lips:

> Si mis párpados, Lisi, labios fueran,
> besos fueran los rayos visüales
> de mis ojos, que al sol miran caudales
> águilas, y besaran más que vieran.
>   Tus bellezas, hidrópicos, bebieran,
> y cristales, sedientos de cristales;
> de luces y de incendios celestiales,
> alimentando su morir, vivieran.
>   De invisible comercio mantenidos,
> y desnudos de cuerpo, los favores
> gozaran mis potencias y sentidos;
>   mudos se requebraran los ardores;
> pudieran, apartados, verse unidos,
> y en público, secretos, los amores. (no.448)

If my eyelids, Lisi, were lips, then the visual rays of my eyes would be kisses and like golden eagles they would look at the sun and kiss more than they saw. They would dropsically drink your beauties and be as crystals, thirsty for crystals; they would live on lights and celestial fires which would nourish their death. Sustained by invisible contact and denuded of body, my faculties and senses would enjoy your favours; our passions would be exchanged silently, and could be united, even while they were apart, and be secret, though in public.

R.M. Price draws attention to the secondary meanings in this context of words like 'desnudos' and 'potencias' which have a carnal significance.[18] The impulse behind this poem — that of a frustrated but aching desire — and the presence of an unmistakable lexical ambiguity testify to a clearly sensual, not spiritual, intent.[19] Beyond this, however, the sonnet can be seen as representative of the implicitly carnal nature of many of Quevedo's love poems in that it contains a range of semantic association and lexical relationship that points clearly in that direction. It is a poem to which consequently I shall return in later chapters; but for the moment I wish to single out the principal image of the second quatrain — that of thirst. Were the lover's eyes lips they would imbibe the lady's charms insatiably: her skin ('cristales'), her eyes ('luces') and her hair ('incendios'). They would be his nourishment. Quevedo returns insistently to these ideas of thirst/drinking and hunger/appetite in his love poetry. The former, especially, is much used as a symbol of desire, both fulfilled and thwarted.

In a *romance* where the poet recounts the details of a dream of sexual fulfilment to the woman who was the subject of the dream (no.440), the reference to drinking comes in a clearly erotic but unusual semantic context. The dreaming lover interrupts the lady's words, of protest presumably, by kissing her, though the verb used is not 'besar' but 'beber':

> Tus voces y tus razones
> me di, Floris, tanta prisa
> a beberlas de tu boca,
> que me excusaba de oírlas. (ll.19-22)

So quickly did I hasten, Floris, to drink your words and reasoning that I excused myself from hearing what you said.

The image of drinking is a focal one in a *silva* which, unusually for Quevedo, contrasts past pleasure and present frustration (no.400). The scene of the lovers' former shared joy was a fountain which is the object of the poet's address throughout the poem. The connection between water, fertility and fulfilment is established over much of the poem by a process of pathetic fallacy. As in Garcilaso's First Eclogue (ll.300-9), the poet notes how weeds grow now where flowers once grew: 'la tierra que dio flores ya da abrojos!' ('The earth which gave flowers now yields thorns!') (l.33). He laments the fact that no longer can he assuage his thirst at this now arid place:

> ¡En qué de partes de tu margen veo
> polvo, donde mi sed halló recreo! (ll.37-8)

In how many places on your bank do I now see dust where my thirst found a place to rest!

It was here that they had made love, though it was but a short-lived joy:

> Ya me viste gozarla,
> y en medio del amor, con mil temores,
> llorar más que la aurora en estas flores. (ll.49-51)

You already saw me enjoy her, and in the midst of our love, with a thousand fears, weep more than the dawn in these flowers.

He proposes turning the fountain into a shrine to his love. It will comprise a statue of a satyr afflicted by perpetual thirst (ll.60-3). The inscription will exhort the passer-by to continue his journey, even if he is thirsty, rather than partake of the water that the *amada* had once drunk: 'corrientes. . . dignas de los dientes/de Aminta' ('waters . . . worthy of the teeth of Aminta') (ll.71-3). If he does not heed this advice, the waters will escape from him, as happened with Tantalus:

> . . . No seas osado
> a obligarlas a huir; ¡ay!, no lo creas,
> cuando otro nuevo Tántalo te veas. (ll.74-6)

Do not be so daring as to force them (the waters) to flee; ah!, do not believe it, when you see yourself another Tantalus.

Apart from figuring as part of an elaborate conceit in praise of the beloved, the reference to Tantalus operates also as a symbol of the lover's frustration and relates to earlier references to drinking and thirst.

The mere frequency of the word 'Tantalus' in Quevedo's poetry does not truly reflect the significance of the myth for him. Apart from the more oblique method of reference as in an *idilio*:

> Tú, que del agua yaces desdeñado,
> con sed burlado, en fuente sumergido. . . (no.390)

You, who lie scorned by the water, with a thirst that is mocked, immersed in a fountain.

the widespread use of imagery associated with thirst and drinking and the recourse to the fountain image in erotic contexts are indications of the importance of this myth. Quevedo associates Tantalus with a fountain almost invariably in his love poetry. There is the *silva* previously considered (no.400), the oblique reference cited above, and the final line of one of the best-known sonnets:

> Tántalo en fugitiva fuente de oro. (no.449)

Tantalus in a fugitive fountain of gold.

The fountain is associated with the fulfilment of love, or at least the expectation or hope of it, in a *canción* in which the poet invites Aminta to share the pleasure of the spring landscape with him (no.389). At the height of the poet's amorous fantasizing, it is the fountain that forms the backdrop for their embraces, providing the harmonious sound of accompanying nature:

> ¡Ay, si llegases ya, qué tiernamente,
> al ruido de esta fuente,
> gastáramos las horas y los vientos,
> en suspiros y músicos acentos! (II.49-52)

Ah!, if you were to come now, how tenderly, to the sound of this fountain, would we while away the hours and the breezes in sighs and the sounds of music!

The semantic link of the fountain and drinking as a metaphor for kissing is again present: 'Tu aliento bebería/en ardiente porfía' ('I would drink your breath with persistent ardour') (ll.53-4).

For the most part, however, the idea of thirst and the image of the fountain are used in negative connections to connote the frustration of the poet's desires, for such is the keynote of Quevedo's amatory verse. By this semantic coupling, fountain-thirst, Quevedo departs from the more common Petrarchist understanding of the fountain image. Close has provided a schematic catalogue of the themes of Quevedo's love poetry and emphasized the similarities between the types of imagery associated with them and those found in the work of those poets whose works, taken together, form a Petrarchist manner as defined by Leonard Forster and

Luigi Baldacci.[20] Among her list there appear aspects of nature, such as fountains and rivers, which are apostrophized in 'set-piece topics of pity' (p.838). In the *silva* which I considered above (no.400), there was such an apostrophe, but the symbolic significance of the fountain, as seen in the quotations from the poem, represents something less conventionally Petrarchist. It is evident that the principal function of imagery associated with water — mainly fountains and rivers — in Petrarchist poetry is to operate metaphorically as a means of describing sorrow, notably by the conceit of tears swelling the volume of water and by ingenious and witty variations of this conceit. There are, indeed, a number of poems by Quevedo that belong to this convention and it would be extremely surprising were it not so.[21] But the relationship of the fountain to thirst as a metaphor for desire has an equal if not greater significance and in this he can be said to depart from the norm. Even in poems of no great emotional weight the link is present. Such is the case in one of the slightest sonnets to Lisi, an occasional poem where the advice to the beloved to imitate the manner of a fountain leads to a request for 'una yerba y una rosa' — symbols that need no explanation — through the idea of fertility:

> Ya que huyes de mí, Lísida hermosa,
> imita las costumbres desta fuente,
> que huye de la orilla eternamente,
> y siempre la fecunda generosa.
>   Huye de mí cortés, y, desdeñosa,
> sígate de mis ojos la corriente;
> y, aunque de paso, tanto fuego ardiente
> merézcate una yerba y una rosa. (no.493)

Since you flee from me, beautiful Lisi, imitate the manner of this fountain, which eternally flows from the bank and always fertilizes it generously. Flee from me courteously and scornfully, let the flow from my eyes follow you and, albeit slowly, may such an ardent fire deserve a plant and a rose from you.

The idea of the fountain as a place where love may be consummated — a *locus amoenus* — and consequently as a symbol of fertility and fulfilment rather than as a retreat for the jilted, unhappy lover relates to a tradition that is older and more popular than Petrarchism. It is characteristically, though not exclusively, indigenous: it is in the *cantigas d'amigo*; in the traditional Spanish lyric — the so-called 'poesía de tipo tradicional'; and in the *romance viejo*, for example that of 'De fonte-frida y con amor' ('Of the Cold Fountain and with Love').

Even when Quevedo refers to suffering by the commonplace of the lover's tears or weeping, he sometimes adds the notion of desire by an allusion to thirst or drinking. An example of this is a powerful expression of his frustrated wishes in the *silva* entitled 'Ansia de amante porfiado'

('Yearning of a constant lover') (no.403). There is here an ironic conceit in that although the water of his tears (i.e., the extent of his suffering) drowns (overwhelms) him, it cannot, however, allay his thirst (desire):

> Sedienta y desvelada
> tengo la vista, sin poder hartarse
> del llanto mismo en que se ve anegada. . . (ll.37-9)

my eyes are thirsty and wakeful, unable to satisfy themselves with the very tears in which they are drowned.

A similar conceit is to be found in a *romance*, 'Alegórica enfermedad y medecina de amante' ('Allegorical Illness and Lover's Medicine') (no.426):

> Témese de hidropesía
> mi ardiente sed, pues se aumenta
> y arde más, aunque mis ojos
> mares de lágrimas viertan. (ll.33-6)

My burning thirst is afraid of dropsy, since it increases and burns more, although my eyes shed seas of tears.

Even through the sea of tears which engulfs him, his desire for the lady is still intense and ever increasing.

A trenchant realization of the idea of anguished frustration is provided by a sonnet from *El Parnaso español* which is entirely based on the myth of Tantalus (no.294). It takes the form of a set-piece exaggeration of the poet's experience by relation to mythology. As so often in the case of such comparisons, the purpose is to make the lover's sufferings seem greater than those of his mythological counterpart:

> Dichoso puedes, Tántalo, llamarte,
> tú, que, en los reinos vanos, cada día,
> delgada sombra, desangrada y fría,
> ves, de tu misma sed, martirizarte.
> Bien puedes en tus penas alegrarte
> (si es capaz aquel pueblo de alegría),
> pues que tiene (hallarás) la pena mía
> del reino de la noche mayor parte.
> Que si a ti de la sed el mal eterno
> te atormenta, y mirando l'agua helada,
> te huye, si la llama tu suspiro;
> yo, ausente, venzo en penas al infierno;
> pues tú tocas y ves la prenda amada;
> yo, ardiendo, ni la toco ni la miro.

You can count yourself lucky, Tantalus, you, who, in the vain kingdoms, every day, a slender, blood-drained and cold shadow, see yourself martyred by your own thirst. You may well rejoice in your suffering (if those people are capable

of joy), since (you will discover) my suffering occupies a greater part in the
kingdom of night. For if you are tormented by the eternal affliction of thirst,
and, as you look at the icy water, it evades you if your sigh calls out to it; I, in
my absence, exceed the sufferings of hell; for you touch and see the cherished
gift, while I, burning for love, neither touch it nor see it.

The relationship of the poet's desire to the thirst of Tantalus is given a twist
in the final tercet. The torment of Tantalus is a condition in which he can see
and touch the water he longs to drink, but Quevedo reverses the particular
psychological nature of Tantalus' punishment in order to highlight his own
fate. The fact that the mythological figure can see and momentarily grasp
the water of which he is deprived is not seen as an especially cruel part of his
torment but, unusually, as a compensating factor. Quevedo refers to the
water that eludes Tantalus as 'la prenda amada', thereby fusing the two
parts of the comparison. The lover, absent from the beloved, but driven by a
strong desire to possess her, is less fortunate: he can neither see nor touch
her. The third element implicit in this comparison is that of drinking, which
corresponds to a stage beyond sight and touch at the amatory level, i.e.,
fulfilment. The characteristic Quevedian link of thirst=desire, drinking=
fulfilment is again established.

Another implication of this sonnet which is important for understanding
the nature of the lover's aspirations in the poetry of Quevedo relates to the
conception of the amatory intent in terms of stages of love. Sight and touch
do not satisfy; nothing short of fulfilment (the quenching of thirst) will
remove the torments of hell. Tantalus sees and touches but even so is not
free of suffering. For most Spanish poets of the Golden Age, including
Quevedo himself on occasion, the mere sight of the beloved would
constitute a supreme boon, the limit of plausible aspiration. This is an issue
to which I shall return below.

For the moment, however, I wish to recall the sonnet to Lisi that
prompted the observations on the semantic field of thirst-fountain-
fulfilment to pursue a related idea, that of nourishment, as in the first tercet:

> De invisible comercio mantenidos,
> y desnudos de cuerpo, los favores
> gozaran mis potencias y sentidos. . . (no.448)

Sustained by invisible contact and denuded of body, my faculties and senses
would enjoy your favours.

Apart from the double meanings already mentioned, the idea of 'comercio'
is worthy of comment. Besides its mercantile significance, which is its
primary significance, though an unusual one here, it also bears the meaning
of an illicit or secret relationship, which is entirely apposite in this
context.[22] The association with commerce is one that will occupy my

attention in a later chapter, but now I wish to concentrate on the juxtaposition, 'comercio mantenidos', where, it seems to me, Quevedo is punning on '*comer*cio' — '*comer*' ('to eat'). The relationship of desire to nourishment is not as common as the coupling of desire with thirst in the amatory verse, though in the moral poetry the view of physical desire not uncommonly involves the image of appetite, hence the 'brutos apetitos' ('brute appetites') of one of the poems of the *Heráclito cristiano* (no.34).

In at least two love poems, Quevedo combines the images of thirst and hunger as correlatives of desire as, for instance, in the first quatrain of a sonnet from *El Parnaso español:*

> No lo entendéis, mis ojos, que ese cebo
> que os alimenta es muerte disfrazada
> que, de la vista de Silena airada,
> con sed enferma, porfiado, bebo. (no.340)

You do not understand, my eyes, that the food which nourishes you is death in disguise which, with the sight of angry Silena, I persist in drinking with a sick thirst.

Even here, the references to love's fatal deception and to desire as a sickness have moral overtones. In the *romance* that is concerned with fulfilment in a dream (no.440), the images of hunger and appetite are used twice, in the first case in juxtaposition with those of wealth and greed — a coupling that offers a parallel to the phrase 'De invisible comercio mantenidos' from the sonnet to Lisi:

> maté la hambre al deseo,
> y enriquecí la codicia. (ll.43-4)

I killed desire's hunger and enriched my greed.

Images of thirst and hunger are frequently used by Quevedo to convey the dire consequences of the failure of his amatory aspirations. Thus they not only symbolize desire but, with appropriate qualifiers, the thwarting of desire. I quote two notable examples though there are many occurrences. There is the opening of one of Quevedo's most impassioned utterances, a sonnet to Lisi dominated by both images:

> En los claustros de l'alma la herida
> yace callada; mas consume, hambrienta,
> la vida, que en mis venas alimenta
> llama por las medulas extendida.
> Bebe el ardor, hidrópica, mi vida. . . (no.485)[23]

In the cloisters of the soul the wound lies silent; but it consumes in its hunger the life that nourishes in my veins a flame that spreads through the marrow. The passion is dropsically drunk by my life.

and the analogy at the start of another sonnet from the same series, where the striking idea of the poet providing nourishment to his own suffering is preceded by the more conventional notion of his tears supplying refreshment for wild beasts:

> Éstas son y serán las postreras
> lágrimas que, con fuerza de voz viva,
> perderé en esta fuente fugitiva,
> que las lleva a la sed de tantas fieras.
> ¡Dichoso yo, que, en playas extranjeras,
> siendo alimento a pena tan esquiva,
> halle muerte piadosa, que derriba
> tanto vano edificio de quimeras! (no.473)

These are and will be the last tears which, with the strength of a voice that has life, I shall lose in this fugitive fountain, which carries them to so many thirsty beasts. Lucky am I who, on foreign beaches and the source of nourishment to such an elusive punishment, should find a merciful death, which destroys such a vain edifice of fancies!

In all there are at least twenty-five poems where the image of either thirst or hunger and closely related ideas occur,[24] which is nearly one poem in eight — a frequency especially significant if comparisons are made with other poets writing in the same tradition. Garcilaso, for instance, uses the idea of thirst and the myth of Tantalus on only one occasion and when he does so, it is in a poem which, as commentators universally acknowledge, expresses an intense physical yearning intermingled with feelings of guilt and remorse at the nature of his emotion: the *Canción* IV.[25] Quevedo's repeated and distinctive use of images of physical necessity as correlatives of love, whether in terms of his understanding of his own motivation and expectation or as the expression of the denial of his hopes, is clearly indicative of an essentially carnal intention that is far more overt than is the case with the vast majority of Spanish Petrarchists. Furthermore, apart from the evidence to be gleaned from an examination of a favoured semantic field, involving myth and symbol, there are numerous examples of a mode of approach and address to the *amada* and references to her that have an unusual boldness and explicitness of erotic intent, and which serve to complement the observations I have made thus far.

This tendency can be seen even in what are ostensibly unexceptional and conventional utterances such as the following occasional sonnet from *Las tres Muscas*:

> Artificiosa flor, rica y hermosa,
> que adornas a la misma primavera,
> no temas que el color que tienes muera,
> estando en una parte tan dichosa.

Siempre verde serás, siempre olorosa,
aunque despoje el cielo la ribera;
triunfarás del invierno y de la esfera,
envidiada de mí por venturosa.
  Cuando caíste de su frente bella,
no te tuve por flor; que, como es cielo,
no esperaba yo dél sino una estrella;
  mas pues cuando se cae la flor al suelo
muestra que el fruto viene ya tras ella,
ver que te vi caer me da consuelo. (no.370)

Artful flower, rich and beautiful, who adorn Spring itself, do not fear that the
colour you have will perish, as it is in such a fortunate place. You will always be
green, always fragrant, although the heavens plunder the bank; you will
triumph over winter and the globe (sun) alike, and I shall envy your good
fortune. When you fell from her beautiful brow, I did not take you for a flower;
for, as she is a heaven, I did not expect anything from it other than a star; but,
because when it falls to earth, a flower shows that the fruit is soon to come after
it, seeing that I saw you fall consoles me.

The intention over most of the poem is to praise the beauty of the beloved
via an address to a flower placed in her hair. This is a common type of
Petrarchist procedure and one that critics hostile to part or all of Quevedo's
love poetry might label as typical of his frivolous vein. The sonnet has a
jealousy conceit. The flower's fortunate location is envied by the poet and
invested with qualities that he ascribes to the beloved: her beauty is
considered immortal and she is compared to the heavens — a highly
unusual term of reference for the beloved in the love poetry, as we shall see.
But the final tercet reveals a marked shift of emphasis: after the hyperbolic
metaphor of the flower being a star (l.11), the poet focusses on a
phenomenon more closely related to the object itself, that of fruit emerging
after the fall of flowers or blossom. This has the effect of converting the lady
from an ideal into an object of desire that the lover longs to possess. The
falling flower is interpreted hopefully as an augury of fulfilled desire. A
mediocre sonnet of vapid eulogy thus has an unexpected conclusion. But
this is by no means untypical of Quevedo. Even in his most conventional
utterances, there not infrequently escapes from him a statement or a
request that hints at a deep-rooted wish for sexual fulfilment, altogether
more direct and urgent than the vague pleas of his contemporaries.
    In one of Quevedo's longest love poems, a *silva* entitled 'Farmaceutria o
medicamentos enamorados' ('Pharmaceutics or Love Potions') (no.399),
the poet ponders on the efficacy of magic as a method of winning the lady's
favours. He invokes Hecate as well as Venus in order to assist him in his
quest (ll.55-60). His intention, as expressed near the start of the poem, is as
follows:

> Quiero a mis solas, Galafrón amigo,
> pues se sujeta a Amor la primavera,
> usar de mis conjuros:sea testigo
> el monte, el valle, el llano y la ribera.
> Aprovecharme quiero del encanto,
> pues no aprovecha con Aminta el llanto.(ll.13-18)

I wish alone, Galafron, my friend, to make use of my spells since spring is given over to love: let the mountain, valley, plain and bank testify. I wish to make the most of enchantment, since tears don't get me anywhere with Aminta.

What is of interest here is the concept Quevedo has of the lover's weeping. Often employed in Petrarchist poetry as an emblem of suffering, frequently associated by metaphor with the natural world and, on occasion, elevated into an expression of constant and dignifying emotion, here it is seen as no more than a means or a ploy to achieve a desired end. It is not so much an attitude that arises out of failure as a stage towards the achievement of success. The lover seems to declare: 'As one course of action has not worked (i.e. weeping), I shall try another, more drastic, one (enchantment)'. The use of the verb 'aprovechar' in this connection is a telling expression of intent.

In such cases, Quevedo reveals a directness, if not a deviousness, that is at variance with the accepted principles of address and reference — in a word, he is indecorous. For poets writing in the courtly-Petrarchist tradition, the idea of fulfilment is either so remote or impossible that lesser goals are established as absolute limits. This could comprise merely an acceptance by the beloved of the poet's suit, or a willingness to engage him in conversation, as so memorably expressed in Herrera's *Elegía* III, or, quite commonly, the possibility for the lover to contemplate the beauty of the beloved.[26] Quevedo too adheres to these conventions, as for instance in a sonnet from *Las tres Musas* that is a free imitation of Petrarch:

> El sueño, que es imagen de la muerte,
> en mí a la muerte vence en aspereza,
> pues que me estorba el sumo bien de verte. (no.359)

Sleep, which is an image of death, for me, outdoes death in bitterness, since it deprives me of the supreme good of seeing you.

and in a *romance*:

> No hallo rosas ni flores
> cuando no miro tu cara,
> que como en ella están todas,
> con ella todas me faltan. (no.432, ll.29-32)

I find neither roses nor flowers when I do not look at your face, for since they are all in it, when I am without it I am without them too.

But in a *silva* entitled 'Himno a las estrellas' ('Hymn to the Stars') (no.401), possibly inspired by a number of poems to stars and the night by Francisco de la Torre whose work was first edited by Quevedo, there is an interesting variation or qualification of the idea of the lady receiving the lover's suit. The poem comprises an extensive apostrophizing and description of the stars (ll.1-48), after which the poet makes his request:

> si amasteis en la vida
> y ya en el firmamento estáis clavadas,
> pues la pena de amor nunca se olvida,
> y aun suspiráis en signos transformadas,
> con Amarilis, ninfa la más bella,
> estrellas, ordenad que tenga estrella. (ll.49-54)

if you loved in life and now you are fixed in the firmament, since the suffering of love is never forgotten, and you still sigh, though changed into constellations, stars, ensure that I may be able to thank my lucky stars with Amarilis, most beautiful of nymphs.

There is nothing exceptional in this generalized request for an improvement in the lover's fate. But there is a further, more specific, plea:

> Si entre vosotras una
> miró sobre su parto y nacimiento
> y della se encargó desde la cuna,
> dispensando su acción, su movimiento,
> pedidla, estrellas, a cualquier que sea,
> que la incline siquiera a que me vea. (ll.55-60)

If one among you looked upon her birth and took charge of her from the cradle, controlling her actions and movements, ask her, stars, whichever one of you it may be, to be disposed at least to see me.

The lover's goal is that the beloved should be prepared to see him and to acknowledge him but, it must be stressed, this is a *minimum* goal, not the limit of his aspiration. He asks that she *at least* receive him, if nothing else be allowed.

Another poem built on a rhetorical framework, a *romance* addressed to Time (no.422), contains a passage which refers to the fulfilment of the lover's desires as a clear aim. Its structure is argumentative and involves the exaggeration of the lover's suffering in a comparison with other experiences. If Time is to be afforded respect, then its deeds should consist of the resolution of the lover's plight, not the lesser achievements commonly attributed to it:

> si quieres que te conozcan,
> si gustas que te confiesen
> con devoción temerosa

> por tirano omnipotente,
>   da fin a mis desventuras,
> pues a presumir se atreven
> que a tus días y a tus años
> pueden ser inobedientes. (ll.29-36)

if you want them to know you, if you would be pleased that they acknowledge you with frightened devotion as an all-powerful tyrant, bring an end to my misfortunes, since they dare to presume that they need not obey your days and years.

But how are the lover's misfortunes to be ended? The central part of the *romance* consists of a series of suggestions in the form of rhetorical questions followed by recommendations to Time. They amount to two possible solutions: either the renunciation of love or its fulfilment. In his commentary and notes on this poem, Price refers to the former solution but overlooks the latter.[27] A detailed consideration of this passage, however, suggests to me that the poet proposes the gratification of his desire as one way of alleviating his suffering. Initially he wonders at the constancy of his unrequited passion ('cuidado'); at how it survives the passing of time:

> ¿Y será bien que un cuidado,
> tan porfiado cuan fuerte,
> se ría de tus hazañas
> y vitorioso se quede? (ll.41-4)

And will it be right that an emotion, as obstinate as it is strong, should laugh at your deeds and end up the victor?

He next refers to the beloved's beauty and disdain and its effect upon him:

> ¿Por qué dos ojos avaros
> de la riqueza que pierden
> han de tener a los míos
> sin que el sueño los encuentre? (ll.45-8)

Why should two eyes, avaricious about the richness that they lose, affect mine so much that they do not find sleep?

He muses ruefully on his lost freedom, entirely the work of the lady who is thief, prison and judge:

> ¿Y por qué mi libertad
> aprisionada ha de verse,
> donde el ladrón es la cárcel
> y su juez el delincuente? (ll.49-52)

And why is my freedom to be imprisoned, where the thief is the prison and the criminal its judge?

There ensues a series of suggestions for the resolution of his problem which,

if fulfilled, would truly demonstrate the power of time. The first proposal
could be read in two ways:

> Enmendar la obstinación
> de un espíritu inclemente. (ll.53-4)

To correct the stubbornness of an unmerciful spirit.

This could be interpreted as an appeal for Time to destroy the persistence
of his passion; 'to correct the indiscipline of his soul', to quote Price.
Alternatively, the appeal could be for Time to ensure that the beloved
herself change by returning his love, since the description,'espíritu
inclemente', could well be applied to her. The following lines provide some
justification for the second interpretation:

> entretener los incendios
> de un corazón que arde siempre;
> > descansar unos deseos
> que viven eternamente,
> hechos martirio de l'alma,
> donde están porque los tiene. . . (ll.55-60)

To allay the fires of a heart that always burns; to put to rest desires that live
eternally, that have become a martyr of the soul, where they dwell because it
possesses them.

Price suggests that 'entretener' should be translated as 'to allay the pain of',
but another of Covarrubias's definitions is 'sustentar una cosa en el modo
que ser puede' ('to support something in the way that is appropriate'), i.e.,
the idea of alleviating or of killing hunger. This would be appropriate if the
phrase is to be understood as implying the satisfaction rather than the
renunciation of desire. In any case the succeeding phrase, 'descansar unos
deseos', enhances this impression: a desire is laid to rest when it is fulfilled.
It is only in the closing lines of this section that the idea of escaping love and
returning to a condition of former freedom ('siendo su patria mi alma') is
unambiguously mooted:

> reprehender a la memoria,
> que, con los pasados bienes,
> como traidora a mi gusto,
> a espaldas vueltas me hiere;
> > castigar mi entendimiento,
> que en discursos diferentes,
> siendo su patria mi alma,
> la quiere abrasar aleve. (ll.61-8)

to reproach memory which, with former joys being treacherous to my
pleasure, stabs me in the back; to punish my understanding which, with
different reasoning, though my soul is its homeland, wishes treacherously to
burn it.

It is important to appreciate the dual aspect of the solution that the poet envisages for his suffering. The idea of fulfilment is given a prominence equal to that of renunciation. In either case, the poet seeks a remedy rather than languish and suffer.

What is evident from the preceding examples is that the lover's pleas and envisaged solutions have a distinctive directness and boldness. To help to confirm this view, a comparison with Quevedo's predecessor, Herrera, is enlightening. Herrera is regarded as a supreme exponent of Spanish Petrarchism and, as such, is a suitable touchstone for thematic comparison. The demands and pleas of the lover in Herrera's poetry are noticeably less daring and ambitious than those of his Quevedian counterpart. For example, the single request in his *soneto* XXVII is 'acoged blandamente mi suspiro' ('gently receive my sigh');[28] while in *soneto* XIV, the two pleas are for the beloved to hear his complaint, followed by the hope of being able to contemplate her beauty, as so often in Herrera, conceived in terms of light: 'Oye la voz de mil suspiros llena. . . Buelve tu luz a mí, buelve tus ojos' ('Hear the voice full of a thousand sighs. . . Turn your light to me, turn your eyes') (p.40). A particularly good comparison is provided by the *Elegía* II, a poem that has many similarities of lexicon and imagery with Quevedo's poetry as it strives to express an emotional experience which is particularly powerful and overwhelming:

> No es amor, es furor jamás cansado;
> rabia es, que despedaça mis entrañas,
> este eterno dolor de mi cuidado. (p.36)

It isn't love, it's a tireless fury; a rage that tears my entrails apart, this eternal grief of my love.

The sarcasm of the succeeding lines has a clear affinity with a sonnet by Quevedo:

> ¡Qué gran vitoria, Amor, i qué hazañas
> atravesar un coraçón rendido,
> un coraçón que dulcemente engañas!

What a great victory, Love, and what an achievement to pierce a heart that is exhausted, a heart you sweetly deceive!

Compare:

> ¡Mucho del valeroso y esforzado,
> y viéneslo a mostrar en un rendido!
> Bástame, Amor, haberte agradecido
> penas, de que me puedo haber quejado. (no.341)

A lot of bravery and valour and you come to show it in one who is exhausted! It is enough for me, Love, to have thanked you for sufferings of which I could have complained.

But in the closing part of Herrera's *Elegía*, where the poet makes a series of pleas to the beloved, the differences between the two poets become conspicuous. For all the suppressed passion, even rage, the lover in Herrera's poem contents himself with the following sequence of pleas:

> Bella Señora, si mi voz cansada
> alcança tanto bien, que no os ofende,
> *oidla blandamente sosegada. . .*
> Si os puede enternecer el dolor mío,
> comiencen a ablandaros mis enojos;
> *no deis ya más lugar a más desvio.*
> *No me neguéis essos divinos ojos. . .* (my italics)

Beautiful Lady, if my weary voice achieves so much bliss that it does not offend you, *listen to it with sweetness and calm. . .* If my grief can make you tender, let my misfortunes start to soften you; *do not allow scope for more indifference. Do not deny me those divine eyes. . .*

The series culminates in the request for an opportunity to see and be seen by the beloved, whose beauty is, in any case, understood in spiritual rather than physical terms, as both the final phrase and earlier allusions to her beauty make clear.

Let us now compare a *canción* by Quevedo that, as with Herrera's *Elegía* II, contains three requests to the *amada* (no.394). The poem falls into two equal parts: in the first, the characteristic tone is a pleading one; in the second, one of lament at the failure of the plea. The requests reveal a gradation — after the address to the beloved, the first appeal is for her to treat him less cruelly:

> Dulce señora mía,
> norte de mi afligido pensamiento,
> luz de mi fantasía,
> principio, medio y fin de mi tormento,
> pues es tuya mi vida,
> no seas con desdenes su homicida. (ll.1-6)

Sweet lady of mine, guide of my afflicted thought, light of my fantasy, beginning, middle and end of my torment, since my life is yours, do not kill it with your disdain.

The second stanza continues in a similar vein: the lady, seen as his guiding star initially, is now viewed as a sun and, unusually for Quevedo, as a source of good, even enlightenment. The request, at the end of the stanza, is that she should not be indifferent to him, that he should not be consigned to oblivion on account of his love:

> Sol que a mis ciegos ojos
> das la luz que Cupido me ha quitado,
> llevando por despojos
> un vivo corazón enamorado,
> pues me tienes rendido,
> no me des por amor eterno olvido. (ll.7-12)

Sun, who to my unseeing eyes, give the light that Cupido has taken away from me, bearing away for spoils a vital, loving heart, since you have me exhausted, do not grant me eternal oblivion for love.

The pleas of the first two stanzas have thus been conventionally directed against the lady's cruelty and indifference. But Quevedo envisages a third stage. After the appeals for less hostility and for her not to forget him, there comes a clear and unexpected plea for his love to be fulfilled, couched in the form of a choice: she should either ensure that his attachment to his love be broken or else accede fully to his request:

> Helada roca fuerte,
> que en el mar amoroso de mis años,
> para darme la muerte,
> te puso el ciego autor de mis engaños,
> mata mi confianza,
> o cúmpleme del todo la esperanza. (ll.13-18)

Strong, icy rock, which the blind perpetrator of my illusions placed in the loving sea of my years, kill my trust or else completely fulfil my hope.

By presenting his demands in this way the poet betrays an obvious exasperation. He seems to admit that he cannot endure a constantly frustrated desire and that he will not be appeased by anything less than the consummation of his passion; the phrase 'del todo' is an important qualifier here. The poem has thus far been constructed so as to highlight each plea: 'no seas. . . homicida', 'no me des. . . eterno olvido', 'mata mi confianza,/o cúmpleme. . . la esperanza'. The last request is structurally focal as well as thematically unexpected, coming at the central point of the poem. The second part of the composition is a melancholy meditation on the consequences of the lover's failure. In the context of the poet's final, daring and obviously unheeded plea, a phrase like 'dándome tal rigor por beneficio' ('granting me such harshness as a boon') (l.22) is probably not so much a contradiction relating to the idea of love as a blessed suffering as a sarcastic comment on the outcome of his amatory aspirations: his reward (some reward!) is her unwavering disdain. In the next stanza there is, I feel, another divergence from a courtly-Petrarchist convention — the idea of the lover's unworthiness:

> El eco está cansado
> de responder al mal que no merezco. . . (ll.25-6)

The echo is weary of responding to the ill I do not deserve. . .

It is not a case here of the lover admitting his unworthiness to be even a jilted lover, as in Herrera's *soneto* XV:

> Porque mi pena es tal, que tanta gloria
> en mí no cabe, i desespero, cuando
> veo qu' el mal no devo merecello;
>   pues venço mi passión con la memoria
> i con la onra de saber penando
> que nunca a Troya ardió fuego tan bello. (p.41)

Because my suffering is such that so much glory cannot be contained in me, and I despair when I see that I ought not to deserve this harm; since I overcome my passion with my memory and with the honour of the grievous knowledge that such a beautiful fire never burned at Troy.

Quevedo's is a more straightforward or literal understanding of 'mal', i.e., he thinks he does not deserve to be made to suffer by being rejected; 'mal' is not to be understood as a synonym of unrequited love (cf. 'cuidado') but at face value with the meaning of pain or suffering. The poet's lament is not wistful and melancholy; it is frustrated and angry.

Another instance of the lover's pleas deviating from the unspecific and the conventional is provided by the following sonnet from *Las tres Musas:*

> Cifra de cuanta gloria y bien espera,
> por premio de su fe y de su tormento,
> el que para adorar tu pensamiento
> de sí se olvidará hasta que muera;
>   reforma tu aspereza brava y fiera
> a oír lo menos del dolor que siento:
> dale, señora, al tierno sentimiento
> en ese pecho ya lugar cualquiera.
>   Pues mi remedio está sólo en tu mano,
> antes que del dolor la fuerza fuerte
> del aliento vital prive a Silvano,
>   intento muda, porque de otra suerte
> llegará tarde, y procurarse ha en vano
> a tanto mal remedio sin la muerte. (no.361)

A sign of so much glory and good is awaited as a reward for his faith and torment by him who, in order to adore your thought, will forget about himself until he dies; change your harsh and cruel bitterness to hear the least part of the grief I feel: lady, now let gentle feelings have a place in that breast. Since my remedy is in your hand alone, before the powerful force of grief deprives Silvano of his life's breath, change your intention because otherwise it will come too late, and it will be vain to seek a remedy without death to so much ill.

Here again, there is evidence of a gradation in the lover's requests: they become increasingly bold. The first quatrain contains several terms that belong to the conventional lexicon of *cancionero* poetry: 'gloria', 'bien', 'fe', 'tormento' and 'adorar'. Love is seen as a worthy but arduous pursuit, demanding self-sacrifice. In the second quatrain, the lover asks, not unusually, that the lady at least heed his plight. It is a request that he repeats in more urgent and physical terms (ll.7-8) — an attitude that is carried over into the first tercet, the metonymic 'mano' following the use of 'pecho'. With the allusion to the hope or the possibility of a 'remedio', it can be seen that the poet has been imperceptibly developing his plea: from the minimal, initial request of a hearing — of inviting the lady to lend an ear to his suffering — to contemplating a solution to the suffering. This is developed further in the final appeal: 'intento muda'. The effect is as though the poet were to say: 'Behave differently towards me; change your conduct; heal my suffering and remedy my unhappiness before it is too late'. The final tercet has the same urgency and impatience that characterized the alternative demands in the *canción* previously considered (no.394). Again, it is as if there were an effort to harrass the lady in order to produce an immediate and, hopefully, favourable response.

   In another sonnet, the conventional plea to the lady is given a subtle but clear twist:

> De tantas bien nacidas esperanzas
> del doméstico amor y dulce vida,
> burlas, ingrata Silvia fementida,
> con desdenes, con celos, con tardanzas.
>
>   No arroje más tu brazo airadas lanzas
> del pecho a la pirámide escondida;
> que ya no dan lugar a nueva herida
> las que en ella te rinden alabanzas.
>
>   Confieso que di incienso eu tus altares
> con sacrílega mano al fuego ardiente
> del no prudente dios preso con grillo.
>
>   Si me castigas dándome esos males,
> no me mates, que un muerto no lo siente:
> dama vida, y así podré sentillo. (no.373)

You mock, ungrateful and false Silvia, so many well-born hopes of a gentle love and a sweet life, with scorn, jealousy and postponement. Let not your arm hurl more angry lances at the hidden pyramid in my breast; for now the praises paid to you there allow no more room for a new wound. I confess that I placed incense on your altars with a sacrilegious hand into the blazing fire of the imprudent god, imprisoned with shackles. If you punish me by giving me those ills, do not kill me, for a dead man does not feel it: grant me life, and then I shall be able to feel it.

The greater part of the poem is not unusual, except perhaps for the reference to 'tardanzas' which suggests both reproach and the prospect of ultimate fulfilment for which the lover impatiently longs. The ideas of praise and worship — not common in Quevedo's love poetry — succeed the lover's complaints. The final tercet develops an idea broached in the second quatrain: that of the lover at a stage of suffering where further cruelty on the lady's part would be superfluous. Indeed, if he is to continue suffering, and by so doing, presumably continue to demonstrate his love, then the lady must not persevere in her mocking scorn. But after the plea directed at what she should *not* do, in effect a paraphrase of the fifth and sixth lines:

> no me mates, que un muerto no lo siente. . .

there is a positive exhortation:

> dame vida, y así podré sentillo.

Behind the façade of a required condition for continuing suffering (and thus proof of love), there is a direct command with clear connotations: 'dame vida'. For the lover's suffering to continue, there must be not only an end to the lady's hostility but, in addition, an effective alleviation of the lover's plight. If 'muerte' is the consequence or the symbol of a protracted denial of fulfilment, then 'vida', its opposite, quite clearly suggests the achievement of fulfilment. The poet concludes with a request that is daring and paradoxical: to continue suffering, his love must be returned. By the play on the accepted symbolic significance of life and death in amatory contexts, he ingeniously and implicitly asks the *amada* to yield to his plea for fulfilment.

Finally, a particularly interesting, if not enigmatic, instance of the tendency to a bolder address than is customary in Petrarchist poetry occurs in a *romance* that describes the torments of an absent lover (no.424). The poem contains ideas that are commonly found in connection with the topic of absence: physical separation but spiritual union (ll.41-4) and, as a principal idea here, the need for communication with the beloved and the inability to achieve it. But by contrast with the poems considered above, the lover in the *romance* rebukes himself at one point for merely daring to address the *amada*:

> Deciros yo mi pasión
> no es esperanza de premio,
> sino acusación y culpa
> que pongo a mis pensamientos. (ll.13-16)

That I should tell you of my passion is not in hope of reward, but an accusation and blame I attach to my thoughts.

But there is an unexpected sequel. The lover previously stated that he was seeking 'sólo audiencia, no remedio' (l.8), but he contradicts that now:

> Oír y no remediar,
> bien es de fiereza extremo:
> que quien escucha las quejas,
> las tiene piadoso miedo. (ll.21-4)

To hear and not to remedy is indeed an extreme of cruelty: for he who listens to complaints has a compassionate fear of them.

He is not content with envisaging the lady as only an audience; to listen and not to remedy his complaint would be an act of extreme cruelty. Within a few lines, then, he has moved from self-recrimination at what he considered to be boldness in merely expressing his feelings to a criticism of the listener for not righting a deficiency. He now expects not only a listener, but one who will act in the way he requires; he seeks fulfilment despite his prior assertion to the contrary. The gesture is only temporary, though. He returns to the self-deprecating and renunciatory vein of the opening: in his humble pose (ll.25-8), the description of his wretched state (ll.29-32) and the apology for too open a display of lament (ll.33-6). What is significant though, is that here, as in so many other places, the voice of desire and exasperation should be heard, if only momentarily, in a clear and startling contradiction.

1 Jaime A. Montesinos, *La pasión amorosa de Quevedo: el ciclo de sonetos a Lisi* (Ph.D. Thesis, New York University, 1972). See *Dissertation Abstracts International,* XXXIII, 11A (1973), 6368-9.

2 *Courtly Love in Quevedo,* 8.

3 *Poesía española,* 516.

4 *Francisco de Quevedo* (Madrid, 1978), 39.

5 In this connection see Keith Whinnom, 'Hacia la interpretación y la valoración de las canciones del *Cancionero general* de 1511', *Filologia,* XIII (1968-9), 361-81.

6 Op. cit., 61-7, 88.

7 *Courtly Love in Quevedo,* 24-31.

8 Op. cit., 301.

9 She argues convincingly that 'Quevedo's love-poetry has a thoroughly Petrarchist pedigree' (art. cit., 836).

10 Emilia N. Kelley draws attention to Quevedo's eclecticism in *La poesía metafísica de Quevedo* (Madrid, 1973), 28-34. She suggests that the creative spirit in him was greater than the scholarly urge: 'Parecen faltarle tiempo y paciencia para profundizar objetivamente en lo que fuere, y su necesidad es siempre la medida de su profundidad. Se le puede achacar falta de perseverancia, pero no de intereses; es, esencialmente, un creador y, como tal, la medida absoluta de su mundo. Frente al estudioso que lucha incesantemente

por comprender e interpretar objetivamente a otros, el creador, al adentrarse en otro intelecto, en otro espíritu, lo adapta, se apropia de lo que le satisface o le intriga y lo hace suyo' (p.34).

11 Art. cit., 836.

12 *Poesia española*, 516-17.

13 *An Anthology of Spanish Poetry 1500-1700. Part II: 1580-1700* (Oxford, 1968), xxvi.

14 See nos.460, 471 and 472. The absence of commitment in the tercets is also noted by Olivares, who writes of a 'lack of emotional reinforcement' and a 'slackening of emotion after the first quatrain. *The Love Poetry of Francisco de Quevedo* (Cambridge, 1983), 92-3.

15 *Rimas*, ed. J.M. Blecua (Madrid, 1972), 123.

16 '"Sutileza del pensar" in a Quevedo sonnet', *Modern Language Notes*, LXXXI (1966), 131-42.

17 *Poesía española*, 516. Olivares suggests, more correctly I feel, that Fabio is the poet's *persona* and that the advice he offers is to himself and that it constitutes 'a rationalization for frustrated desire' (op. cit.,24).

18 *An Anthology of Quevedo's Poetry*, ed. R.M. Price (Manchester, 1969), 106. The ambiguity of the poem — its conflicting spiritual and sensual implications — is also noted by Olivares (op. cit., 94-6).

19 A slightly different view is taken by Arthur Terry, 'Thought and Feeling in Three Golden-Age Sonnets', *Bulletin of Hispanic Studies*, LIX (1982), 241-3.

20 Art. cit., 838.

21 See for example no.351. Dámaso Alonso (*Poesia española*, 503) believes that such compositions are of poor quality and early works of the poet.

22 'Por alusión se toma también por trato y comunicación familiar, y de ordinarió secreta entre dos personas'. *Diccionario de la lengua castellana . . . compuesto por la Real Academia Española* (Madrid, 1729).

23 Blecua (*Poesía original*, xcvii) sees these lines as distinctively Quevedian. They constitute 'la huida de la retórica de su tiempo y el hallazgo de raras y delicadas expresiones,llenas de la más asombrosa modernidad'.

24 Nos.294, 299, 306, 310, 311, 314, 340, 345, 387, 389, 390, 395, 400, 403, 421, 426, 440, 448, 449, 467, 471, 473, 474, 483, 485, 500.

25 See R.O. Jones, *A Literary History of Spain. The Golden Age: Prose and Poetry* (London, 1971), 38.

26 See Green, 'Courtly Love in the Spanish *Cancioneros*', p.63; J.M. Aguirre (ed.), Hernando del Castillo, *Cancionero general* (Salamanca, 1971), 21; Herbert Moller, 'The Meaning of Courtly Love', *Journal of American Folklore*, LXXIII (1960), 39-52.

27 Ed. cit., 107-8.

28 *Poesías*, ed. Vicente García de Diego (Madrid, 1970), 57.

CHAPTER II

The Consequences of Love: Suffering

Emilia N. Kelley's observation that suffering is an ever present condition in Quevedo's love poetry is one that can be readily endorsed;[1] indeed, only if suffering were not to have this key role would there be cause for surprise and comment. The relationship of love to suffering or death is one that continually occurs in poetry. Therefore, by her statement Kelley involves Quevedo in a vast community of poets stretching from antiquity to the present day. Nor is this relationship confined to poetry or, for that matter, literature. It is not merely a convention at the heart of certain literary phenomena, movements or schools, such as courtly love or Romanticism, but something that responds to an altogether more deep-rooted and unconscious understanding of the nature and implications of love which may also be seen in the other arts and even popular culture.[2]

Uncontroversial too, at first sight, is Kelley's reiteration of Green's thesis that the basis and presentation of the lover's plight owe much to courtly love. I quote Green: 'Courtly love is by nature a love of *penas*, of "blessed suffering", of nonattainment, of *have* and *have-not* . . . It is thus a love of paradoxes, of impossibility, an "amour lointain".'[3] The prominence of suffering as an inescapable part of the amatory experience because of an emphasis on the negative, unfulfilled aspect of love is generally regarded as the most significant feature of and inheritance from the Provençal poets. Huizinga sees this new focus on suffering in love as marking an important turn in the history of European civilization.[4] In the poetry of succeeding centuries, a cult of suffering is developed in which suffering is a positive factor, a proof of love and constancy — in essence, a proof of identity. The oxymoron, 'blessed suffering', quoted by Green, is easily explicable. Suffering for the courtly lover has a purpose and a value, as much as it does for the Christian.[5] It refines, dignifies and elevates and is to be preferred to not suffering, hence not experiencing love.[6] The frequently paradoxical rationalizations of love in the work of the *cancionero* poets and the rarified atmosphere of ennobling suffering in a poem like Herrera's *Elegía* III bear witness to this emotional reality. The poetry of Petrarch provides a distinctive enrichment of the phenomenon. Beyond the lament, one detects a note of melancholy consolation. It has been said of Petrarch that he seems at times to indulge or wallow in his suffering; the condition of 'dolendi voluptas' is á recurring one in the *Canzoniere*.[7]

That the spirit as well as the substance of the Petrarchan manner dominates Spanish love poetry of the Golden Age with increasing significance is a truth that requires no demonstration. The strains of the wistful lament are to be heard from Salicio's song through Herrera to the sonnets of Villamediana at the start of the seventeenth century. Everywhere there is to be found a certain transcendental or at least a transforming quality that derives from the knowledge that suffering has its compensations because of its origin and its nature — a feature encouraged by Neoplatonic ideas. In his study of Herrera's love poetry, Oreste Macrí refers to what Italian critics have termed *petrarquismo mayor* (*'greater Petrarchism'*), a designation that Macrí applies to a select band of poets, ranging from the Middle Ages to the present day, among them Quevedo as well as Herrera. This *petrarquismo mayor* 'está por encima de las academias, arcadias y casuísticas de escuela: que es solución pura del naturalismo y del doctrinalismo en la *teoría del corazón humano,* virgen e inmune de sus mismas implicaciones cronológicas y retóricas; liberación de la pasión misma, música y color; *lengua poética* absoluta e independiente del sujeto lírico, la cual por sí misma habla en la identidad fonética y semántica del recuerdo y la presencia, de la fantasía y la realidad; alta conmemoración de lo humano en la responsabilidad unívoca del poeta lírico, en el tiempo en que vive su lucha expresiva — melódica y conceptual — con el Eros, como símbolo de lo demónico de nuestra ambigua naturaleza' ('is above the academies, Arcadies and scholastic casuistry: for it is a pure solution of naturalism and doctrinalism in the *theory of the human heart,* unaffected by and immune from its attendant chronological and rhetorical implications; freedom from passion itself, music and colour; *a poetic language* that is absolute and independent of the subject of the lyric, a language which of its own accord speaks in a phonetic and semantic identity of recollection and presence, of fantasy and reality; a lofty celebration of what is human in the univocal responsibility of the lyric poet, at the time in which it lives its expressive — melodic and conceptual — struggle with Eros, as a symbol of the demonic in our ambiguous natures').[8] A few lines from Herrera's *Elegía* II, quoted in the previous chapter as an example of parallels with and divergences from Quevedo, testify to the transcendental and liberating power of love even in suffering. These lines have a radiant and hymn-like quality that dwarfs the suffering, although suffering is an integral part of the superior experience implied here:

> Nací para inflamarm' en la pureza
> d' aquellas vivas luzes qu' al sagrado
> cielo ilustran con rayos de belleza.
>   I de sus flechas todo traspassado,
> por gloria estimo mi quexosa pena,

> mi dolor por descanso regalado.
> Tal es la dulce Luz que me condena
> al tormento, i tal es por suerte mía
> de mi enemiga la beldad serena. (pp.36-7)

I was born to be inflamed in the purity of those vital lights that illuminate the sacred sky with rays of beauty. And, totally transfixed by their arrows, I consider my plaintive suffering as a glory, and my grief as a pleasant repose. Such is sweet Luz (Light), who condemns me to torment, and such, for my good fortune, is the serene beauty of my enemy.

In an impressionistic vein, Dámaso Alonso, focussing on the conventional aspects of Quevedo's love poetry, attempts to evoke the wistful and nostalgic mood which he sees as characteristic of this part of the poet's output. He envisages it as a world full of tenderness and beauty, rather like a Pre-Raphaelite dream: 'Siempre envuelve en nuestra imaginación un halo a estas mujeres cantadas por un poeta. Nos imaginamos la frente victoriosa, los rizos rubios desordenados por el viento, la risa, el mohín, los ojos, que ahora incitan, ahora se burlan, ahora se apartan despectivos. Y se nos iluminan días lejanos, soles muertos. Y sentimos una ternura por la vida, adensada en el amor, concentrada o simbolizada por una bella mujer. ¡Qué hermosa, la vida!' ('Always implicit in our minds is a halo to these women of whom the poet sings. We imagine the victorious forehead, the blonde ringlets ruffled by the breeze, the laughter, the pout, the eyes which by turns incite, mock and turn scornfully away. And far-off days, dead suns are illuminated for us. And we feel a tenderness towards life, condensed in love, and concentrated in or symbolized by a lovely woman. How beautiful is life!').[9]

Both this impression and Macrí's understanding of *petrarquismo mayor*, though they represent different modes of approach, can be related to the notion of a blessed suffering that Green and Kelley see as being at the heart of Quevedo's love poetry. But this is an interpretation that has been challenged. Mas, nothing if not iconoclastic in his assessment of critical views of Quevedo's amatory verse, suggests that one of A.J. Denomy's definitions of courtly love — that of the ennobling force of human love — does not appear to any significant degree in Quevedo.[10] In his study, Pozuelo Yvancos, departing from his overall thesis that Quevedo's love poetry lacks thematic novelty, suggests that in the case of the topic of blessed suffering, Quevedo parts company with tradition and, specifically, with poets like Petrarch and Herrera.[11] If a single statistic can demonstrate anything, then the fact that in ninety-one love sonnets (i.e., all the love sonnets except those to Lisi) there are only two expressions of the blessed suffering paradox (nos. 340 and 357) would seem a confirmation of Pozuelo Yvancos's view. As corroboration, one could quote attitudes to suffering in other poets that we do not find in Quevedo. There is, for instance, Lupercio Leonardo de Argensola's acceptance of suffering and its constraints:

> Aprueba y dobla el daño mi paciencia,
> pues no puedo quejarme de su furia,
> por no culpar ni resistir su gusto.[12]

My patience approves and doubles the pain, since I cannot complain of her fury so as not to blame or resist her pleasure.

and the same poet's recognition that with the passing of time, it becomes bearable — a habit:

> No temo los peligros del mar fiero
> ni de un scita la odiosa servidumbre,
> pues alivia los hierros la costumbre,
> y al remo grave puede hacer ligero. (p.49)

I do not fear the perils of the fierce sea nor the horrid servitude of a Scythian, since custom allays the irons and can make the heavy oar seem light.

The lover in one of Herrera's sonnets, burdened though he is by the overwhelming weight of amatory disappointment, nonetheless concludes that he could not face the prospect of alleviation, so alien is happiness to him. I quote the tercets:

> No es justo, no, que siempre quebrantado
> me oprima el mal, i me deshaga el pecho
> nueva pena d' antiguo desvario.
>   Mas ¡ô! que temo tanto el dulce estado,
> que (como al bien no esté enseñado i hecho)
> abraço ufano el grave dolor mío. (p.43)

No, it is not right that, shattered as I always am, the ill should oppress me and that a new suffering of a former delirium should destroy my breast. But I fear the sweet condition so much that (as I am neither instructed in happiness nor made for it) I proudly embrace this grievous pain of mine.

There are interesting differences too between a sonnet by Quevedo, 'Es hielo abrasador, es fuego helado' ('It is burning ice, an icy fire') (no. 375), and one by Camões, 'Amor é fogo que arde sem se ver' ('Love is a fire which burns invisibly'), on which it is clearly based, both of which are definitions of love.[13] While there are evident similarities of substance and structure, the Quevedo sonnet, significantly, omits any reference to love as a bitter-sweet experience which figured in Camões's sonnet. On the other hand, Quevedo introduces elements that are not present in Camões. These are negative ideas such as love as an illness, as a coward and as an abyss.

But apart from such isolated details of omission or divergence, there are other ways in which the absence of blessed suffering is a notable and distinctive feature of Quevedo's amatory verse. These not only relate to an avoidance of predictable verbal formulae and their replacement by a more personal and trenchant idiom, but also impinge upon an understanding of individual experience and its place in a wider context. In other words, apart from Pozuelo Yvancos' thoroughly convincing analysis of the *means* by which a particularly intense and unrelieved suffering is expressed, there are areas to be explored where the absence of the *spirit* of blessed suffering or the ennobling power of love has an effect on common themes and topics of amatory verse.

One of the features that most sharply distinguishes sixteenth-century Spanish love poetry from that of the previous century, apart from technical and metrical factors, is the importance attached to nature. This difference is not merely one of decoration: that the lover now has a backdrop for his utterances. It affects the register, indeed the substance of the utterance so that the experience that emerges from a poem by Garcilaso or Cetina is recognizably and definably different to that of the poetry found in Hernando del Castillo's *Cancionero general*, published and reprinted frequently in the lifetime of Garcilaso. Terms like 'obsessive intensity', 'tormented obsession', 'impersonality', 'narrow virtuosity' and 'claustrophobic'[14] which hint at a limited, introspective and even neurotic apprehension of love are appropriate for this *cancionero* poetry but not for the work of Spanish Petrarchists. Nature, as understood by Petrarch and his followers, was the source of a double liberation: not only to the suffering soul but also to the creative imagination. It offered opportunities to the poet in his capacity both as a practitioner of his art and as a lover. The idea of liberation is especially significant. Gustavo Agrait states how nature in Garcilaso's Second Eclogue, one of the poet's most troubled and anguished products, offers freedom and relief: 'Efectivamente la nota más destacada y persistente en estas estancias es la de libertad. El paisaje descrito, el noble ocio a que se entrega el personaje, esas "aves sin dueño con canto no aprendido", todos los ingredientes, en suma, contribuyen a crear una atmósfera de holgura, de generoso abandono natural: el solitario y amable refugio que jamás gozó el poeta en los breves e inquietos años de su vida' ('Indeed the most outstanding and persistent note in these verses is that of freedom. The description of the landscape, the noble diversions to which the character surrenders himself, those "uncaged birds who have not been taught to sing", all the ingredients, in short, go towards the creation of an atmosphere of comfort, of a complete abandon to nature: the solitary and cherished refuge which the poet never enjoyed in the few and troubled years of his life').[15]

Close recognizes the opportunities offered to poets by nature, as part of her argument that factors such as imagery and the rhetorical character of Petrarchism are not mere embellishments but correspond to something fundamental: 'the setting of the poet's lament against a background of nature . . . opens dimensions of pathos, plangent tenderness, and pictorial fancy unknown in *cancionero* poetry'.[16]

It is my contention, however, that Quevedo's conception of the role of nature does not, as a rule, conform to the various positive functions that other Petrarchists attach to it, whether it be liberation, alleviation, refuge or beauty. In the first place, the pastoral vein is one that Quevedo does not find appropriate for his presentation of the amatory experience. In addition to providing a stylized background, pastoral involves a particular attitude to experience in which nostalgia and consolation figure prominently. Furthermore, though this is a trend, albeit a significant one, rather than a norm, nature in the love poetry of Quevedo is conceived as a conflicting and negative force rather than as a receptive and consoling element. In Petrarchist poetry, nature is usually sympathetic notwithstanding the variety of depiction. A barren, desolate location would correspond to the mood of the lover and serve to correlate his despair and anguish.[17] An idyllic setting, a *locus amoenus*, would act as a source of consolation and alleviation, momentarily relieving the lover's sorrow. A classic instance of this is the opening of Nemoroso's lament in Garcilaso's First Eclogue.[18]

But this note of wistful resignation, suggestive perhaps of the poet's acceptance of the place of suffering in his experience, is rarely to be found in Quevedo's poetry. In the cycle of poems to Lisi, where nature as a setting as opposed to a source of analogy and metaphor is in any case uncommon, there are two sonnets with similar themes and structures that stress the difference or the incongruity between the poet and the outer world:

> Ya tituló al verano ronca seña;
> vuela la grulla en letra, y con las alas
> escribe el viento y, en parleras galas,
> Progne cantora su dolor desdeña.
>   Semblante azul y alegre el cielo enseña,
> limpio de nubes y impresiones malas;
> y si a estruendo marcial despierta Palas,
> Flora convida al sueño en blanda greña.
>   La sed aumenta el sol, creciendo el día;
> de la cárcel del yelo desatado,
> templa el arroyo el ruido en armonía.
>   Yo solo, ¡oh Lisi!, a pena destinado,
> y en encendido invierno l'alma mía,
> ardo en la nieve y yélome abrasado. (no. 466)

Already a raucous sign has given out Spring's title; the crane makes an inscription with its flight, and the wind writes with its wings, and, in garrulous finery, Procne scorns her grief with her song. The sky reveals a blue and joyful aspect, devoid of clouds and bad impressions; and if Pallas awakens to the clamour of war, Flora invites sleep in a soft shank of hair. The sun increases one's thirst as the day grows; the stream, released from the prison of ice, tempers its noise into harmony. I alone, oh Lisi!, destined to suffering and with my soul in an inflamed winter, burn in the snow and freeze as I burn.

> Colora abril el campo que mancilla
> agudo yelo y nieve desatada
> de nube obscura y yerta, y, bien pintada,
> ya la selva lozana en torno brilla.
>   Los términos descubre de la orilla,
> corriente, con el sol desenojada;
> y la voz del arroyo, articulada
> en guijas, llama l'aura a competilla.
>   Las últimas ausencias del invierno
> anciana seña son de las montañas,
> y en el almendro, aviso al mal gobierno.
>   Sólo no hay primavera en mis entrañas,
> que habitadas de Amor arden infierno,
> y bosque son de flechas y guadañas. (no.481)

April colours the countryside that is stained by the sharp ice and the snow, released from a dark, stiff cloud, and now the lush wood, bright with colour, shines around. The stream, soothed by the sun, discovers the limits of the shore; and the voice of the brook, articulated on the pebbles, calls the breeze to compete with it. The final absences of winter are the age-old sign of the mountains, and a warning to bad government in the almond tree. Only in my entrails, that, inhabited by love, burn as hell and are a wood of arrows and scythes, is there no Spring.

The arrival of spring is not reflected in the lover's experience. The final tercet, in both cases, serves to highlight the incompatibility of nature with the inner world (respectively 'alma' and 'entrañas') of the lover and thus to stress his isolation and desolation. A similar process is to be found in one of Quevedo's most detailed evocations of nature, in a *romance* (no.439) first published in 1637 in Jorge Pinto Morales' collection, *Maravillas del Parnaso*, where the refrain states the lack of harmony between the lover and the natural world:

> yo solo, Floris, preso y desterrado,
> con pena y llanto, sin el dueño mío,
> borro la primavera, turbo el río,
> enciendo el monte y entristezco el prado. (ll.17-20)

I alone, Floris, imprisoned and exiled, in suffering and lamentation, without my lady, blot the Spring, stir up the river, set fire to the mountain and sadden the meadow.

There is an inability on the part of the lover to relate inner grief to the outer world. By failing to define and locate that suffering he reveals that he can neither come to terms with it nor have any hope of assuaging it.

This tendency is also conspicuous in a number of poems centred on a favourite Petrarchist topic: the reference and, frequently, the address to streams or rivers, which fulfil an analogical and metaphoric function. A conceit almost invariably arising from the topic is that of the lover's tears causing the river to swell. This conceit, which again depends upon a view of the natural world as receptive and sympathetic, is, at best, susceptible to subtle variation, at worst, to preposterous wit. It may well invite poets to a tongue-in-cheek attitude. But as Forster points out, when Petrarch writes 'fiume che spesso del mio pianger cresci' ('river who grow deep with my weeping'), addressing the river Sorgue, there can be no doubt that he is serious.[19] There is a similar dignity in a *cultista* sonnet by Villamediana where the river-tears conceit operates in terms of reciprocal harmony and where the lover's lament is transfigured by the sweetness of art:

> Las no cuajadas perlas deste río,
> que en urna breve su cristal desata,
> undoso plectro son, cuerdas de plata,
> que alternan voz y llanto con el mío.
>
> Fortuna, pues, común, común desvío,
> a bien conforme vínculo nos ata,
> grillos de yelo en margen pone ingrata,
> cuando a yerros vincula mi albedrío.
>
> Articulado, pues, el sentimiento
> en líquida tïorba, en triste canto,
> quejas damos recíprocas al viento.
>
> Dulce de Orfeo emulación, en cuanto
> animadas sus aguas con mi acento,
> su caudal enriquecen con mi llanto.[20]

The uncongealed pearls of this river, which dissolves its crystal in a brief urn, are a wavy plectrum with strings of silver, that alternate voice and weeping with mine. A common fate, then, a common indifference, ties us to a truly similar bond, it cruelly places icy shackles on the bank when it shackles my free-will with irons. Our feelings, then, are expressed in a liquid lute, and in a sad song, we utter mutual complaints to the wind. When its waters are vitalized with my notes, they enrich their flow with my weeping, in sweet imitation of Orpheus.

In the following sonnet by Francisco de la Torre, the river is viewed as a source of momentary respite. It provides some alleviation to the lover by allowing him to unburden himself and by acting as an outlet for his sadness:

> Claro y sagrado río, y tu ribera
> de esmeraldas y pórfidos vestida,
> corto descanso de una amarga vida,
> que entre amor y esperança desespera.

> Cierto mal, bien incierto, ausencia fiera,
> gloria passada y gloria arrepentida,
> tienen tan acabada y combatida
> la triste vida, que la muerte espera.
>   Tú, que lavas el monte y las arenas
> rojas de mi Cyteron soberano,
> lleva mi voz y lástimas contigo.
>   Alivia tú, llevándolas, mis penas;
> assí veas su rostro tan humano,
> quanto yo despiadado y enemigo.[21]

Clear and sacred river, whose bank is clothed in emeralds and porphyries, a brief rest in a bitter life, which despairs between love and hope. A certain ill, an uncertain good, a harsh absence, a glory that has gone and a glory that I repent, have so exhausted and assailed my sad life that it hopes for death. You, who wash the mountain and the red sands of my sovereign Cithaeron, bear my voice and complaints off with you. Alleviate my sufferings by carrying them away; thus may you see her face to be as human as I saw it merciless and hostile.

In the same poet's *Endecha* I, the river is both a confidant and refuge for the unhappy lover. An individual touch here is the contrast with the sea which symbolizes the turmoil of the lover's experience:

> Cristalino río,
> manso y sossegado,
> mil vezes turbado
> con el llanto mío:
> oye mis querellas
> amorosamente,
> sin que tu corriente
> se turbe con ellas.
> Sólo a ti me buelvo,
> el furor huyendo
> deste mar horrendo
> que en mi mal rebuelvo. (p.82)

Crystalline river, soft and peaceful, a thousand times disturbed by my lament: hear my complaints lovingly, without your current being disturbed by them. To you alone I turn, fleeing the fury of this horrendous sea, which I disturb in my misfortune.

The idea of a receptive nature in the guise of a river is, admittedly, present in Quevedo as at the opening of a sonnet from *El Parnaso español* where there is an implication of the Orpheus legend:

> Esforzaron mis ojos la corriente
> de este, si fértil, apacible río;
> y cantando frené su curso y brío:
> ¡tanto puede el dolor en un ausente! (no.318)

My eyes reinforced the flow of this peaceful though fertile river; and as I sang, I halted its vigorous course: so much can pain achieve in one who is absent!

But when Quevedo employs rivers as a referent, there are repeatedly expressions of that same divorce between the poet and the natural world that we saw previously. The sonnet that immediately follows the one just quoted in *El Parnaso español* offers such a case:

> Frena el corriente, ¡oh Tajo retorcido!,
> tú, que llegas al mar rico y dorado,
> en tanto que al rigor de mi cuidado
> busco (¡ay, si le hallase!) algún olvido.
>   No suenes lisonjero, pues perdido
> ves a quien te bebió con su ganado;
> viste de mi color desanimado
> los cristales que al mar llevas tendido.
>   Pues en llantos me anegan mis enojos,
> con el recién nacido sol no rías,
> ni alimente tu margen sino abrojos.
>   Que no es razón que, si tus aguas frías
> son lágrimas llovidas de mis ojos,
> rían cuando las lloran ansias mías. (no.319)

Halt your flow, oh meandering Tagus!, you, who reach the rich and golden sea, while I seek (if only I could find it) to forget awhile the harshness of my love. Do not sound pleasing, since you see him who drank you with his flock now lost; you saw the crystals of my lifeless colour, these that you carry off to the sea. Since my sufferings drown me in tears, do not laugh with the newly-risen sun, and may your bank only nourish thorns. For it is not right, if your cold waters are tears that have rained from my eyes, that they should laugh when they are the tears of my afflictions.

As with the two poems by Francisco de la Torre, the poet seeks an escape from his suffering (ll.3-4). But there is no indication that he can achieve it. Instead, attention is drawn to differences and points of conflict between the lover and the natural world. It would be fitting, argues the poet, that in order to match his mood the river-bank should be adorned with weeds — a conceit of receptive nature that recalls some lines of Nemoroso's lament in Garcilaso's First Eclogue.[22] But the poem concludes by stressing through the antithesis of laughter and tears the lack of harmony between poet and nature; the river is oblivious of the lover's plight as it blithely moves on, its sweet sounds at odds with the lover's tears which Quevedo, conventional at least in this detail, suggests are responsible for its very flow.

A similar antithesis is present in the quatrains of a sonnet to Lisi:

> Aquí, donde su curso, retorciendo,
> de parlero cristal, Henares santo,
> en la esmeralda de su verde manto

> ya engastándose va, y ya escondiendo,
>   sentí, molesta soledad viviendo,
> de engañosa sirena docto canto,
> que, blanda y lisonjera, pudo tanto,
> que lo que lloro yo, lo está riendo. (no.463)

Here, where, meandering on its course of eloquent crystal, the holy Henares, in the emerald of its green mantle, is now prominent and the next moment hidden, I heard, as I dwelt in tiresome solitude, the wise song of the deceiving siren, who, soft and pleasing, could achieve so much that what I lament she laughs at.

The setting is idyllic, pleasing to eye and ear alike. But the lover, though momentarily beguiled by the scene, refuses to consider the distraction as a welcome relief; it is a deceptive and hollow consolation. The sweet sounds of the river lull him into a false sense of ease of mind but, ultimately, these sounds seem like mocking laughter. By his withdrawal into the natural world he is cast into tiresome isolation, unlike the poet-lover in pastoral literature.

In a sonnet from *Las tres Musas* speculatively dated as early as 1599 by Astrana Marín on account of an allusion to the Henares, there is another contrast — between tears and song:

> Detén tu curso, Henares, tan crecido,
> de aquesta soledad músico amado,
> en tanto que, contento, mi ganado
> goza del bien que pierde este afligido;
>   y en tanto que en el ramo más florido
> endechas canta el ruiseñor, y el prado
> tiene de sí al verano enamorado,
> tomando a mayo su mejor vestido.
>   No cantes más, pues ves que nunca aflojo
> la rienda al llanto en míseras porfías,
> sin menguárseme parte del enojo.
>   Que mal parece, si tus aguas frías
> son lágrimas las más, que triste arrojo,
> que canten, cuando lloro, siendo mías. (no.362)

Suspend your course, that has grown so much, Henares, the cherished musician of this lonely place, while happily my flock enjoys the good that this afflicted one has lost; and while the nightingale sings his dirges on the most flowery branch, and the meadow has made the summer fall in love with it, taking May for its best dress. Sing no more, since you see I never loosen the rein of weeping in my wretched constancy, nor does any part of my pain diminish. For, if your cold waters are mostly the tears that I sadly shed, it seems bad to sing as I weep, for they are mine.

The poet rejects the idea — indeed the convention — that the sound of the flowing river should accompany his lament. It is far from the spirit of the well-known refrain from Spenser's *Prothalamion*: 'Sweet Thames, run softly, till I end my song'. The poet develops the conventional address to the river to suspend momentarily its flow in order to heed his complaint into a plea that it should flow no more. The summer landscape is radiant and fertile; the second quatrain presents a particularly intense and joyous picture of the natural world. But equally intense is the lover's suffering, expressed in a phrase that straddles the ninth and tenth lines of the poem. The antithesis of the conclusion provides a condensed version of the contrast between the lover and nature described earlier. It is also implied that art or poetry does not afford relief or an outlet to the lover.

Another sonnet from the series to Lisi confirms the impression received from Quevedo's 'river' poems of a lover alienated not only from his beloved but also from nature. It provides another instance of how a set-piece topic can be significantly modified. It is based on the idea of the river as a conveyor of the lament:

> Aquí, en las altas sierras de Segura,
> que se mezclan zafir con el del cielo,
> en cuna naces, líquida, de yelo,
> y bien con majestad en tanta altura.
>   Naces, Guadalquivir, de fuente pura,
> donde de tus cristales, leve el vuelo,
> se retuerce corriente por el suelo,
> después que se arrojó por peña dura.
>   Aquí el primer tributo en llanto envío
> a tus raudales, porque a Lisi hermosa
> mis lágrimas la ofrezcas con que creces;
>   mas temo, como a verla llegas río,
> que olvide tu corriente poderosa
> el aumento que arroyo me agradeces. (no.447)

Here, in the lofty ranges of Segura, whose sapphire mingles with that of the sky, you are born in a liquid cradle of ice and in true majesty at such a height. You are born, Guadalquivir, from a pure fountain, where the light flow of your crystals twists its current along the ground after it hurled itself over a hard cliff. Here I send the first tribute in tears to your torrents so that you may offer my tears, with which you grow, to beautiful Lisi; but I fear, since you arrive in her sight as a river, that your powerful flow might forget the increase that, as a brook, you thanked me for.

Again a conventional starting-point is given a negative slant. The lover's tears swell the river — a sympathetic relationship. But the poet continues by expressing the fear that his complaint may be overwhelmed by the sheer volume of the water. His lament will not only be unheeded, it will be unheard. There is a suggestion here, as in previous examples, of a failure on the part of the lover to unburden his soul. Beyond the denial to nature of any consoling or creative power, there is the impression that the lover is thwarted not only by having his suit rejected, but also because he is deprived of the capacity for merely expressing his suffering.

The beauty of nature, then, neither distracts nor consoles; it serves only to intensify anguish, sometimes by ironic contrast (laughter-tears, tears-song). Such an understanding of nature is consistent with the fact that the lover in Quevedo's poetry is less susceptible to fluctuations in love than in the work of his contemporaries. There are fewer satisfactions short of the ultimate goal (as shown in the previous chapter), fewer improvements of fortune, even if momentary or illusory, and less by way of compensation through art or nature. The unchanging quality of suffering, as well as its persistence, is a well-marked feature.

One myth that most profoundly expresses the idea of a receptive nature is that of Orpheus, where the poet and nature are linked by the poet's art in a harmonious relationship. In view of its particular suitability as a referent for the amatory condition,[23] it can be said to occur infrequently in Quevedo's love poetry — not unexpectedly in the light of the preceding pages. There are five occurrences as compared with nine in non-amatory verse, which is, admittedly, a larger unit but a less likely location for the myth. One of the five occurrences refers to the part of the Orpheus legend that involves the recovery and second loss of Eurydice (no.407). Of the remaining four instances, one amounts to no more than a parenthetical allusion in a sonnet that explores an area of Neoplatonic theory (no.321) and thus has an insignificant role in that sonnet. In a poem in *octavas*, an *idilio* (no.390), the myth is incorporated into a passage where nature is receptive and where, unusually for Quevedo, though conventionally, the poet attains some degree of consolation:

> Las aves que leyeren mis tristezas
> luego pondrán en tono mis congojas,
> y cantarán mi mal en las cortezas
> al son que hiciere el aire con las hojas.
> Cualquier viento, templado a mis ternezas,
> de las cuerdas, Amor, que no me aflojas
> (pues del tormento son que se conspira),
> fabricará con mis suspiros lira.
> Allí serán mis lágrimas Orfeos,
> y mis lamentos, blandos ruiseñores;
> suspenderé el infierno a mis deseos,
> halagaré sus llamas y rigores . . . (ll.9-20)

The birds that read of my sadness will then set my griefs to music, and they will sing of my misfortunes on the barks of trees to the sound that the breeze would make among the leaves. Any wind, tuned to my tender laments, will make with my sighs a lyre of the strings, Love, which you do not loosen for me (since they are part of the conspiracy of my torment). There, my tears will be Orpheusus, and my laments, sweet nightingales; I shall suspend hell with my desires, I shall beguile its flames and rigours.

But this is the sole allusion to the Orpheus myth associated with sympathetic nature in the whole of Quevedo's love poetry. He does, however, treat the myth in this common way in non-amatory contexts, as this extract from an ode to Don Jerónimo de Mata makes clear:

> Bien con voz dolorosa pudo Orfeo,
> por divertir su ausencia y su deseo,
> músico suspender, regalar tierno
> las penas del infierno . . . (no.291)

Indeed, with a dolorous voice, Orpheus, the musician, to relieve his absence and desire, was able to suspend, to soothe the sufferings of hell.

This is a classic example of the Orphean myth *vis à vis* the power of art, in this case its capacity to subdue the forces of evil. But in two love sonnets the same aspect of the legend is given a negative slant. One of these is an imitation of a sonnet by the Italian poet, Luigi Groto, whose work forms one of the principal direct sources of Quevedo's poetry:[24]

> Si el abismo, en diluvios desatado,
> hubiera todo el fuego consumido,
> el que enjuga mis venas, mantenido
> de mi sangre, le hubiera restaurado.
> Si el día, por Faetón descaminado,
> hubiera todo el mar y aguas bebido,
> con el piadoso llanto que he vertido,
> las hubieran mis ojos renovado.
> Si las legiones todas de los vientos
> guardar Ulises en prisión pudiera,
> mis suspiros sin fin otros formaran.
> Si del infierno todos los tormentos,
> con su música, Orfeo suspendiera,
> otros mis penas nuevos inventaran. (no.299)

If the abyss, dissolved in floods, had consumed the whole fire, the one that dries my veins, kept going by my blood, would have restarted it. If the day, misled by Phaeton, had drank all the sea and waters, my eyes would have renewed them with the merciful tears that I have spilt. If Ulysses could keep all the legions of the winds in prison, my endless sighs would create others. If all the torments of hell were suspended by Orpheus and his music, my sufferings would invent new ones.

This sonnet has an unusual structure: enumeration rather than development.[25] It comprises a series of hypotheses which serve to highlight the extent of the lover's suffering. The Orpheus myth is the final analogy. The effectiveness of the mythological figure's art or music is negated, however, as the lover's sorrow eclipses the consoling beauty of the playing of Orpheus. A more expressive denial of the magical quality of Orphean music and the consequent impossibility for any alleviation of the burden of suffering is to be found in a sonnet from *El Parnaso español*, in which the Orpheus myth occupies a focal position as a source of identification for the lover:

> A todas partes que me vuelvo veo
> las amenazas de la llama ardiente,
> y en cualquiera lugar tengo presente
> tormento esquivo y burlador deseo.
>   La vida es mi prisión, y no lo creo;
> y al son del hierro, que perpetuamente
> pesado arrastro, y humedezco ausente,
> dentro en mí propio pruebo a ser Orfeo.
>   Hay en mi corazón furias y penas;
> en él es el Amor fuego y tirano,
> y yo padezco en mí la culpa mía.
>   ¡Oh dueño sin piedad, que tal ordenas,
> pues, del castigo de enemiga mano,
> no es precio ni rescate l'armonía! (no.297)

Everywhere I turn, I see the threats of the burning flame, and wherever I am, I find before me a disdainful torment and a mocking desire. Life is my prison, and I cannot believe it; and to the sound of irons, whose weight I perpetually drag along, and which, in my absence, I soak, within my own self I try to be Orpheus. In my heart are furies and punishments, in it, Love is a fire and a tyrant, and I suffer my own offence within myself. Oh merciless lord, who thus ordain, then, that harmony is neither a prize nor a ransom from the punishment of a hostile hand.

The poet seeks to establish an equivalence between his emotions and the experiences of Orpheus in hell. The imagery is of a kind regarded as characteristic of Quevedo's 'desgarrón afectivo' — intense, violent and suggestive of an extreme of emotion.[26] Various lexico-syntactical patterns such as the chiasmus of the fourth line and the parallel between hell and Love in the ninth and tenth lines enhance the expressive vigour. But the principal means by which the potency of suffering is suggested comes from the poet's arousal of a certain expectation in the reader which he then disappoints. The allusion to Orpheus in hell leads us to expect a mood of eventual or partial alleviation: that the torment in the poet's heart — the metaphorical hell — can be assuaged just as the torments of hell were suspended by the playing of Orpheus. But no such process occurs, although, interestingly, as Close has pointed out, in a sonnet by Marino that offers a parallel to if not a source of Quevedo's poem, the lover succeeds in achieving some solace.[27] In his treatment of the myth in this sonnet, Quevedo does not develop it truly as an analogy by emphasizing similarity, but rather as a point of contrast, with the result that there is a clear divergence from the essential point of the myth.

It has been frequently noted that the expression of suffering offers the most striking lexical and stylistic novelties in Quevedo's poetry, often because of a tendency to unusual physical realizations of the experience.[28] In the previous chapter I alluded to his predilection for images based on thirst and nourishment as vehicles for expressing the symptoms and effects of love. Common too are processes whereby feelings are related to the body. Emotional turmoil and sorrow are experienced in the poet's very bones, blood, marrow and veins, the last of these being particularly prominent. The word 'venas' occurs on fourteen occasions in the love poetry. It has two principal associations or, to put it another way, it is mainly to be found in two, differing, contexts. In the cycle of poems to Lisi, with a single exception (no.485), it is present in sonnets where the poet praises his love and wonders at, even celebrates, his constancy. It occurs with these positive associations in two of the anniversary sonnets (nos. 471 and 491) and in the most eloquent example of this attitude: the sonnet 'Cerrar podrá mis ojos la postrera' ('The last [shadow] will close my eyes') (no.472).

Outside the series to Lisi, however, the poet makes the word 'venas' function in an unusual and distinctive manner on a number of occasions. Let us first consider one of a number of sonnets attacking love:

> Si tu país y patria son los cielos,
> ¡oh Amor!, y Venus, diosa de hermosura,
> tu madre, y la ambrosía bebes pura
> y hacen aire al ardor del sol tus vuelos;
>   si tu deidad blasona por abuelos
> herida deshonesta, y la blancura
> de la espuma del mar, y a tu segura
> vista, humildes, gimieron Delfo y Delos,
>   ¿por qué bebes mis venas, fiebre ardiente,
> y habitas las medulas de mis huesos?
> Ser dios y enfermedad ¿cómo es decente?
>   Dignidad y cárcel de sentidos presos,
> la dignidad de tu blasón desmiente,
> y tu victoria infaman tus progresos. (no.310)

If your country and homeland are the heavens, oh Love!, and your mother is Venus, goddess of beauty, and you drink pure ambrosia, and your flight fans the heat of the sun; and if your divinity boasts for grandparents a lewd wound and the whiteness of sea foam, and Delphi and Delos humbly moaned in your sure sight, why, then, do you drink my veins, burning fever, and inhabit the marrow of my bones? How can it be decent to be both a god and an illness? Dignitary and prison of captured senses, the dignity is belied by your shield, and your actions discredit your triumph.

The poem is based on a comparison, though unlike the sonnets on Tantalus (no. 294) and Orpheus (nos. 297 and 299), one in which the lover belittles rather than exaggerates his experience. Why should Cupid, descended from the gods, nourished on their food, an inhabitant of their lofty abode, pay attention to the hapless lover? Points of contrast are clearly established and rhetorically presented: if Cupid's native place is the heavens, why should he choose to dwell in the poet's marrow? If he can feed on ambrosia, why does he, like a fever or an illness, partake of the lover's blood? Quevedo does not use 'sangre' here, as might be expected in view of the verb 'beber', but 'venas' — the receptacle of blood. He thereby establishes a punning contrast between Cupid's mother, 'Venus', his original nourisher and the lover's 'venas', which now suprisingly are the god's source of sustenance. The verb 'beber' serves to clarify the conceit, connecting and contrasting Cupid's divine upbringing with his present inferior role, and thus reflecting the argumentative thrust of the sonnet.

The plausibility of such an interpretation can be confirmed by reference to other poems. There is an allusion to 'Amor' and 'venas' in the exasperated utterance directed at Cupid in a sonnet from *El Parnaso español.* I quote the quatrains:

> ¡Mucho del valeroso y esforzado,
> y viéneslo a mostrar en un rendido!
> Bástame, Amor, haberte agradecido
> penas, de que me puedo haber quejado.
> ¿Qué sangre de mis venas no te he dado?
> ¿Qué flecha de tu aljaba no he sentido?
> Mira que la paciencia del sufrido
> suele vencer las armas del airado. (no.341)

A lot of bravery and valour and you come to show it in one who is exhausted! It is enough for me, Love, to have thanked you for sufferings of which I could have complained. What blood from my veins have I not given you? What arrow from your quiver have I not felt? Note that the patience of the sufferer is apt to overcome the weapons of the aggressor.

Here there is an internal rhyme ('penas'-'venas') which underlines the relationship of Cupid ('Amor') with the lover ('penas') whose blood ('venas') is once more sought by the god of love. It is as though the lover's suffering were the god's life-blood, the cause of his existence; and, in the light of the 'venas-Venus' pun already perceived in one poem, one could hazard an interpretation which sees the lover's 'venas' as supplanting 'Venus', Cupid's mother, as a provider of blood (i.e., life).

Of interest too is the following attack on the god of love:

> ¿Tú, dios, tirano y ciego Amor? Primero
> adóraré por dios la sombra vana.

> Hijo de aquella adúltera profana,
> dudoso mayorazgo de un herrero;
>   viejo de tantos siglos embustero,
> lampiño más allá de barba cana;
> peste sabrosa de la vida humana,
> pajarito de plumas de tintero,
>   ¿dejas libre a Floralba, y en sus manos
> me prendes, donde ardiendo en nieve, enjugo
> mis venas con incendios inhumanos?
>   Si quieres coger fruto, dios verdugo,
> aprende a labrador de los villanos:
> que dos novillos uncen en un yugo. (no.327)

You, a god, tyrannical and blind Love? I will sooner worship as a god the vain shadow. Son of that profane adulterer, the doubtful heir of a blacksmith; a deceitful old man of so many centuries, soft-cheeked beyond the hoary beard; delicious plague of humanity, a little bird of inkwell plumes, do you leave Floralba in freedom and trap me in her hands where, burning in snow, I dry up my veins with inhuman conflagrations? If you want to pluck fruit, executioner god, learn from a peasant farmer: that two bulls are harnessed to a yoke.

The poet upbraids Cupid for failing to ensure that the beloved be as smitten by love as he is, although the metaphor employed in the final tercet is not a conventional one, such as darts or arrows, but a rustic one, in Price's words, 'a coarse analogy'.[29] Though the phrase 'coger fruto' is directed at Cupid, its erotic association is obvious and provides another instance of the evident carnal aspiration of the Quevedian lover. The quatrains take the form of a vehement demythification. Cupid's physical attributes are grossly ridiculed, while unflattering mention is made of his parentage: the son of an adulterous liaison, hence the 'dudoso mayorazgo' of the cuckolded Vulcan. Quevedo does not name these mythological figures but instead refers indirectly to them. Again there is an implied pun on Venus ('aquella adúltera profana') and 'venas' (l.11). The latter image is again associated with the intensity of the poet's suffering, caused by the thwarting of his amatory hopes. The pun thus embodies a contrast between a wanton Venus who succeeds in gratifying her desires, and the poet who cannot, though it is his clear goal.[30] The metaphor 'coger fruto' now appears more apt.

The semantic field involving the play on 'Venus' and 'venas' is broadened on four occasions by the inclusion of a related pun, one that alludes to Vulcan, Venus' husband. This particular punning relationship is a highly distinctive feature: the word 'volcán' ('volcano') occurs four times in Quevedo's love poetry; on *each* occasion the word 'venas' is juxtaposed. Ostensibly there is no connection between the words. Pozuelo Yvancos comments on the spatial or visual incongruity created by the juxtaposition in the case of one of the four occurrences (though he does not, apparently, notice how the feature is repeated): 'Estas asociaciones son poderosísimas, pues atraen el espacio amplio del volcán a estrecho canal de unas venas que terminan explotando de rabia' ('These associations are very powerful, as they attract the broad space of the volcano to the narrow channel of veins that end up by exploding with rage').[31] He describes the juxtaposition as a novelty; but more than that, it is a mannerism, indeed a habit. We can discount the alliteration produced by the initial consonants of the two words since this would be too insignificant to constitute an effect and thus to be a factor to account for the coupling. The image of the volcano is clearly linked to the Petrarchan commonplace of love as a fire, and is a more vivid and violent realization of that metaphor. The image conjured up is one of veins throbbing with the force of the lover's blood, and it makes for a powerful expression of unrequited and suppressed passion. But the decisive element in explaining Quevedo's consistent recourse to the coupling is the double pun whereby 'venas' = 'Venus' and 'volcán' = 'Vulcano'. Let us now consider some of the contexts in which these puns occur.

They are present in a sonnet from *El Parnaso español*:

> Arder sin voz de estrépito doliente
> no puede el tronco duro inanimado;
> el robre se lamenta, y, abrasado,
> el pino gime al fuego, que no siente.
>   ¿Y ordenas, Floris, que en tu llama ardiente
> quede en muda ceniza desatado
> mi corazón sensible y animado,
> víctima de tus aras obediente?
>   Concédame tu fuego lo que al pino
> y al robre les concede voraz llama:
> piedad cabe en incendio que es divino.
>   Del volcán que en mis venas se derrama,
> diga su ardor el llanto que fulmino;
> mas no le sepa de mi voz la Fama. (no.322)

Even the hard and lifeless tree trunk cannot burn without the strident sound of suffering; the oak laments, and the burnt pine, that cannot feel, whimpers in the fire. And you command, Floris, that my sensitive and living heart, an obedient victim at your altars, should be dissolved as a mute cinder in your ardent flame? May your fire grant me what the devouring flame allows the pine and the oak: it is proper for a divine conflagration to be merciful. Let the weeping I thunder express the ardour of the volcano that overflows in my veins; but may my voice be unknown to Fame.

In this poem, the lover strenuously refutes what he sees as the *amada*'s unreasonable demand for discretion and silence, as his direct and indignant questions reveal. The 'volcán-venas' conceit suggests an undeclared but overwhelming passion that threatens to break into an unburdening lament.[32] Here, as elsewhere, Quevedo creates a particular kind of tension: between convention or the reader's expectation and an individual register or rebellious voice. The topic of the lover's silence and discretion — a *sine qua non* of courtly and Petrarchist poetry — is challenged. There is that same note of rebelliousness here as there was in those sonnets on love, desire and renunciation discussed in the previous chapter. A parallel can also be established with the sonnet 'Si mis párpados, Lisi, labios fueran' (no. 448) where the constraints on the amatory relationship caused by the limited possibilities for communication are overcome by the bold and erotically motivated hypothesis. There are, admittedly, cases where silence is accepted as necessary, though even here, there is some evidence of a modification of the convention as in a sonnet to Lisi where the imperative of silence is counterbalanced by the necessity of expression, hence the dilemma caused by the conflicting claims of restraint and approach:

> ¿Cómo es tan largo en mí dolor tan fuerte,
> Lisis? Si hablo y digo el mal que siento,
> ¿qué disculpa tendrá mi atrevimiento?
> Si callo, ¿quién podrá excusar mi muerte?
>   Pues ¿cómo, sin hablarte, podrá verte
> mi vista y mi semblante macilento?
> Voz tiene en el silencio el sentimiento:
> mucho dicen las lágrimas que vierte. (no.451)

How is such a strong pain so long-lasting in me, Lisi? If I speak and state the ill I feel, what excuse will my boldness have? But how, without speaking to you, will my eyes and haggard face be able to see you? Feeling has a voice in silence: much is said by the tears it sheds.

What there is seldom, if ever, in Quevedo is that willing, unquestioning acceptance of the convention of silence and its transformation into a positive experience, as the almost devotional tone of the quatrains of the following sonnet by Villamediana reveals:

> ¡Oh cuánto dice en su favor quien calla,
> porque, de amar, sufrir es cierto indicio,
> y el silencio el más puro sacrificio
> y adonde siempre Amor mérito halla!
>   Morir en su pasión, sin declaralla,
> es de quien ama el verdadero oficio,
> que un callado llorar por ejercicio
> da más razón por sí, no osando dalla.[33]

Oh, how much does he who is silent say in his favour, because suffering is a sure indication of loving, and silence, the purest sacrifice wherein Love always finds merit. To die with one's passion, without declaring it, is the act of one who loves the true role, for the exercise of silent weeping gives a better account of itself by not daring to provide it.

A sonnet from the series to Lisi casts further light on the 'volcán-venas' coupling:

> ¿Ves con el polvo de la lid sangrienta
> crecer el suelo y acortarse el día
> en la celosa y dura valentía
> de aquellos toros que el amor violenta?
>   ¿No ves la sangre que el manchado alienta;
> el humo que de la ancha frente envía
> el toro negro, y la tenaz porfía
> en que el amante corazón ostenta?
>   Pues si lo ves, ¡oh Lisi!, ¿por qué admiras
> que, cuando Amor enjuga mis entrañas
> y mis venas, volcán, reviente en iras?
>   Son los toros capaces de sus sañas,
> ¿y no permites, cuando a Bato miras,
> que yo ensordezca en llanto las montañas?(no.497)

Do you see the earth rise up with the dust from the bloody struggle and the day grow shorter in the jealous and hardy courage of those bulls enraged by love? Do you not see the blood that the spotted one breathes; the steam that comes from the broad brow of the black bull, and the tenacious stubborness with which the enamoured heart is shown? Well, if you see it, oh Lisi!, why do you wonder when Love dries up my entrails, and my veins are a volcano that breaks out in anger? Are the bulls capable of their rage and you do not allow me, when you look at Bato, to deafen the mountains with my weeping?

Here the principal theme is jealousy and the idea that the rejected lover must accept his treatment uncomplainingly. As in the sonnet considered above (no.322), the beloved is questioned very pointedly about what the lover interprets as an unreasonable demand. He claims that it is only natural that he should express anger at what he considers an unjust slight. The image that forms the point of comparison — that of bulls — not only correlates the vehemence of the lover's rejection but also points very clearly to the nature of the emotions that he entertains which are carnal, if not lustful.[34] The idea of jealousy bears very much on the myth of Venus and Vulcan, punningly alluded to in the juxtaposition in the eleventh line, and particularly that aspect of the myth which concerns Vulcan as a wronged husband, cuckolded by Venus with several lovers, notably Mars. Jealousy, indignation and a sense of hurt pride are common to the lover's experience and to the mythological relationship referred to in the sonnet.

What emerges from J.M. Cossío's study of the myth of Vulcan is that the majority of Golden Age poets viewed the god as a figure of fun.[35] Quevedo himself reveals a similarly jocular attitude to cuckolds in various of his works and indeed treats Vulcan as a burlesque figure in two of his satirical poems.[36] But the view of Vulcan in the love poetry shows none of these traits even though a sardonic and burlesque approach towards Cupid and Venus and a process of demythification are prominent in some love poems. In two poems where the 'venas-volcán' coupling occurs, there is an indication of a degree of identification between the poet and Vulcan. In the case of the sonnet I have just considered (no.497), Pozuelo Yvancos draws attention to a close grammatical relationship whereby 'volcán' is in apposition to the understood 'yo'; indeed, he refers to a 'volcán-poeta' to emphasize this degree of identification, though he does not relate 'volcán' to Vulcan as I do.[37] The same syntactic isolation is to be found in another sonnet that has the coupling. This is in the nature of an occasional poem, wittily exploiting fire and snow metaphors that arise from Aminta's covering her eyes with her hand. Only the quatrains need be quoted:

> Lo que me quita en fuego, me da en nieve
> la mano que tus ojos me recata;
> y no es menos rigor con el que mata,
> ni menos llamas su blancura mueve.
>   La vista frescos los incendios bebe,
> y, volcán, por las venas los dilata;
> con miedo atento a la blancura trata
> el pecho amante, que la siente aleve. (no.306)

What the hand that hides your eyes takes away from me in fire, it gives back to me in snow; and the rigour with which it kills is not less, nor does its whiteness fan fewer flames. My eyes drink the fresh fires, and as a volcano it spreads them through the veins; the enamoured breast regards the whiteness with attentive fear, for it feels it to be treacherous.

The volcano image is in close relation to the poet's observation of the beloved's action and the beauty of her skin. The conceit derives from the idea of the eyes drinking in the fires (i.e., physical beauty arousing his passion). Here the grammatical link of 'vista' and 'volcán' through apposition relates to the lover in terms of his response ('beber', as so often) to a physical presence. Through the faculty of his sight, he is converted into a volcano.

The emotional or psychological implications underlying Quevedo's unique use of this punning relationship require some consideration because it amounts to a mannerism. One might, for instance, point to an autobiographical factor: the lameness common to Vulcan and Quevedo.[38] A particularly profitable line of inquiry is suggested by the fact that the name 'Vulcano' is totally absent in Quevedo's love poetry, despite the several punning allusions in conjunction with 'venas-Venus'. There thus seems to be a form of hidden association or identification. As we have already seen, the Quevedian lover's understanding of and reaction to suffering are distinctively bleak; the experience is one that affords little by way of consolation, for love is neither a blessed suffering nor an elevating emotion. The sense of hurt and of the lover being cheated, because love and its consequences are not for him what they may be for others, finds an appropriate image in the figure of Vulcan. Further, in several poems, Quevedo describes the lover and his aspirations not so much as an object or cause of indifference or scorn as one of mockery.[39] This adds to the idea of a persona much damaged by the consequences of his desires. The veiled nature of the allusions to Vulcan testifies to the dilemma of many poets: the conflicting requirements of poetry as an act of unburdening and purgation and of that psychological reserve that does not wish to reveal the most sensitive and painful areas of experience. It goes without saying that the dilemma is highly conducive to creativity.[40]

The question of motive needs also to be applied — less speculatively than my preceding observation on the myth of Vulcan — to the whole issue of the lover's suffering and its distinctive and intense treatment. There are two related questions here which have been partially answered, at least by implication, but which it is helpful to formulate at this juncture. Firstly, do Quevedo's departures from convention represent more than stylistic and linguistic independence or, in other words, is there a body of communicated experience that is substance not style? Secondly, why should suffering offer less by way of consolation or compensation to the lover in Quevedo's poetry than to his counterpart in the work of the poet's contemporaries? The answer broadly resides in this chapter and the preceding one taken together. There are causes and effects in the relationships between the lover's expectation, his frustration, and his concept of the beloved — the last-mentioned a factor to be developed in the next chapter. There is thus a wider area of amatory experience into which the view of suffering fits and in the context of which it needs to be understood. For example, it is possible to establish a parallel between the *extent* of the lover's carnal wishes and expectations (as outlined in the previous chapter) and the *extent* of his suffering — a consequence of the failure of specific aspirations. Desire and suffering therefore operate in direct proportion to each other. Suffering in love could be more readily accommodated into a purposeful pattern of experience if, for example, one of two conditions were to be fulfilled: either that desire be sublimated into a lofty and ultimately spiritual experience, or that the lover's amatory goal be less than physical union with his beloved. The failure of the Quevedian lover both to transcend physical desire and to compromise short of it corresponds to and, in large measure, accounts for similar shortcomings in his response to suffering. An illuminating insight, by way of concluding illustration, of how the lover in Quevedo's poetry differs in his response to his experience of unhappy love is provided by the theme of lost liberty: the lover looking back over his life and longing to return to a condition when he was free of love.

As a point of comparison, examples drawn from three other poets should prove representative. Poems like Herrera's *soneto* XL: 'Viví gran tiempo en confusión perdido' ('I lived a long time, lost in confusion'), where the lover succeeds in freeing himself from love and its harmful effects, are rare. More common is the depiction of an unequal struggle where the poet's recovery of liberty is seen as an unlikely or impossible goal. This struggle allows for great variety of approach and emphasis. In Herrera's *soneto* XXXIV, the lover endeavours only half-heartedly to renounce love and his failure is not unwelcome:

> Venció las fuerças el Amor tirano,
> cortó los niervos con aguda espada
> d' aquella dulce libertad amada,
> que sin vigor suspiro siempre en vano.
> Él me buelve i me trae por la mano
> a do mi error i perdición l' agrada;
> mas ya la vida, de su mal cansada,
> osa tornar s' al curso usado i llano:
> pero es flaca osadía, i con la muerte
> luchando, abraço alegre el dulce engaño,
> i me aventuro en el desseo i pierdo.
> Que yo no puedo ser al fin tan fuerte,
> que contraste gran tiempo a tanto daño;
> ni en tal terror me vale ya ser cuerdo. (p.67)

Tyrannical Love overcame my strength, and cut, with a sharp sword, the nerves of that sweetly cherished freedom for which, without strength, I always sigh in vain. He brings me back and takes me by the hand to the place where he is pleased by my error and perdition; but now my life, weary of its misfortune, dares to return to the accustomed and simple path: but this is but a feeble boldness, and struggling with death, I joyfully embrace the sweet illusion, and I venture into desire and am lost. For I cannot ultimately be so strong that I resist so much ill for long; nor in such a terror does it avail me now to be wise.

The sonnet is a particularly successful realization of the contradictions experienced by the lover and of his vacillations. Freedom, as he enjoyed it once, is sweet but not tempting, even if constantly half yearned for. His love is seen in terms of wrong moral action and a source now of weariness. The idea that he may return to his former way of life is but a feeble aspiration, however, and his perseverance in loving is a source of joy. The conclusion that an awareness of his plight ('cuerdo') is of no avail is not to be thought of as a tragic defeat, but more as a willing acceptance of suffering. The mood is melancholic and wistful.

In two sonnets by Lope de Vega, the emphasis is on the idea of love as a truancy or aberration, but also as infinitely desirable and ultimately unavoidable despite the poet's awareness of his moral deficiency. This is shown in the puns in the tercets of one of these sonnets. The lover hopes to isolate himself from the overwhelming temptations of love by his absence, but to no effect:

> Marcio, ausentéme y en ausencia un día
> miráronme unos ojos y mirélos,
> no sé si fue su estrella o fue la mía.
>   Azules son, sin duda son dos cielos
> que han hecho lo que un cielo no podía;
> vida me da su luz, su color celos.[41]

Marcio, I absented myself and one day, in my absence, some eyes looked upon me and I looked at them, I know not if it was her star or my lucky stars. They are blue, they are, without doubt, two heavens that have brought about what one Heaven could not; her light gives me life, its colour makes me jealous.

The contrast of 'dos cielos' (eyes) and 'un cielo' (heaven) is a pungent expression of the lover's moral defeat. In the other sonnet, there are references to a moral awareness and to an expectation that the poet will renounce love. But postponement becomes rejection as once again the lady's eyes overcome his good intentions:

> Ya vengo con el voto y la cadena,
> desengaño santísimo, a tu casa,
> porque de la mayor coluna y basa
> cuelgue de horror y de escarmiento llena.
>   Aquí la vela y la rompida entena
> pondrá mi amor, que el mar del mundo pasa
> y no con alma ingrata y mano escasa,
> la nueva imagen de mi antigua pena.
>   Pero aguárdame un poco, desengaño,
> que se me olvidan en la rota nave
> ciertos papeles, prendas y despojos.
>   Mas no me aguardes, que serás engaño,
> que si Lucinda a lo que vuelvo sabe
> tendráme un siglo con sus dulces ojos. (p.145)

I arrive at last with my pledge and my chains, holiest of disillusions, at your house, so that I may hang them, full of horror and as a warning at the base of the highest column. Here my love will place the sail and the broken mast, for the new image of my former suffering passes over the sea of the world not with an ungrateful soul and a meagre hand. But wait for me just a moment, disillusion, because I have forgotten about some papers, articles and spoils in the shattered ship. But do not wait for me, as you will be an illusion, for if Lucinda knows for what I return, she will detain me for a century with her sweet eyes.

In these two sonnets, the focus is on love as sweet but wrong; while in the Herrera sonnet it was on love as an acceptable suffering. The following sonnet by Lupercio Leonardo de Argensola provides a different slant:

> Temí, señora, con razón mi daño,
> cuando Amor con razón me persuadía,
> porque bien sospechaba que encubría
> con falso rostro algún efecto extraño.
> A tiempo el alma descubrió su engaño,
> mas no se resistió de parte mía;
> ni el áspero desdén con mano fría
> despertó, como suele, al desengaño.
> Entonces bien pudiera por ventura;
> agora no, que ocupa el otro extremo,
> rendida la razón, que estaba en medio.
> Ya perdí la esperanza de la cura,
> ya los consejos son lo que más temo,
> ya ni el mal es sufrible ni el remedio.[42]

I had every reason, lady, to fear for my misfortune when love persuaded me with reason, because he knew that I concealed with a false face some strange emotion. In time, the soul discovered its deceit, but for my part there was no struggle; nor did bitter scorn rouse me, as it usually does, with a cold hand to disillusionment. Once, indeed, I could fortunately do so; but now my defeated reason, which was in the middle, has gone to the other side. Now I have lost the hope of being healed, now the advice is what I fear most, and now neither the illness nor its remedy is tolerable.

Here the conclusion takes the form of a dilemma: love brings suffering but so would the removal of love, and if anything, the prospect of not loving is a bleaker one than that provided by the pain attendant upon loving.

In Quevedo's approach to the conflict between present suffering in love and past freedom from it, the predominant mood is exasperation and impatience. One sonnet alone could be considered unexceptional:

> Ya que no puedo l'alma, los dos ojos
> vuelvo al dulce lugar, donde, rendida,
> dejé mi antigua libertad, vestida
> de mis húmedas ropas y despojos.
> ¡Oh, si sintiera ya los lazos flojos
> en que tirano Amor la tiene asida,
> o el desengaño tardo de mi vida
> a su prisión burlara los cerrojos!
> A ti me fuera luego, y de tu techo
> las paredes vistiera, por honrarte,
> con duro lazo, por mi bien, deshecho.
> Mas hállome en prisión tan de su parte,
> ¡oh libertad!, que faltas a mi pecho
> para poder sin Fili desearte. (no.300)

Now that my soul no longer avails me, I turn my eyes to the sweet place where, in its weariness, I left my former freedom, clothed in my damp garments and my rags. Oh, if only I regretted the weak bonds with which Love has it in its grasp, or if only the belated disillusion of my life could mock the padlocks of its cell! Then I would go to you and I would clothe the walls, from the roof, in your honour, with the tight bond that has been released for my well-being. But I am so much a prisoner on her behalf, oh freedom!, that you are missing in my breast for me to be able to desire you without Filis.

This has a clear similarity with the second Lope sonnet quoted above: the easily defeated hope for disillusionment, seen as a good but unavailing intention in Lope and as no more than a hypothesis (ll.5-11) in Quevedo. There are also lexical similarities deriving from the poets' use of the same metaphor for freedom and disillusionment and activities related to them: the hanging of the spoils of the anticipated or hypothetical victory over passion on walls and from ceilings.[43]

In several other poems by Quevedo there is a different emphasis. As a rule, the argument is to the effect that if the lover enjoyed freedom from love, he would no longer have to endure the intense and unwelcome suffering. Unlike the lover in the sonnets by Herrera and Lope quoted above, he is motivated by an aversion to love as suffering rather than by an awareness of love as 'engaño': as a truancy or as an error. For him there is neither the experience of love as a pleasurable aberration nor as an acceptable and thus blessed suffering. A sonnet from the *Cancionero antequerano* provides a key to Quevedo's reaction in a particularly striking manner. I quote the quatrains:

> Piedra soy en sufrir pena y cuidado
> y cera en el querer enternecido,
> sabio en amar dolor tan bien nacido,
> necio en ser en mi daño porfiado,
>   medroso en no vencerme acobardado,
> y valiente en no ser de mí vencido,
> hombre en sentir mi mal, aun sin sentido,
> bestia en no despertar desengañado. (no.379)

I am a stone in suffering pain and love, and wax in tenderly loving, wise in loving such a well-born pain, a fool in being obstinate in my misfortune, a fainthearted coward in not overcoming myself and brave in not being overcome by myself, manly in feeling my misfortune, though it is senseless, a beast in not waking up disillusioned.

The poet's contradictory views of his experience in suffering are thrown into sharp relief by the semantico-structural pattern. The final line of the two quatrains stands in antithesis both to the preceding three lines and, more directly, to the immediately preceding line, thus highlighting the opposing attitudes: 'sabio-necio', 'hombre-bestia'. The implication here is that the lover is 'necio' and a 'bestia' *because*, from another viewpoint, he is 'sabio' and an 'hombre'. In other words, there is a causative as well as contrasting function between the third and fourth lines of both quatrains, for a close examination of what the poet criticizes so vehemently reveals that it is related to the notion of love as suffering: 'dolor tan bien nacido' (i.e., blessed suffering) and 'mal . . . sin sentido'. It is the fruitless, self-abnegating aspect of the experience of thwarted love that is being condemned. It is an illusion (1.8) in the sense of not being able to grant him the fulfilment that he seeks.

A similar impatience is discernible in a sonnet from *Las tres Musas* which has justifiably attracted critical attention:

> Dejad que a voces diga el bien que pierdo,
> si con mi llanto a lástima os provoco;
> y permitidme hacer cosas de loco:
> que parezco muy mal amante y cuerdo.
>
> La red que rompo y la prisión que muerdo
> y el tirano rigor que adoro y toco,
> para mostrar mi pena son muy poco,
> si por mi mal de lo que fui me acuerdo.
>
> Óiganme todos: consentid siquiera
> que, harto de esperar y de quejarme,
> pues sin premio viví, sin juicio muera.
>
> De gritar solamente quiero hartarme.
> Sepa de mí, a lo menos, esta fiera
> que he podido morir, y no mudarme. (no.360)

Allow me to shout aloud about the happiness I am losing, if I can incite you to pity with my weeping; and let me act like a madman, for I seem a very bad lover as I am sane. The net I break and the prison I bite, and the tyrannical rigour that I adore and touch are but little to show my suffering if I recall, to my misfortune, what I once was. Listen to me everyone: allow me at least, fed up of waiting and complaining, to die insane since I lived without reward. I want to have my fill only of shouting. Let this beast know of me, at least, that I managed to die and did not change.

Various commentators have pointed to the poem's lexical vigour and originality.[44] The surprising juxtaposition in the fourth line derives from the traditional view of the lover as one whose reason has been overcome by passion. Hence to speak of past freedom, to consider its loss as a misfortune greater even than the miseries of the demented lover is, in a sense, to betray the role. The lover's experiences should dominate, indeed exclude, other experiences. A wise man ('cuerdo') in this context cannot be anything other than an unrepresentative lover ('mal amante'). The key to the motive for the lover's backward glance at his lost freedom is to be found in the first tercet. Here again is a clear expression of exasperation. The tenth line has

> Mas después que te vi, señora mía,
> supe, siendo mortal, sujeto a muerte,
> hacer contra mí proprio un dios tan fuerte,
> que pone al cielo ley su valentía.
>   Supe de Amor, en el tormento y potro,
> después de darte victoriosas palmas,
> hallar en la afición para las almas
> el pasadizo que hay de un cuerpo a otro. (ll.41-8)

But after I saw you, my lady, though I am mortal and subject to death, I was able to establish against myself a god who was so powerful that his courage imposes law upon the heavens. In the torment and rack of love, after giving you the palms of victory, I was able to discover in the affection for the souls the channel that there is from one body to another.

But it is not this temporary fulfilment of desire that arouses thoughts of a time free of love — a contrast which would of course be motivated by a moral impulse — but the lover's plight as rejected lover. The anguished reaction provoked by thoughts of a happier past finds expression in an outburst reminiscent of a sonnet (no.360) considered above. In the *idilio* we read:

> haced que amando a Tirse viva amado,
> y que tratable de mi amor la vea.
>   Cuando de que me vi libre me acuerdo,
> cuya memoria en daño me redunda,
> por romperla, sacudo la coyunda,
> y la maroma, por soltarme, muerdo. (ll.15-20)

ensure that as I love Tirse I too am loved, and that I see her amenable to my love. When I remember that I was free, the memory of this redounds to my misfortune, and I shake the tether in order to break it and I bite the string to release myself.

The word 'tratable' is worthy of comment. Like 'comercio' and 'sueldo', it has mercantile associations and, by extension, carnal overtones, especially if Covarrubias' definition of the phrase 'muger de mal trato' as 'la que no es casta y recogida' ('she who is not chaste and modest') is borne in mind.

The remainder of the poem is concerned for the most part with another contrast, one that is not unusual in poetry of this period, namely that between innocence and the experience of love:

> Antes que te rindiera mis despojos
> y antes te mirara, gloria mía,
> yo confieso de mí que no entendía
> el secreto lenguaje de los ojos.
>   Pasaba el tiempo en ejercicios rudos,
> el oro despreciando y los zafiros;
> nunca les hallé lengua a los suspiros,
> porque pensé hasta agora que eran mudos. (ll.25-32)

> Before I surrendered my spoils to you and before I looked at you, my glory, I must confess, for my part, that I did not understand the secret language of the eyes. I spent my time in simple pursuits, scorning gold and sapphires; I never found an utterance for sighs because, until then, I thought they were mute.

But this is not love as an unconsummated desire, which is the poet's present reality. It refers to the period in the past when his love was returned. It is with this experience that the bitter-sweetness of love — an unusual oxymoron for Quevedo — is associated, as is also the poet's past fear that he might lose or renounce love:

> Jamás imaginé llegar a estado
> que temiendo le fuese concedido
> remedio a mi dolor, tan bien nacido,
> no le osase pedir desesperado. (ll.37-40)

> I never imagined that I should reach a condition where, fearing that a remedy be granted to my pain, so nobly born, I should not dare to request it, though I be in utter despair.

These are common features in Golden Age love poetry (e.g., Garcilaso's *Canción* IV), but they normally appear in the context of unrequited love. In the case of Quevedo's *idilio*, however, it is the fulfilment of the lover's desires that prompts such an understanding.

As a final observation, it is worth mentioning how, in his description of the joys and mysteries of a fulfilled love, the lover reveals emotions not often found in Quevedo's work. There is a note of tenderness in an inspired allusion to the lady's tears and their effect upon the lover:

> Y antes que viera del Amor las lides,
> nunca pude creer que se tornaba,
> en cada mujer débil que lloraba,
> cada pequeña lágrima un Alcides. (ll.33-6)

> And before I saw the struggles of love, I never could believe that every tiny tear in every fragile weeping woman would become a Hercules.

The experience of fulfilment seemingly brings with it an insight and a compassion rare in Quevedo, and there is a consequent enrichment of the poem's emotional fabric. The result is, moreover, entirely consistent with the poet's whole approach to suffering in love. For what is to be found in this poem, as in so many others, is no wallowing in sorrow, no resignation to fate, but an overwhelming sense of bewilderment and injustice at the rejection of his love. Feelings of tenderness cannot be associated with the denial of the poet's desires; only with their fulfilment do such feelings emerge. As the extraordinary lexical and stylistic resources of this and other poems reveal, the thwarting of the lover's deep-rooted and clear amatory aspirations is not tolerated; the prisoner of love does not languish, he lashes out.

1 Op.cit., 67.

2 In 'The Philosophy of Compositon', where he discusses the creation of his poem 'The Raven', Poe writes: 'Now, never losing sight of the object — *supremeness* or perfection at all points, I asked myself — "Of all melancholy topics what, according to the *universal* understanding of mankind, is the *most* melancholy?" Death, was the obvious reply. "And when," I said "is this most melancholy of topics most poetical?" From what I have already explained at some length the answer here also is obvious — "When it most closely allies itself to *Beauty*: the death then of a beautiful woman is unquestionably the most poetical topic in the world"'. *The Works of Edgar Allan Poe*, 8 vols. (Philadelphia, 1905), V, 187. The durability and transformations of the Romeo and Juliet story is a classic instance of the popular appeal of the same syndrome, as Erich Segal's best-seller, *Love Story,* has recently demonstrated. In a Radio Three programme on the music of Samuel Barber, responses were elicited from two performers of his music regarding his well-known *Adagio for Strings*: one reaction was that the music suggested love, the other that it was about death.

3 *Courtly Love in Quevedo*, 10.

4 *The Waning of the Middle Ages* (London, 1924); rpt. (Harmondsworth, 1965), 104.

5 See Roger Boase, *The Origin and Meaning of Courtly Love. A Critical Study of European Scholarship,* (Manchester, 1977), 109.

6 'La cárcel de amor, cuyo valor simbólico es evidente, con todas las penas que llevaba consigo, era preferible a la insulsa libertad disfrutada por los no enamorados'. Aguirre, ed.cit., 23.

7 Leonard Forster, *The Icy Fire* (Cambridge, 1969), 3.

8 *Fernando de Herrera* (2nd ed.) (Madrid, 1972), 475.

9 *Poesía española*, 514.

10 Op.cit., 301, 303.

11 Op.cit., 181, 183.

12 Ed.cit., 63.

13 See my article, 'Camões and Quevedo: Some Instances of Similarity and Influence', *Bulletin of Hispanic Studies*, LIX (1982), 106-8; and Dámaso Alonso, *Ensayos sobre poesía española,* (Madrid, 1944), 175-6.

14 See Jones, op.cit., 29-33.

15 *El* Beatus Ille *en la poesía lírica del Siglo de Oro* (Río Piedras, 1971), 78.

16 Art.cit., 838-9.

17 See, for example, the *Canção* IX by Camões.

18   Corrientes aguas puras, cristalinas,
            árboles que os estáis mirando en ellas,
            verde prado de fresca sombra lleno,
            aves que aquí sembráis vuestras querellas,
            hiedra que por los árboles caminas,
            torciendo el paso por su verde seno:
               yo me vi tan ajeno
               del grave mal que siento
               que de puro contento
            con vuestra soledad me recreaba . . .
          (Poesías castellanas completas, ed. E.L. Rivers (2nd ed.) (Madrid, 1972), 128.

19 Op.cit., 64.

20 *Obras*, ed. J.M. Rozas (Madrid, 1969), 158.

21 *Poesías*, ed. A. Zamora Vicente (Madrid, 1969), 8.

22   La mala hierba al trigo ahoga, y nace
en lugar suyo infelice avena;
    la tierra, que de buena
    gana nos producía
    flores con que solía
quitar en solo vellas mil enojos,
produce agora en cambio estos abrojos,
ya de rigor d'espinas intratable.
    Yo hago con mis ojos
crecer, lloviendo, el fruto miserable. (p.130)

23 See Pablo Cabañas, *El mito de Orfeo en la literatura española* (Madrid, 1948).

24 See J.G. Fucilla, 'Some Imitations of Quevedo and Some Poems Wrongly Attributed to Him', *Romanic Review*, XXI (1930), 229-32; and *Estudios sobre el petrarquismo en España* (Madrid, 1960), 201-9.

25 Compare a sonnet by Boscán that begins 'O gran fuerça d'amor, que assí enflaqueçes'. *Obras poéticas I*, ed. M. de Riquer, A. Comas and J. Molas (Barcelona, 1957), 199.

26 See Dámaso Alonso, *Poesía española, passim*, and Close's reservations on this view (art.cit., 844).

27 Art.cit., 843-5. Marino's sonnet opens thus: 'Vero inferno è 'l mio cor, che non attende'.

28 See Blecua, *Poesía original*, xcvi-xcvii.

29 Ed.cit., 105.

30 'Lust, the life of desire, is by far the most common interpretation of Venus in the Middle Ages . . . Venus represents the life of *voluptas*, desire, which Paris, the man of the senses, chooses over Juno, the active life, and Pallas-Minerva, the contemplative life or wisdom'. Joan M. Ferrante, *Woman as Image in Medieval Literature* (New York, 1975), 155.

31 Op.cit., 193.

32 Compare the close of Samuel Daniel's sonnet, 'These plaintive verse, the posts of my desire':
    These lines I use to unburden mine own heart;
    My love affects not fame, nor 'steems of art.
(*The Penguin Book of Elizabethan Verse*, ed. Edward Lucie-Smith (Harmondsworth, 1965), 78)

33 Ed.cit., 83.

34 See Green, *Courtly Love in Quevedo*, 12.

35 *Fábulas mitológicas en España* (Madrid, 1952), 888.

36 Nos. 680 and 709.

37 Op.cit., 193.

38 Quevedo's lameness was the source of much cruel humour for his enemies. A libel entitled *Al poema delirico de don Francisco de Quevedo* refers to him as 'Vulcano, de los cielos abatido, cojo de haber caído'. See Ayala, art. cit., 103. His comments on Quevedo's physical defects, the mockery they provoked and Quevedo's reaction to it lend support to the idea I develop here. I shall return to this issue also in the Conclusion.

39 See for example nos. 297, 358, 373, 390 (l. 58).

40 The peculiar problems confronting modern Spanish poets such as Lorca, Cernuda and Prados concerning their homosexuality and the transformation of their experience into poetry offers an interesting comparison.

41 *Poesías líricas I*, ed. José F. Montesinos (Madrid, 1960), 127.

42 Ed.cit, 54.

43 Compare Horace's Fifth Ode:
       . . . me tabula sacer
       uotiva paries indicat uuida
       suspendisse potenti
       uestimenta maris deo. (ll. 13-16)
   ('The votive tablet on the temple wall indicates/ that I have hung up my soaking clothes as a
   dedication/to the god that rules the sea.') See David West, *Reading Horace* (Edinburgh,
   1967), 100.

44 Kelley, op.cit., 72-3; Pozuelo Yvancos, op. cit., 185-7; Dámaso Alonso, *Poesía español,*
   545-6; Olivares, op.cit., 61-3.

45 In a note on the occurrence of the word in an *idilio* to Lisi (no. 509), González de Salas
   states that 'esta voz aquí tiene grande expresión de afecto'. See Blecua, *Poesía original,*
   537. Olivares states that 'hartar' is 'often a euphemism for sexual fulfillment' (op.cit., 62).

CHAPTER III

The Object of Love : Beauty

Nothing in the whole field of Renaissance love poetry would appear to offer less scope for distinctiveness than the description of the beloved. Pozuelo Yvancos refers to 'la petrificación del retrato en la tradición lírica cortesana' ('the petrification of the portrait in the courtly lyric tradition');[1] Leonard Forster speaks of the Petrarchist lady as 'physical and spiritual perfection' whose 'individual beauties can be added together to make an icon of perfection', while the lady's beauties were 'codified';[2] and Gary J. Brown sums up the task of the Renaissance poet in this regard as follows:

> The Renaissance poet seeking to praise his lady undertook a task that was founded upon a tradition of feminine encomium initially forged by the efforts of classical, troubadour, 'dolce stil novo', and Petrarchan poets. Such praise followed established conventions of imagery as well as the tenets of epideictic rhetoric. When Garcilaso, Herrera, Lope, Góngora, Quevedo, and their contemporaries descriptively praised their ideal ladies, they were well aware of the rhetorical nature of their exercise, and, reflecting the imitative canons of their epoch, they reacted just as much — or even more — to the examples of previous poets than to the actual beauty of the woman. As such, the laudatory sonnet, given its rhetorical design of praise for the purpose of inspiring admiration of beauty and emulation of virtue, necessarily imposed stylized roles upon the poet's speaking voice and addressee, encouraging an equally conventional response from the audience.[3]

From the above quotations, two points clearly emerge: that the mode of detailing the lady's qualities is a highly stylized one and that she represents an ideal of beauty, a symbol of perfection. In her study on the role of woman in medieval literature, Joan M. Ferrante refers to the lady of the courtly love lyric as a 'super-personification, the source and repository of all good qualities'.[4] But this unanimity in assessing the response of love poets of several centuries towards the object of their aspiration and praise should be qualified in the case of Spanish literature by remembering that the reference to the beloved — the expressive means of enunciating her qualities — underwent a significant change in the second quarter of the sixteenth century. While the *cancionero* poets praised the beauty of their *amadas*, they were unconcerned about detailing this beauty; in their verse they do not dwell on the lady's various physical attributes as do Petrarchist poets. In *cancionero* poetry, beauty is taken for granted and allusions to it are normally cursory, as the first two examples chosen by Green in his section on beauty in his study of the *cancioneros* reveal:

> Con la beldad me prendistes,
> con la gracia me robastes,
> con la bondad me feristes
> al punto que me mirastes.
>
> Vuestra beldad escogida
> causa que seays así,
> no queriendo, bien querida
> de muchos e más de mí.[5]

With your beauty you captured me, with your grace you stole me, with your
goodness you wounded me as soon as you looked at me.
Your perfect beauty is the reason you are thus, though you do not love, you
are much loved by many and most of all by me.

As important as beauty are the abstract qualities or the virtues of the
beloved and these figure prominently in the encomium. In the following
example from a poem by Hugo de Urries, entitled 'De la dama', the allusion
to physical beauty is but one factor in the poet's eulogy:

> Estrema gracia tenedes,
> e muy noble condición;
> los buenos vuestros facedes
> e los malos atraedes
> a conocer la razón;
> vos sois la pura virtut,
> vos sois la graciosidat. . .
> Linda sois e bien apuesta,
> sentida e moderada,
> e a quien se vos acuesta
> siemple dais sabia respuesta,
> e nunca vos cuesta nada. . .
> Divina sois, e humana,
> discreta e atrativa,
> gentil e mucho lozana,
> e no por cierto ufana,
> desdeñosa ni pasiva.[6]

You have grace in abundance and are most noble; you make the good your
own and draw the wicked to know reason; you are pure virtue, you are
grace. . . You are pretty and elegant, sensitive and restrained, and to the one
who approaches you, you always give a wise reply and it is never an effort for
you. . . You are divine and human, discreet and attractive, charming and most
proud, but not at all haughty, scornful or unmoved.

Even in what Green terms a 'picture' of some detail, from a poem by
Fernando de la Torre, the portrait is essentially one of abstract qualities.
What is stressed is the ennobling effect of the lady's attributes on the lover:
that her virtue encourages him to strive towards an equal level of moral
achievement. The poet is primarily a eulogist:

De nuevo soy amador
y amado segund creo,
de dona de grand aseo,
digna de mucho loor.
    Y digna de ser amada,
segund su mucha veldad,
y digna de ser loada
sobre todas en verdad. . .
    Y digna de ser querida
de gentiles amadores,
y digna de ser servida
su velleza por amores. . .[7]

Again I am a lover, and loved, or so I think, by a lady of great refinement,
worthy of the highest praise. And worthy to be loved as befits her great beauty,
and worthy, indeed, to be praised above all others. . . And worthy to be
courted by refined lovers, and whose beauty is worthy to be served by love. . .

The Petrarchist innovations can hardly be said to have made the *amada*
more real; that, in any case, was not the poet's aim. On the contrary, the
beloved has become more of an ideal, in a sense less human than the
beloved in *cancionero* verse. But she has become a detailed ideal whose
physical beauty is defined in a stylized and almost entirely metaphorical
fashion. The function of these metaphors is not the achievement of visual
realism, even though they derive from a visual inspiration, but eulogy. They
serve to convey the value and perfection that the lady represents; based on
physical beauty and expressed in concrete metaphor, they nonetheless
point ultimately to the same abstract emphases found in *cancionero* verse.
Such an approach and expressive process lend themselves readily to the
incorporation or discovery of a spiritual dimension: the Neoplatonic
tendency, latent already in Petrarch, was to be cultivated increasingly in
sixteenth-century poetry under the guidance of writers such as Bembo and
Castiglione. Thus apart from the common metaphors for merely physical
attributes such as hair, cheeks or skin, poets would focus on, for example,
the lady's eyes, which they would relate to both the physical and spiritual
sphere. Ortega y Gasset noted something of this phenomenon in poetry of
an earlier period, in the work of Dante, when he commented on the Tuscan
poet's mystical understanding of Beatrice's smile: 'Dante de la boca y la
pupila toma sólo la mística electricidad de la sonrisa que saluda. Esta
sonrisa que va a aparecer tantas veces en la obra posterior de Dante, este
disiato riso es la sonrisa gótica que perpetúan las oscuras vírgenes de
piedra en los portales de las catedrales europeas' ('Dante takes only the
mystical electricity of the welcoming smile from the mouth and the pupil.
This smile, which is to figure so much in the later work of Dante, this *disiato*

riso, is the Gothic smile perpetuated by the obscure stone Virgins in the hallways of European cathedrals').[8]

Two sonnets by Quevedo, juxtaposed by González de Salas in the first edition of the poet's work, reveal this same transcendental apprehension of the beloved's beauty (nos.333, 334). Their Neoplatonic affiliations are evident, as Pozuelo Yvancos has indicated.[9] The first conceives the lady's eyes as prime movers ('primeros mobles son vuestras esferas'):

> Las luces sacras, el augusto día
> que vuestros ojos abren sobre el suelo,
> con el concento que se mueve el cielo,
> en mi espíritu explican armonía.

The sacred lights, the auspicious day that your eyes open up on the earth, with the concord that heaven moves, they explain the harmony in my spirit.

while in the second, the mysterious beauty of the lady invites a mode of appreciation that goes beyond the visual and demands a more penetrating and spiritual insight:

> Esa benigna llama y elegante,
> que inspira amor, hermosa y elocuente,
> la entiende l'alma, el corazón la siente,
> aquélla docta y éste vigilante.
>   Los misterios del ceño y del semblante
> y la voz del silencio que, prudente,
> pronuncia majestad honestamente,
> bien los descifra mi respeto amante.

That benign and elegant flame that, by its beauty and eloquence, inspires love is understood by the soul and experienced by the heart, the former wise, the latter attentive. My respectful love deciphers well the mysteries of the frown and the countenance and the voice of silence which prudently utters a decorous majesty.

I differ, however, from Pozuelo Yvancos in my contention that such utterances are not as characteristic of Quevedo as he implies, just as the sonnets that express a Neoplatonic renunciation of physical desire are not numerous, and, in any case need to be interpreted carefully so that their full significance as poems is understood.

In the following sonnet by Herrera, there is a blend of Petrarchist description and Neoplatonic philosophy in the idealization of both the physical and spiritual attributes of the beloved:

> Ardientes hebras, do s' ilustra el oro
> de celestial ambrósia rociado,
> tanto mi gloria sois i mi cuidado,
> cuanto sois del Amor mayor tesoro.

Luzes, qu' al estrellado i alto coro,
prestáis el bello resplandor sagrado,
cuanto es Amor por vos más estimado,
tanto umilmente os onro más i adoro.
Purpúreas rosas, perlas d' Oriente,
marfil terso i angélica armonía,
cuanto os contemplo, tanto en vos m' inflamo;
i cuanta pena l' alma por vos siente,
tanto es mayor valor i gloria mía;
i tanto os temo, cuanto más os amo. (p.66)

Burning strands, where gold, moistened by celestial ambrosia shines forth, you are as much my glory and my concern as you are Love's greatest treasure. Lights, who lend the beautiful, sacred radiance to the starry and lofty choir, the more love is esteemed by you, the more humbly do I honour and adore you. Purple roses, pearls of the Orient, polished ivory and angelic harmony, the more I gaze upon you, the more I become inflamed by you, and the greater the suffering of my soul for you, the greater my achievement and my glory, and the more I fear you, the more I love you.

I wish to single out two features of this sonnet. Firstly, the repeated trend towards the spiritual experiencing of love. This is evident in the qualification of the lady's physical attributes: her hair is not only golden and seemingly aflame, but appears to the poet as 'de celestial ambrósia rociado'; while the Petrarchist enumeration of the attraction of her cheeks, teeth and neck in the first tercet is completed, not by a further physical or facial metaphor, but by the phrase 'angélica armonía'. In the second place, the lover's sadness and misfortune is offset by the mere experience of being able to contemplate this beauty (l.11), by a consequent awareness of its transcendental implication and by the poet's ability (if not duty) to celebrate the beloved's beauty. Hence the paradoxes: 'mi gloria sois i mi cuidado': 'cuanta pena. . . siente,/tanto es mayor valor i gloria mía'; 'tanto os temo, cuanto más os amo'.

By comparison, here is a sonnet to Lisi by Quevedo that, apart from an initial lexical similarity, is created along similar lines. It is an idealized Petrarchist portrait with Neoplatonic overtones:

Crespas hebras, sin ley desenlazadas,
que un tiempo tuvo entre las manos Midas;
en nieve estrellas negras encendidas,
y cortésmente en paz de ella guardadas.
Rosas a abril y mayo anticipadas,
de la injuria del tiempo defendidas;
auroras en la risa amanecidas,
con avaricia del clavel guardadas.
Vivos planetas de animado cielo,

por quien a ser monarca Lisi aspira,
de libertades, que en sus luces ata.
   Esfera es racional, que ilustra el suelo,
en donde reina Amor cuanto ella mira,
y en donde vive Amor cuanto ella mata. (no.443)

> Curly strands, untied with abandon, which once Midas held in his hands; black stars aflame in snow and courteously kept in her peace. Roses that bring forward April and May, protected from the ravages of time; daybreaks that dawn in her laughter, greedily retained by the carnation. Vital planets in a bustling sky, of whom Lisi aspires to be the monarch, of freedoms that she ties in her lights. She is a rational sphere that lights the earth, in which love reigns wherever she looks, and in which love lives wherever she kills.

The lady's facial beauties are listed conventionally, although the metaphors have become more precious and extravagant. The golden hair, the snow-white skin, the eyes like stars, the cheeks like roses and the carnation lips lead to an image that has a clear Neoplatonic association — the circling planets. The word 'luces' (l.5) was also present in Herrera's sonnet (l.11), but, unlike Herrera, Quevedo does not develop the spiritual aspect or allow it to predominate. On the contrary, Lisi's eyes are interpreted in a non-transcendental sense as snares to trap the lover — a common Petrarchist metaphor expressing enslavement by love. The final tercet, which sums up Lisi's beauty and its effect, likewise contains a cosmogonic metaphor (l.12) that hints at a concept of the beloved as a sublime and spiritual force. But the penultimate line is ambivalent: is 'Amor' a cosmic allusion or a reference to Cupid? This forms an effective transition to the courtly-Petrarchist antithesis of life and death in the last line, highlighted by the semantico-structural parallels with the previous line ('reina'='vive'; 'mira'≠'mata'). Ultimately the lady is not considered as a source of enlightenment and thus as an object of praise, as would be consistent with a Neoplatonic approach, and which, in view of the cosmogonic imagery, the reader would expect here. On the contrary, she is seen as the cause of extreme suffering, as a death-dealing agent. This denial of the transcendental, this turning-away from the spiritual, is a characteristic of Quevedo's love poetry, as is the way in which he seems to tease the reader by arousing an expectation only to disappoint it.

    There are at times in Quevedo's love poetry indications of a tendency to attach negative qualifiers to words or images that of themselves possess a positive and potentially spiritual connotation. Thus, in an occasional poem whose title — 'Quéjase del rigor de una hermosura, que no le miró por mirar a un hombre muerto que tenían en público para que le reconociesen' ('He complains of the coldness of a beautiful lady, who did not look at him because she was looking at a dead man laid out in public so he could be recognized') (no.404) — is an apt enough reflection of its frivolous character, the poet refers to the lady's eyes as 'belicosas luces' ('belicose lights') (l.43). Allusions to the *amada*'s eyes as stars or lights are common in Petrarchist-Neoplatonist poetry as an epitome of beauty; indeed in Herrera, they acquire a metonymic function, as evidenced by his predilection for pseudonyms such as Luz and Estrella. To attach the epithet 'belicosas' to the metaphor 'luces' is to contradict any lofty or transcendental implication; it offers a clear contrast to the 'luces sacras' ('holy lights') of the first line of one of the genuine Neoplatonic utterances (no.333). In a *canción* (no.395) from *Las tres Musas*, the effect of the lady's beauty is diametrically opposed to the connotations in the poems that see love as a spiritual and elevated experience. The lover compares his suffering to that of a man on his death-bed; his punishment resides in the cruelty of his mistress — an alternative to the visions of hell — and is ordained by her beauty, the cause of his particular hell:

> Y como aquel que expira,
> vecina la mortaja y sepultura,
> tristes visiones mira
> en mi muerte. Así ordena tu hermosura
> que vea tu enojo eterno
> en vez de las visiones del infierno. (ll.37-42)

And like the man who is dying, on the verge of his shroud and tomb, look at sad visions in my death. Your beauty thus ordains that I should see your eternal anger instead of the visions of hell.

As a further point of comparison with Herrera, I turn to a sonnet to Lisi, probably influenced by Góngora, in which the lover ponders on the beauties of his mistress in a miniature he carries in a ring:

> En breve cárcel traigo aprisionado,
> con toda su familia de oro ardiente,
> el cerco de la luz resplandeciente,
> y grande imperio del Amor cerrado.
> Traigo el campo que pacen estrellado
> las fieras altas de la piel luciente;
> y a escondidas del cielo y del Oriente,
> día de luz y parto mejorado.
> Traigo todas las Indias en mi mano,
> perlas que, en un diamante, por rubíes,
> pronuncian con desdén sonoro yelo,
> y razonan tal vez fuego tirano,
> relámpagos de risa carmesíes,
> auroras, gala y presunción del cielo. (no.465)

In a tiny cell, I have imprisoned, with all its family of burning gold, the gleaming circle of light and the great empire of Love enclosed. I carry the starry meadow where the lofty beasts of shining skin graze; and, hidden from the heavens and the Orient, a day of light and better birth. I carry the whole Indies on my hand, pearls that, in a diamond, through rubies, scornfully utter sonorous ice, and utter at times a tyrannical fire, crimson flashes of laughter, dawns, finery and the presumption of heaven.

The quatrains outline the radiance and sublimity of Lisi's beauty; again the point of reference is the cosmos, and the description is rich and the metaphors ingenious.[10] But whereas in the Herrera sonnet and in the sonnet to Lisi previously considered (no.443) the utterance was structured in such a way as to indicate a movement from a particular physical beauty to an universal understanding — a classic Platonic trend — here the reverse is true. After the celestial association of the second quatrain, it is as though the poet's gaze turned downwards. The focus changes to a terrestrial one as he compares Lisi's beauty to the Indies and details this by means of conventional Petrarchist metaphors, e.g., the reference to precious stones. There is a further change, too. As in the other sonnet to Lisi, the lady is seen, not as a source of praise and cause of rejoicing, but as a cruel and disdainful tyrant. There is in these poems a tendency analogous to the ambivalence encountered in the ostensibly Neoplatonic sonnets considered in Chapter I. In both cases there is a shrinking away from what appears conventionally prescribed, whether ennoblement or celebration.

It can be asserted with some confidence that, with the exception of a handful of sonnets to Lisi, Quevedo does not dwell on the spiritual potential of the lady's beauty, especially if we compare him with Herrera. Further minor exceptions are provided by two small groups of poems: the madrigals and the poems written in Castilian metres. In the former, the tone is mainly frivolous; the purpose of the poem is frequently to exploit a conceit or a paradox for wit and surprise, as my comments in an earlier chapter on one of these poems, 'El día que me aborreces, ese día' (no.410), will have revealed.[11] There are, however, in the madrigals, surprisingly perhaps, several descriptions of the beloved in ideal spiritual terms, though these are in no sense anything other than superficialities and clichés borrowed from Neoplatonism. One could cite the reference to the beloved's eyes as 'vivas luces' ('live lights') (no.405), allusions to her as 'mi sol divino' ('my divine sun') (no.414) and as 'luz clara del cielo, /firmamento que vives en el suelo' ('clear light of the sky, firmament, who live on the earth') (no.407); there is a description of how the lady gazing at her reflection in a mirror adds 'sol con tu cara, estrellas con tus ojos' ('sun with your face, stars with your eyes') (no.408). One would not seek to attribute to these phrases a density of meaning and seriousness equal to the spiritual earnestness of the two sonnets considered previously (nos.333,

334), although the preponderance of such expressions in what is arguably the lightest, least heart-felt part of Quevedo's amatory verse — occasional, even performance, poems — can be interpreted as more evidence of the unimportance of the spiritual vein in the love poetry.

Apart from his *romances,* Quevedo wrote only eight poems in traditional Castilian metres (nos.415-21, 441). As Close states, here Quevedo makes much use of *cancionero* style and topics and the mood is again, in her opinion, light-hearted.[12] But in this group too there is an emphasis on a spiritual concept of beauty that is generally absent from the sonnets and the longer poems in Italianate forms. One may quote a phrase such as 'hermosura celestial' ('celestial beauty') (no.421, l.12); the following passage from a poem in *quintillas* (no.415) that celebrates the beauty of the lady's eyes:

> Quien os ve, claras estrellas
> de amor, si humano se atreve
> a mirar luces tan bellas,
> no paga lo que las debe,
> si no se muere por ellas. (ll.26-30)

If a human being could dare to look at such beautiful lights, then whoever sees you, bright stars of love, does not pay his due to them unless he dies on their account.

and a more extended passage from a poem in *redondillas* (no.418), where the effect of the beloved's eyes is compared to the action of the sun on the clouds and earth beneath:

> ... me alumbran desde ese cielo
> los dos soles de tus ojos?
> Mas en todo se parecen
> tus luces a las de Apolo:
> que abrasan de lejos sólo
> y en su esfera resplandecen.
> Y con sus rayos lucientes,
> se levantan de la tierra
> las nubes que el aire encierra,
> la nieve y rayos ardientes.
> Que los sutiles vapores
> suben al fuego y se encienden,
> y en rayos vueltos descienden
> de las partes superiores. (ll.23-36)

... the two suns of your eyes illuminate me from that sky? But in everything, your lights resemble those of Apollo: for they only burn from afar and they shine in their own sphere. And with their glowing rays, the clouds enveloped in air, the snow and burning rays rise up from the earth. For the tenuous vapours climb to the fire and are set on fire, and, converted into rays, they descend from the upper regions.

This metaphor, together with the allusion to the reciprocal movement between earth and the sun ('se levantan. . . descienden'), recalls one of the inspired analogies of Aldana's *Carta para Arias Montano*, one of the great Neoplatonic meditations of the sixteenth century.[13]

What is also noticeable in these eight poems is that ideas such as the lover's renunciation of physical desire and the willing acceptance of constraints upon his aspirations occur frequently; among this handful of poems there are as a consequence numerous expressions of the paradox of blessed suffering.[14] These attitudes have been shown to be uncharacteristic of the lover in Quevedo's poetry. However, the coexistence in these eight poems of all these exceptional aspects of the nature, consequences and object of love relates to and confirms the reasons for the absence of the blessed suffering syndrome in Quevedo, i.e., that there are connections, causes and effects between the various strands that make up the total amatory experience. As an afterthought, it is of interest that Quevedo reserves his most conventional courtly-Petrarchist vein for poems written in the traditional indigenous forms, whereas the Italianate poems are, by comparison, more individual in their approach to common themes or topics. It is tempting to form a hypothesis whereby this distribution reveals that he viewed what could be termed mainstream Petrarchism — the Petrarchism of Garcilaso, Francisco de la Torre, Herrera, early Góngora — as an archaic element and associated it, aptly enough, together with the *cancionero* features Close refers to, with the older Hispanic verse-forms. The *romances* conform to this division in their adherence to a more conventional understanding and expression of experience and to a frequently frivolous atmosphere, though, as the previous chapters have shown, this is not without exception.

The theme of the lover's reason being overcome by the lady's beauty is a common one in Golden Age love poetry. In his first sonnet to Lisi, Quevedo gives it a characteristically negative slant:

> ¿Qué importa blasonar del albedrío,
> alma, de eterna y libre, tan preciada,
> si va en prisión de un ceño, y, conquistada,
> padece en un cabello señorío?
>   Nació monarca del imperio mío
> la mente, en noble libertad criada;
> hoy en esclavitud yace, amarrada
> al semblante severo de un desvío.

Una risa, unos ojos, unas manos
todo mi corazón y mis sentidos
saquearon, hermosos y tiranos.
   Y no tienen consuelo mis gemidos;
pues ni de su vitoria están ufanos,
ni de mi perdición compadecidos. (no.442)

Of what use is it to boast of free-will, of a soul that is eternal, free and so valued, if it goes in the prison of a frown and, defeated, suffers in an imperious strand of hair? My mind was born the monarch of my empire and brought up in noble liberty; today it lies in slavery, lashed to the harsh expression of her indifference. One laugh, those eyes, those hands, plundered with their beauty and tyranny the whole of my heart and my senses. And my moans are inconsolable; for those attributes of hers are neither proud of their victory nor compassionate with my defeat.

As both Kelley[15] and Close[16] have indicated, there is here a contrast between the greatness of the soul and the insignificance of the physical attributes responsible for its defeat. A sonnet by Camões, on which the Quevedo poem may well be based,[17] concludes positively by stating paradoxically that the glory of being overcome by such beauty offers the lover a victory greater than that of the lady, his vanquisher. I quote the tercets:

Mas porém, se vos tinha prometido
o vosso alto destino esta vitória,
ser-vos tudo bem pouco está sabido.
   Que posto que estivesse apercebido,
Não levais de vencer-me grande glória;
maior a levo eu de ser vencido.[18]

However, if your lofty destiny had promised you this victory, it is clear that it all means very little to you. For since it was predestined, you do not have much glory for being my vanquisher; I have the greater glory for being the vanquished.

Quevedo's conclusion, by contrast, is bitter. Not only is the lover defeated but, to rub salt in the wound, the *amada* takes no pleasure in her victory.

   Sonnets by Medrano and Lupercio Leonardo de Argensola provide further divergences from Quevedo's approach. The similarities between the two sonnets are evident. I cite Medrano's first:

Tus ojos, bella Flora, soberanos,
y la bruñida plata de tu cuello,
y ese, embidia del oro, tu cabello,
y el marfil torneado de tus manos,
   no fueron, no, los que, de tan ufanos
quanto unos pensamientos pueden sello,
hiçieron a los míos, sin querello,
tan a tu gusto vitorioso llanos.

> Tu alma fue la que vençió la mía,
> que spirando con fuerça aventajada
> por ese corporal apto instrumento,
>   se lançó dentro en mí, donde no avía
> quien resistiese al vencedor la entrada,
> porque tuve por gloria el vencimiento.[19]

It was not your sovereign eyes, beautiful Flora, and the burnished silver of your neck, and that hair of yours, envied by gold, and the curved ivory of your hands, no, not those that, as proud as thoughts can be, made my thoughts, unwillingly, so prone to your victorious pleasure. It was your soul, which, breathing with greater strength through that apt corporeal instrument, hurled itself into mine and overcame it, for there was no one to resist the conqueror's entry because I took defeat for victory.

> No fueron tus divinos ojos, Ana,
> los que al yugo amoroso me han rendido;
> ni los rosados labios, dulce nido
> del ciego niño, donde néctar mana;
>   ni las mejillas de color de grana;
> ni el cabello, que al oro es preferido;
> ni las manos, que a tantos han vencido;
> ni la voz, que está en duda si es humana.
>   Tu alma, que en tus obras se trasluce,
> es la que sujetar pudo la mía,
> porque fuese inmortal su cautiverio.
>   Así todo lo dicho se reduce
> a solo su poder, porque tenía
> por ella cada cual su ministerio.[20]

It was not your divine eyes, Ana, which handed me over to the yoke of love; nor the rosy lips, the sweet nest of the blind child, where nectar abounds; nor the cheeks of scarlet hue; nor the hair which is to be preferred to gold; nor the hands which have overcome so many; nor the voice which one may doubt to be human. Your soul, that is revealed in your deeds, is what was able to subjugate mine, so that its enslavement might be for ever. Thus all that has been said can be reduced to its power alone, because it administered each one itself.

The principal point of divergence between Medrano and Argensola on the one hand and Quevedo on the other is that in the former instances, it is emphasized that what was instrumental in engineering the lover's defeat was the soul of the beloved, and not her physical charms, considerable though these were. In both sonnets, the structure helps to create this emphasis: the notion that a moral or spiritual element is being challenged and eventually dominated by a superior force, but one that by its nature is similar. This is at the opposite extreme to the argument of the Quevedo sonnet, where an eternal spiritual attribute is unexpectedly conquered by seemingly trivial physical ones.

Another topic of Petrarchist poetry is that of the portrait of the beloved. According to J.M. Rozas[21] two themes were often associated with it: that no painter could be able to reproduce such beauty, and that the lady's beauty was indelibly imprinted on the poet's soul — the latter, an idea that has Neoplatonic overtones and one treated by Garcilaso in his *soneto* V ('Escrito 'stá en mi alma vuestro gesto') ('Your face is written in my soul') and by Villamediana in his sonnet 'Ofensas son, señora, las que veo' ('What I see, lady, are offences'):

> Sólo yo tengo aquel [traslado] tan peregrino
> en que el original no está agraviado,
> hecho en mi corazón por vuestra mano. (p.114)

> The only [copy] I have is that rare one in which the original is not spoilt, the one created in my heart by your hand.

In one of the few poems in which he deals with this topic, Quevedo explores neither of the areas mentioned above but develops the idea that the portrait is indistinguishable from the lady:

> Tan vivo está el retrato y la belleza
> que Amor tiene en el mundo por escudo,
> que, con mirarle tan de cerca, dudo
> cuál de los dos formó Naturaleza.
>   Teniéndole por Filis, con presteza,
> mi alma se apartó del cuerpo rudo,
> y viendo que era su retrato mudo,
> en mí volví, corrido con tristeza.
>   En el llevar tras sí mi fe y deseo
> es Filis viva, pues su ser incluye,
> con cuyo disfavor siempre peleo.
>   Mas su rigor aquesto lo destruye,
> y que no es Filis al momento creo,
> pues que de mí, mirándome, no huye. (no.364)

> So life-like is the portrait and the beauty that Love has as its shield in the world that, when I look at it so closely, I am unsure as to which of the two was shaped by nature. Taking it to be Filis, my soul speedily departed from the coarse body, and on seeing that her portrait did not speak, I returned to myself, confused and sad. It is the living Filis in that it carries my faith and desire after it, since it includes her essence, with whose disfavour I always struggle. But its rigour destroyed that idea, and, at the moment, I do not think it is Filis, as she looks at me and does not flee from me.

The overall intention is not to praise the lady's beauty; this factor appears only at the start of the sonnet. The tercets, in particular, are concerned with a different issue: that of possession and the lover's regret at the elusiveness of the *amada;* there is a suggestion that he responds vehemently to her attitude (1.11). This amounts to a divergence from the more conventional function of the portrait sonnet, which is primarily celebration. Even in anti-Petrarchist sonnets by Lope de Vega and Shakespeare, the eulogistic aspect still predominates.[22] Quevedo, however, shifts the focus from the beauty and attractions of the beloved to a preoccupation with the fulfilment of his own desires. Again, the reader is teased in that the poet arouses the expectation of a specific kind of development by his reference to a conventional vehicle — the portrait sonnet — only to surprise by contradiction or significant variation as here. A similar process is to be found in a sonnet, first published in the *Cancionero antequerano*, which, though not a true portrait sonnet, starts by paying homage to the beauty of the lady who steps into a river which serves as a mirror of her beauty:

> Tú, rey de rios, Tajo generoso,
> que el movimiento y calidad hurtaste
> al cuerpo de alabastro que bañaste,
> gentil en proporción, gallardo, hermoso. . . (no.378)

You, king of kings, fertile Tagus, who stole the movement and essence from the alabaster body, elegantly proportioned, graceful and beautiful, that you bathed. . .

But by the final tercet, the lover's emotional reaction has been put on an equal footing with the *amada*'s charms; it is as though they compete for the principal focus of the sonnet:

> ora, sueltas del hielo tus corrientes,
> le des espejo, sólo te suplico
> que, cuando quiera en ti ver sus despojos,
> junto con su hermosura representes
> mi llanto con que creces y estás rico:
> vean siquiera mis lágrimas sus ojos.

Now that your current is freed from the ice, all I ask you is that you give her a mirror so that, when she wishes to see her spoils in you, you reveal together with her beauty my weeping, with which you grow and are wealthy: let her eyes see my tears at least.

The final impression is not that of the lady as a motive for encomium, but rather as a source of desire and painful reminder that desire cannot be fulfilled — an attitude that also underlies the preceding sonnet (no.364).

In the treatment of the 'Carpe diem' or 'Collige virgo rosas' topic, there is not in Quevedo that mood of wistful melancholy and a celebration, whether poignant or ironic, of a fragile beauty, such as we find in Renaissance poets like Garcilaso, Ronsard and Góngora. In two sonnets (nos.304, 338), as Pozuelo Yvancos has demonstrated,[23] Quevedo departs radically from convention by inverting the perspective on time. Instead of evoking future decay from the standpoint of the present, he alludes to a fading or lost beauty and invites the lady to muse on present decline and past glory. A further unusual feature in Quevedo's treatment of the topic is the bitterness and sense of vengeance which characterize the lover's approach.[24] This is especially marked in an *idilio* (no.384), which obeys the normal temporal perspective and which Pozuelo Yvancos consequently does not discuss. The poem contains exhortations characteristic of the topic: the frequent use of the imperative 'goza' and the invocation for lover and beloved to fulfil their love before it is too late:

> Coronemos con flores
> el cuello, antes que llegue el negro día. (ll.61-2)

Let us crown our necks with flowers before the dark day arrives.

There is also, initially, a Petrarchist description of the beloved, such as we find in sonnets by Garcilaso and Góngora ('oro. . .trenzas, perlas . . . labios') ('gold . . . tresses, pearls . . . lips'). But the lover's attempt to persuade his mistress leads him to a bitter conclusion. He envisages a time when she will rue her former disdain:

> Y vendrá la triste hora
> en que, mustio el semblante idolatrado,
> que invidiaba la aurora,
> dirás: '¿Por qué en mi tiempo celebrado
> no tuve este deseo agradecido,
> o ya no tengo el rostro que he tenido?' (ll.31-6)

And the sad hour will come when, with your idolized face, once envied by dawn, now withered, you will say: 'Why, in the past when I was celebrated, did I not gratify this desire, or do I no longer have the face I once had?'

He muses on the prospect of being able to derive satisfaction from her future decay and misfortune. When she is at death's door, the lover, rejected in the past, will achieve a vengeful compensation. The double meanings of 'gozar' and 'paraíso' underline the turning of the tables:

> Pero cuando, obstinada,
> llegues a los umbrales de la muerte,
> si con la voz turbada
> me llamares, iré gozoso a verte;
> y Fabio gozará en tu paraíso,
> ya que no lo que quiere, lo que quiso. (ll.49-54)

But when, obstinate as you are, you reach the threshold of death, if you were to call me with a troubled voice, I shall go joyously to see you; and Fabio will take pleasure in your paradise, seeing that he no longer wants what he wanted once.

Earlier in the poem, too, in his description of the lady, the lover maliciously looks for premonitions of decline in her youthful beauty, in a spirit of animosity rather than of mere warning:

> En tu rostro divino
> ya se ven las pisadas y señales
> que del largo camino
> dejan los pies del Tiempo desiguales;
> y ya tu flor hermosa y tu verano
> padece injurias del invierno cano. (ll.13-18)

In your divine face there can be seen now the footsteps and the indications that the uneven tread of Time leaves on the long road; and now your beautiful flower and your summer suffer the ravages of hoary winter.

The telescoping of time here is reminiscent of Quevedo's extraordinary realizations in his moral and metaphysical poetry,[25] but in this case, it is prompted by a sense of exasperation and an inability or unwillingness to come to terms with thwarted amatory aspirations — an attitude characteristic of the lover in Quevedo's love poetry.

In this poem, Quevedo twice uses the image of winter to correlate the idea of the beloved's fading beauty. This is not an unusual metaphor in such contexts, as Garcilaso's 'Carpe diem' sonnet reveals,[26] though imagery based on snow and ice is also used greatly in love poetry to refer to aspects of the lady's beauty and attitude: her white skin and her coldness towards the lover. But the use of the word 'invierno' would not, of itself, connote beauty. The opening of this sonnet from *El Parnaso español* thus produces a sense of surprise:

> Hermosísimo invierno de mi vida,
> sin estivo calor constante yelo,
> a cuya nieve da cortés el cielo
> púrpura en tiernas flores encendida;
>   esa esfera de luz enriquecida,
> que tiene por estrella al dios de Delo,
> ¿cómo en la elemental guerra del suelo
> reina de sus contrarios defendida?
>   Eres Scytia de l'alma que te adora,
> cuando la vista, que te mira, inflama;
> Etna, que ardientes nieves atesora.
>   Si lo frágil perdonas a la fama,
> eres al vidro parecida, Flora,
> que siendo yelo, es hijo de la llama. (no. 328)

Most beautiful winter of my life, constant ice without summer heat, to whose snow the heavens kindly grant purple ablaze in soft flowers; how can that enriched sphere of light, which has as its star the god of Delos, reign protected from its enemies in the warring elements of the earth? You are the Scythia of the soul that adores you, when it inflames the eyes that look at you; the Etna that treasures burning snows. If your reputation would excuse the fragile association, you are like glass, Flora, for it is ice and yet an offspring of the flame.

With hindsight it can be seen that the winter metaphor in the first line is a piece of Petrarchist shorthand; the image is a condensed one that incorporates the ideas of disdain and beauty that the following lines clarify. But the initial impression is that 'invierno' is an unusual term of reference and address to the lady; indeed it has an ambivalence in that it is mainly used as a negative signifier, and this impression is not altogether dispelled by the explanatory phrases that follow. The second quatrain, however, has an unequivocal radiance in its comparison of the beloved to the sun and in its cosmogonic allusions. The uncommon metaphor, 'Scytia', probably alludes, because of the geographical remoteness of the place, to the beloved's distance from the aspiring lover.[27] The reference to Etna and its 'ardientes nieves' is complex. It can be seen as a version of the Petrarchist 'icy fire' oxymoron and it also serves to encapsulate the dominant and contrasting images thus far in the sonnet: winter (ice, snow) from the first quatrain and the sun from the second — a contrast alluded to in 'elemental guerra' and 'contrarios'. The conclusion is unexpected. The cold-heat or fire-ice contrast has been the main feature in the development of the poem, and this antithetical process is completed by the conceit whereby Flora, compared previously to Etna, is now compared to glass in that this, like the volcano, while seeming to be ice, is the product of fire. But this comparison, as the poet knows full well, is anything but flattering: 'si lo frágil perdonas a la fama'. But despite the poet's disclaimer, which suggests that the comparison is a source of decorative wit, the final tercet is not to be dismissed as mere ingenuity. It adds nothing to the praise of the lady's beauty or to her powerful effect upon the poet, but it is consistent with the ambivalent mood created by the winter metaphor in the first line, and it serves to enhance that ambivalence. The beloved, then, is compared initially to winter and ultimately to glass — neither conventional nor complimentary! It is reasonable to assume that here there is an attack on the beloved. Very often, the praise of beauty yields to a more pressing experience: the feeling of impatience with amatory circumstances that finds an outlet, in this case, in a deliberate ambiguity. Joan Ferrante's definition of the dual function of the lyric lady in courtly literature is worth quoting: 'She is an ideal being the poet adores, but she is also a real woman whom the poet wishes to possess, because his love is both sexual desire that seeks fulfillment in bed and mental yearning that finds its satisfaction in contemplating the image it has formed'.[28] In Quevedo, as in no other

Spanish poet of the Golden Age with the exception of Aldana, one is constantly reminded of this two-fold aspect — 'sexual desire' and 'mental yearning'; if anything, in his amatory work the former is rather more to the fore than the latter.

I have already drawn attention to Quevedo's recourse to terms associated with money and trading as metaphors for aspects of the amatory experience, notably 'sueldo' (no. 403) and 'comercio' (no. 448). Reference has also been made to the frequency of metaphors based on thirst and hunger as correlatives of sexual aspiration. The implied pun 'comer-comercio' links both signifiers and in like manner the appropriateness of the noun 'codicia' as a term embracing desire, appetite and avarice has been commented on by Robert ter Horst.[29] These three elements are encapsulated in a few lines from the *romance* (no. 440) that describes the lover's dream of consummation:

> Dime una hartazga de cielo
> en tan altas maravillas;
> maté la hambre al deseo,
> y enriquecí la codicia. (ll.41-4)

I got myself a fill of heaven with such lofty marvels; I killed desire's hunger and enriched my greed.

In another *romance*, the burlesque 'Alegórica enfermedad y medicina de amante' (no. 426), there is a clear link between desire, thirst and the desired object, the beloved described in Petrarchist terms as gold and precious metals:

> Témese de hidropesía
> mi ardiente sed, pues se aumenta
> y arde más, aunque mis ojos
> mares de lágrimas viertan.
>   Soles me han muerto, y también
> sereno de dos estrellas;
> mucha nieve en cuerpo y manos;
> mucho incendio de oro en trenzas.
>   Por beber yo con la vista
> en labios, coral y perlas,
> preciosa muerte me aguarda,
> después de rica dolencia. (ll.33-44)

My ardent thirst is afraid of dropsy, since it increases and burns more, even though my eyes shed seas of tears. Suns have killed me, and also, a clear sky with two stars; a lot of snow in body and hands; a lot of fire in golden tresses. Because I have drunk with my eyes at lips, coral and pearls, a precious death awaits me after a rich illness.

In the following fanciful *romance* (no. 423), there is a direct comparison between the lover who gazes on the lady's beauty and an avaricious merchant:

> Gaste el Oriente sus minas
> con quien avaro las rompa,
> que yo enriquezco la vista
> con más oro a menos costa. (ll.13-16)

Let the Indies waste their mines on him who, in his greed, destroys them, for I enrich my sight with more gold at less cost.

The conceit is achieved by the juxtaposition of the literal and metaphorical meaning of gold which, in the former instance, represents the object of the explorer's quest, and, in the latter, is the Petrarchist code-word for the beloved's hair which, metonymically, suggests her whole beauty.

The same comparison forms the basis of a sonnet to Lisi whose title ('Procura cebar a la codicia en tesoros de Lisi') ('He seeks to feed his greed on Lisi's treasures') contains the doubly significant term, 'codicia':

> Tú, que la paz del mar, ¡oh navegante!,
> molestas, codicioso y diligente,
> por sangrarle las venas al Oriente
> del más rubio metal, rico y flamante,
>   detente aquí; no pases adelante;
> hártate de tesoros, brevemente,
> en donde Lisi peina de su frente
> hebra sutil en ondas fulminante.
>   Si buscas perlas, más descubre ufana
> su risa que Colón en el mar de ellas;
> si grana, a Tiro dan sus labios grana.
>   Si buscas flores, sus mejillas bellas
> vencen la primavera y la mañana;
> si cielo y luz, sus ojos son estrellas. (no. 445)

You, oh navigator!, who disturb the peace of the sea in your greed and determination to bleed the veins of the Indies of their blondest metal, rich and brilliant, stay where you are; do not proceed further, glut yourself of treasures, quickly, where Lisi combs the slender threads that flame in waves on her forehead. If you seek pearls, her laughter proudly discovers more than Columbus in their sea; if it is scarlet, her lips could give scarlet to Tyre. If you seek flowers, her beautiful cheeks defeat the spring and the morning; if a sky and the light, her eyes are stars.

There is a clear parallel between this sonnet and one by Lupercio Leonardo de Argensola, which not only establishes a comparison between the lover and the gold-seeker, but which has an initial structural and rhetorical similarity:

¡Oh tú, que a los peligros e inconstancia
del mar te obligas, y en el viento esperas
ver del indio tostado las riberas,
y envuelta en sus arenas tu ganancia!
    Sin huir de tu patria tal distancia,
coger perlas finísimas pudieras,
si a Fili los divinos ojos vieras
tristes, vertiendo dellas abundancia.
    Pero no quiso Amor que avara mano
las viese, ni dejó llegar alguna
a parte donde ser robada pueda;
    que en su tesoro las encierra, ufano
de ver que aunque hoy más triunfe la fortuna,
esto, que es mucho, por ganar le queda.[30]

Oh you, who force yourself on to a perilous and unpredictable sea, and hope to see the shores of the sun-drenched Indies in the wind, and your profit buried in its sands! Without having to flee so far from your homeland, you could gather the finest pearls if you saw the divine, sad eyes of Filis shedding them in abundance. But Love did not wish that a greedy hand should see them nor did it allow a single one of them to get to where it could be stolen; for it encloses them in its treasure, proud to see that, although fortune triumphs most today, it still has this, which is much, left to obtain.

The metaphors of the lover as merchant, the beloved as gold or riches and the amatory experience as a hazardous sea journey constitute an allegory. The comparison is based on a common topic in moral poetry of the period: the scorn of wealth and ambition and an aversion to the dangers associated with them. These themes are to be found in poems as diverse as Luis de León's *Vida retirada* and Góngora's *Soledad primera*. The source is classical. Pindar, Catullus, Ovid and Horace all write of man's fatal fascination with the sea, often in connection with material ambition. The following passage from Horace's *Epistles* is particularly apt in the context of the Quevedo and Argensola sonnets quoted above:

inpiger extremos curris mercator ad Indos,
per mare pauperium fugiens, per saxa, per ignes:
ne cures ea, quae stulte miraris et optas,
discere et audire et meliori credere non vis?

You speed to the farthest Indies,/ A tireless trader, cross oceans and rocks and fire/ In your flight from poverty; will you not listen and learn/ And trust one wiser than you, till you cease to care/ For what, in your folly, you crave for now and admire?

In the same poet's ode, *Ad Pyrrham*, the sea journey is a metaphor for the poet's love-affair with Pyrrha, now ended, while he scoffs at his rival's ignorance of the sea and its dangers and, by analogy, of women and love:

> ... heu quotiens fidem
> mutatosque deos flebit et aspera
> nigris aequora uentis
> emirabitur insolens,
>   qui nunc te fruitur credulus aurea,
> qui semper uacuam, semper amabilem
> sperat, nescius aurae
> fallacis, miseri, quibus
>   intempta nites: me tabula sacer
> uotiva paries indicat uuida
> suspendisse potenti
> uestimenta maris deo.

Many's the time/he will weep because the gods have turned against him,/he will gasp at the black winds and rough seas:/little does he know./At the moment he is full of your golden beauty/he imagines you are always going to be at his service,/always loveable. He doesn't know that the wind changes./ I'm sorry for the poor devils/who are attracted by your radiance, but have no experience of it./The votive tablet on the temple wall indicates/that I have hung up my soaking clothes as a dedication/to the god that rules the sea. (See West, op. cit., 100-7.)

Among Spanish poets, Medrano, an accomplished and occasionally inspired imitator of Horace, makes much of passages that refer to mercenary ambition and the perils of seafaring. The final stanza of his *Ode* XII ('Ya, ya, y fierna y, 'ermosa') offers a clear parallel to both the Quevedo and Argensola sonnets:

> ¿Quién trocará, prudente,
> por quanto el Inga atesoró, el cabello
> de Amarili? ¿y por todo el rico Oriente?:
> quando ella tuerçe — ¡oh, cómo ermosa! — el cuello
> a mis ardientes besos, y, rogada,
> con saña fácil niega
> lo que ella, más que el mismo que le ruega,
> dar quisiera, robada.[31]

Who, if he is prudent, will exchange the hair of Amarilis for all the Inca's treasure? and for all the riches of the Indies? when she turns — oh, how beautifully! — her neck to my ardent kisses, and when asked, with ready anger denies what she, more than the very one who asks her, would wish to give, though it has been stolen.

It has a sensuality that is quite striking. Quevedo's sonnet, though less explicit, has something of this same quality. Whereas Argensola's sonnet has a certain coldness and an essentially spiritual orientation, Quevedo is more detailed in his evocation of the *amada*'s charms; the brief cameo of Lisi combing her hair hints at an intimacy that the Argensola sonnet lacks.

Beneath the Petrarchist facade there is an implicit voyeuristic pleasure. Additionally, the use of the blunt imperative, 'hártate', which, as so often, involves the idea of appetite and its satisfaction, suggests the extent of the lover's arousal by Lisi's action.[32]

The parallel between the lover and the gold-seeker is, of course, by no means unique to Quevedo, although nobody exploited as much as he the analogies between the two. The transformation of the Petrarchist metaphors for beauty from symbols of perfection and absolute value into concrete goals is consistent with Quevedo's concept of the lover's understanding of his experience and his approach to the beloved. This perceptible shift of emphasis in the poet-lover's response to beauty is borne out in the conceit that appears in a sonnet to Lisi which is a highly sophisticated, almost precious, realization of the Petrarchist code. It describes Lisi's hair and neck bedecked with carnations. I quote the quatrains:

> Rizas en ondas ricas del rey Midas,
> Lisi, el tacto precioso, cuanto avaro;
> arden claveles en su cerco claro,
> flagrante sangre, espléndidas heridas.
> Minas ardientes, al jardín unidas,
> son milagro de amor, portento raro,
> cuando Hibla matiza el mármol paro
> y en su dureza flores ve encendidas. (no.501)

You curl in rich waves of King Midas, Lisi, the touch that is as precious as it is greedy; carnations burn in her bright ring, flagrant blood, splendid wounds. When Hybla tinges the smooth marble and sees flowers ablaze on its hardness, burning mines, joined to the garden, are a miracle of love, a rare portent.

The conventional metaphor of gold is replaced here by 'minas', the location of gold. By qualifying it with 'ardientes' — as the flowers in Lisi's hair make it seem on fire — Quevedo creates a novel effect. Góngora's use of the 'minas' image is less cryptic than Quevedo's when, in his sonnet, 'Ya besando unas manos cristalinas', he refers to 'aquel cabello/que Amor sacó entre el oro de sus minas' ('that strand of hair that Love extracted from among the gold of his mines').[33] Quevedo omits the term linking hair and mines (i.e., gold) and the effect of the conceit he has created is to transfer the focus from the sheer golden beauty of the hair to an awareness of it as an object to be sought and possessed; or, in other words, from an object that is visually pleasing and a source of praise into one that is visually arousing (the double meaning of 'ardientes' is significant in this connection) and a source of desire. The reference to Midas, which has a phonetic resemblance to 'minas' (compare my remarks on 'venas-Venus' on page 54), underlines the idea of physical aspiration. The poet imagines the touch of Midas to be responsible for the golden colour of Lisi's hair, a hyperbole that has sensual suggestions with the implication of the lover passing his hands through the beloved's hair, or at least wishing he could do so. The adjective 'ardientes' and the phrase 'espléndidas heridas', which also has a double meaning — the visual effect created by the flowers and the metaphor of wounding alluding to the love-smitten poet — serve to involve the lover very much in the scene. The 'contemplative passivity' that Gary J. Brown sees as one of the stylized roles in the sonnet of enumerative praise is inapposite here,[34] while his characterization of sonnets of praise by Herrera and Góngora could be justifiably applied to the above sonnet by Quevedo: '[They] illustrate the dynamism that becomes possible in a sophisticated eulogy, and both exemplify the dramatic means by which poets managed to personalize a weakened tradition' (p.44). The abiding impression of the Quevedo sonnet is that of beauty as an object of specific passion rather than of detached praise.

The phrase 'ondas ricas del rey Midas' from the sonnet just considered is akin to the opening line of another, again to Lisi's hair: 'En crespa tempestad del oro undoso' ('In a curly storm of gold') (no.449). In this poem, the identification of the lover with Midas is more marked; the mythological king is one of no fewer than five such figures in apposition to the poet's heart ('mi corazón, sediento de hermosura') ('my heart, thirsty for beauty'):

> Avaro y rico y pobre, en el tesoro,
> el castigo y la hambre imita a Midas,
> Tántalo en fugitiva fuente de oro.

Greedy and rich and poor, in the treasure, the punishment and hunger, it imitates Midas, Tantalus in a fleeing fountain of gold.

Quevedo utilizes the Midas myth and the near-homophone 'minas' on a number of occasions in his amatory verse.[35] These repeated analogies and images for beauty and for the response that it provokes are not conducive to eulogy, but rather to an expression of the hazards experienced in the striving towards the goal of love — the possession of the desired object. The myth (Midas) and the conceit ('minas') bring to the forefront the notion of insatiable greed. Thus the merchant's lust for riches together with the metaphors of hunger and nourishment combine to create a complex and closely woven pattern of imagery that covers a broad semantic field. An entire amatory scenario can be envisaged: the beauty of the beloved arouses in the poet an intense but frustrated desire to possess her; it is analogous to the gold-seeker's frantic and perilous adventure in search of gold in distant mines; while the lover's discovery and contemplation of the lady's beauty recalls Midas — surrounded by the object for which he yearned, but thwarted in his desires for fulfilment. Both he and the lover remain 'hungry'.

But apart from providing more proof of the overt carnal aspirations of the lover in Quevedo's poetry, this summary also contains moralistic implications, and in view of Quevedo's constant utilization of images from the moral poetry relating to the futility of wealth, these implications have to be carefully considered. One connotation of the amatory-moral analogy is that gold (both literally and metaphorically) is neither an object of value and perfection nor a worthwhile cause for endeavour. It is a negative signifier that engenders a course of action that is reckless and vain. This intrusion by the moralist into the lover's apprehension of experience and of the object of his striving can be matched by the existence of a reverse process in Quevedo's moral poetry, where the moralist's field of reference is frequently invaded by diction and imagery drawn from the lover's experience.

For example, the myth of Midas appears in a moral sonnet where gold has a clearly pejorative significance:

> Si Venus hizo de oro a Fryne bella,
> en pago a Venus hizo de oro Fryne,
> porque el lascivo corazón se incline
> al precio de sus culpas como a ella . . .
>   En pálida hermosura, enriquecidas
> sus facciones, dio vida a su figura
> Fidias, a quien prestó sus manos Midas.
>   Arde en metal precioso su blancura;
> veneren, pues les cuesta seso y vidas,
> los griegos su pecado y su locura. (no. 102)

If Venus made beautiful Phryne of gold, Phryne made Venus of gold in return so that the lewd heart might lean to the cost of her sins as well as to her . . . Phidias, to whom Midas lent his hands, gave life to her shape in pale beauty and with enriched features. Her whiteness burns in precious metal; since it costs them their sanity and life, let the Greeks venerate her sin and their madness.

The comparison between the beauty of golden hair — in this instance, that of a courtesan, Phryne, who was the model for the statue of Venus — and gold as a source of greed is one that has been seen to occur frequently in the love poetry. The association of the courtesan with Venus is reminiscent of the view of the latter as wanton and lascivious in love sonnets referred to in the previous chapter. The idea of worshipping a golden image and the development of this idea in the conclusion, together with the notion of madness, bring to mind the courtly lover's occasionally blasphemous references to his lady. The allusion to Midas occurs in connection with the creation of the golden image. Just as in a love sonnet (no.443) the poet envisaged Lisi's hair passing through Midas' hands, whence their special quality, so here his touch is seen as contributing to the making of the statue.

If the link between gold as a metonym of the beauty of the beloved and as a source of avarice is borne in mind, then Quevedo's moral verse — whether phrases or complete poems[36] — has surprisingly frequent amatory associations. One could decode the reference in a moral sonnet to riches as 'rubia calamidad, púrpura ardiente' ('blonde calamity, burning purple') (no.61) in terms of an allusion to the lady's beauty. The phrase 'rubia calamidad' evokes the golden hair that leads the lover to his doom, as for instance in the sonnet 'En crespa tempestad del oro undoso' (no.449). The 'púrpura' image is employed quite commonly in Petrarchist love poetry to refer to the lady's lips, as for example in a sonnet to Lisi: 'tu labio,/ elocuente rubí, púrpura hermosa' ('your lip, an eloquent ruby, a beautiful purple') (no.501). The epithet 'ardiente' is unusual in this context, but it is a standard term of reference for passion (compare 'minas ardientes' in this respect).

In a moral sonnet on the futile and illusory nature of wealth, after the initial message, there is a line that has obvious amatory overtones and which may be compared to the phrase 'púrpura ardiente', considered above:

> Quitar codicia, no añadir dinero,
> hace ricos los hombres, Casimiro:
> puedes arder en púrpura de Tiro
> y no alcanzar descanso verdadero. (no.42)

What makes men rich, Casimiro, is the removal of greed, not the accumulation of money: you can burn in Tyrian purple and not attain a true repose.

Apart from the verb 'arder' and its clear amatory suggestion, the phrase 'púrpura de Tiro' has many echos in the love poetry, for example in a sonnet to Lisi where the intention is to stress the perils involved in her beauty: 'Doctas sirenas en veneno tirio/con tus labios pronuncian melodía' ('Learned sirens in Tyrian poison sing a song with your lips') (no.484); while in the sonnet that directly compares the lover and the merchant (no.445), there is, as we have seen, an explicit parallel: 'si [buscas] grana, a Tiro dan sus labios grana'.

The similarities between the moral and amatory verse remain even when the semantic field is broadened. The use of thirst as a symbol of desire, and dropsy as one of unfulfilled and insatiable desire, represents a distinctive feature of Quevedo's love poetry. The lust for wealth and gold is sometimes correlated by these symbols in the work of various poets. From Quevedo's verse, one could cite the final tercet of a sonnet on true and false riches:

> No creas fácil vanidad gallarda:
> que con el resplandor y el lustre miente
> pálida sed hidrópica del oro. (no.88)

> Do not believe an easy, graceful vanity: for, with its radiance and gloss, a pale, dropsical thirst for gold is deceiving.

The avarice of the gold-seeker is likewise described in the phrase, 'a tu codicia hidrópica obediente' ('obedient to your dropsical greed') (no.136, l.26). The idea of insatiability is conveyed also by the myth of Tantalus. The final tercet of the sonnet, 'En crespa tempestad del oro undoso' (no.449) interrelates the myths of Tantalus and Midas. The subject is 'mi corazón':

> Avaro y rico y pobre, en el tesoro,
> el castigo y la hambre imita a Midas,
> Tántalo en fugitiva fuente de oro.

As Midas suffered hunger as a part or as a consequence of his punishment, so did Tantalus. The gold that was the former's curse (hence 'rico y pobre') is the source (the beloved's hair) of the lover's varying emotions. It is finally incorporated into a description of the fountain desired by Tantalus to assuage his thirst.[37]

One of the most striking examples of the interplay between the literal and metaphorical meanings of gold is the elaborate and piquant parallel provided by the satirical *letrilla*, 'Poderoso caballero es don Dinero' ('Sir Money is a Powerful Gentleman') (no.660), a version of which appeared as early as 1603 in Espinosa's anthology, *Flores de poetas ilustres de España.*[38] Gold is personified as 'don Dinero' and, in a parody of a traditional genre (e.g., as represented by Góngora's *romancillo*, 'La más bella niña'), the lovesick girl confides in her mother. The satire is thus double-edged in that Quevedo, by this parody, draws attention to what he saw as the mercenary instincts of women.[39] The poem contains much play on the colour of gold ('amarillo', 'quebrado') and the names of coins ('doblón', 'real', 'blanca', 'cuarto') for effects of double meaning. From these, one might single out the phrase, 'porque en las venas de Oriente / todas las sangres son reales' ('because in the veins of the Indies, all blood is royal') for the parallel it affords with lines from a sonnet to Lisi:

> por sangrarle las venas al Oriente
> del más rubio metal, rico y flamante. (no.445)

The poem also contains a witty allusion to the Indies and to how the wealth obtained there brings no benefit to Spain, serving only to repay the debts incurred to Genoese bankers:

> Nace en las Indias honrado,
> donde el mundo le acompaña;
> viene a morir en España,
> y es en Génova enterrado. (ll.11-14)

He is born with honour in the Indies, where everyone attends him; he comes to die in Spain and is buried in Genoa.

Perhaps more than his contemporaries, Quevedo related the stock classical and Horatian topic of avaricious gold-seekers specifically to the rash enterprises of his fellow-countrymen. Quevedo's hostility to the conquest and exploitation of the New World is a strange blend of enlightenment and reaction. In poems like the 'Sermón estoico de censura moral' ('Stoic Sermon of Moral Censure') (no.145) and the celebrated 'Epístola satírica y censoria' ('Satirical and Censorious Epistle') (no.146) addressed to Olivares, the protest against the discovery of the New World is particularly shrill, while his whole work is dotted with scathing references to the Indies.[40] The predominance of such pejorative allusions is a feature that distinguishes Quevedo from his contemporaries and predecessors. One could contrast Aldana's evocative reference to the Indies at a high point of his *Carta para Arias Montano* as a jubilant, even ecstatic, metaphor for the soul's discovery and knowledge of God:

> ¡Oh grandes, oh riquísimas conquistas
> de las Indias de Dios, de aquel gran mundo
> tan escondido a las mundanas vistas![41]

Oh, the great, the richest conquests of the Indies of God, of that great world so hidden from the worldly gaze!

Together with the duplication of imagery and phraseology between the lover and the moralist mentioned above, and the ambivalence which has been detected in Quevedo's presentation of the lover's attitude to the lady, one is perhaps justified in viewing suspiciously the allusions to her as 'Indias'. It has already been shown (see page 80) how, in a sonnet to Lisi (no.465), the reference to the Indies represents what could be termed a descent from the celestial understanding of beauty to an essentially visual or terrestrial one. Other occurrences of the Indies metaphor in the love poetry are associated both with a flippant presentation of the *amada*'s charms (nos.429, 431) and, in one case, with an obscene connotation. This occurs in a *romance* (no.440) to which I have alluded several times, where the poet dreams he is making love to his mistress:

De beso en beso me vine,
tomándote la medida,
desde la planta al cabello,
por rematar en las Indias. (ll.49-52)

From kiss to kiss, I proceeded, to get the full measure of you, from your feet to
your head, and I finished off in the Indies.

An interesting postscript to my comments on the significance of the
metaphors of gold and the Indies is provided by Octavio Paz in an ingenious
socio-historical thesis which involves the formulation of what he terms a
'sun-excrement' duality.[42] Quevedo he sees as 'el poeta excremental'
(p.33) — an interpretation subsequently pursued by Goytisolo[43] — by
contrast with Góngora whom he describes as 'el poeta solar'. Of direct
relevance to this chapter is the fact that Paz does not go to Quevedo's
burlesque works for illustration, but instead selects the love sonnet quoted
above, in which the lover contemplates a portrait of the lady in a ring. This
poem prompts Paz to hazard the following interpretation of gold — wealth
of the Indies and symbol of the Petrarchist lady alike: 'El oro del Nuevo
Mundo y su brillo infraterrestre de letrina ciclópea pero asimismo el
resplandor intelectual del erotismo neoplatónico: la amada es luz, Idea. En
este relámpago grabado arden la herencia petrarquista y el oro de los ídolos
precolombinos, el infierno medieval y las glorias de Flandes e Italia, el cielo
cristiano y el firmamento mitológico con sus estrellas, flores que pacen "las
fieras altas de la piel luciente" ' ('The gold of the New World and its
subterranean brilliance of a Cyclopean latrine but, at the same time, the
intellectual splendour of Neoplatonic eroticism: the beloved is light, Idea.
In this picture of lightning there shines the Petrarchist inheritance and the
gold of the pre-Columbine idols, the hell of the Middle Ages and the glories
of Flanders and Italy, the translucent sky and the mythological firmament
with its stars, flowers that are pasture for the "lofty beasts of shining skin"')
(pp.33-4). And below, directly comparing riches and excrement, he writes:
'Para Swift el excremento es un tema de meditación moral; para Quevedo,
una materia plástica como los rubíes, las perlas y los mitos griegos y
romanos de la retórica de su época. El pesimismo de Quevedo es total: todo
es materia para el incendio' ('For Swift, excrement is a subject for moral
meditation; for Quevedo, plastic matter, like the rubies, pearls and the
Greek and Roman myths of contemporary rhetoric. Quevedo's pessimism
is total: everything is material for the inferno.') (p.34).

Paz's imaginative interpretation represents, I would suggest, more an
intuitive grain of truth than a tenable view of the motives underlying
Quevedo's treatment of common metaphors for beauty; it is part of a much

broader frame of reference and necessarily involves the use of provocative generalization. But his insight is not invalid. Something of the negative side clearly emerges in the lover's approach to the beloved and in his descriptions of her; there is not that total respect which is conventionally prescribed for the expression of this aspect of amatory reality. As this chapter has shown, there are, variously, irreverence, indignation and exasperation, deriving mainly from the motive behind the lover's attitude. It is possession, not praise, that determines the approach, and this leads to a variation in, or even distortion of, the conventional vehicle of eulogy. The apparent intrusion of the moralist, both in specific and implicit parallels,[44] suggests that the pursuit of love and beauty is not worthwhile — an attitude that on closer examination is not based on a moralist's aversion to love, despite the terminology and imagery, but on a lover's anger at having his aspirations rejected, hence the negative rationalization of the beloved and the pursuit of desire. This process is reminiscent of Juan Ruiz's denunciation of love in the *Libro de Buen Amor (Book of Good Love)* — an attack motivated by failure in love, as Don Amor quickly realizes, rather than by moralistic considerations.

A final thought. At the opening of his study on Quevedo's love poetry, Green rejects the views of various critics who speak of a transformation, if not a revolution, in the nature of love and in the approach to woman in Baroque or seventeenth-century literature. He takes exception to claims that the Baroque woman was no longer surrounded by 'una exquisita aureola de distancia' ('an exquisite halo of distance') and that 'love, supposedly, had been emptied of its ideal content'. Perhaps in the light of observations made in this and preceding chapters, one may wonder whether these critics are as far as Green believes from discovering the essence and motive at least of Quevedo's love poetry.[45]

1 Op. cit., 119.

2 Op. cit., 9.

3 'Rhetoric in the Sonnet of Praise', *Journal of Hispanic Philology*, I (1976-7), 34-5.

4 Op. cit., 66-7

5 'Courtly Love in the Spanish Cancioneros', 81.

6 Quoted by Aguirre, ed. cit., 59.

7 'Courtly Love in the Spanish Cancioneros', 50-1.

8 *Estudios sobre el amor* (11th ed.) (Madrid, 1970), 19; see also 178-9: 'En el siglo XIV,

Dante resume siglo y medio de "cortesía" cuando de Beatriz desea sólo el gesto, que es la carne cuanto expresa alma. A Dante le enamora la sonrisa — el *disiato riso* — de la mujer exemplar, que es para él "fin y perfección del amor"'.

9 Op. cit., 77-80.

10 See Crosby's analysis of this sonnet in *Poesía varia*, 251-2. Olivares (op. cit., 67-70) pays particular attention to the use of metaphors and conceits in the poem.

11 In my article, 'Concerning the Authenticity of Two Madrigals Attributed to Quevedo', *Bulletin of Hispanic Studies*, LXI (1984), 483-90, I discuss the stylistic and structural features of Quevedo's madrigals.

12 Art. cit., 836.

13   Puede del sol pequeña fuerza ardiente
desde la tierra alzar graves vapores
a la región del aire allá eminente,
   ¿y tantos celestiales protectores
para subir a Dios alma sencilla,
vernán a ejercitar fuerzas menores? (ll.118-23)
(*Poesías*, ed. E.L. Rivers (Madrid, 1957), 61.)

14 Nos.415, (l.10), 417 (ll.16-20), 418 (l.61), 419 (ll.11-12), 421 (ll.3, 31-2, 38-9, 49).

15 Op. cit., 70-1.

16 Art. cit., 841-3.

17 See my article, 'Quevedo and Camões', 115-16.

18 *Obras completas I*, ed. Hernâni Cidade (3rd ed.) (Lisbon, 1962), 194.

19 *Vida y obra de Medrano II*, ed. Alonso and Reckert (Madrid, 1958), 23.

20 Ed. cit., 59-60.

21 See Villamediana, *Obras*, 114.

22 See Lope's sonnet 'Bien puedo yo pintar una hermosura' (ed. cit., 168) and Shakespeare's sonnet 'My mistress' eyes are nothing like the sun'.

23 Op. cit., 209-21.

24 Ibid., 211, 220.

25 Notably the sonnets that begin '"¡Ah de la vida!" . . . ¿Nadie me responde?' (no.2) and '¡Fue sueño ayer; mañana será tierra!' (no.3).

26 Compare his *soneto XXIII*:
     coged de vuestra alegre primavera
el dulce fruto antes que'l tiempo airado
cubra de nieve la hermosa cumbre.
              (ed. cit., 59)

27 The name Scythia was applied to very different countries or regions at different times. Though Herodotus understood Scythia to comprise the south-eastern part of Europe, between the Carpathian Mountains and the River Don, he believed the Scythians to have been of Asiatic origin and that they were driven out of their Asian homeland by the Massagetae.

28 Op. cit., 67.

29 'Death and Resurrection in the Quevedo Sonnet: "En crespa tempestad"', *Journal of Hispanic Philology*, V (1980-1), 41-9.

30 Ed. cit., 57.

31 Ed. cit., 131-6.

32 Compare the use of the related noun ('hartazga') in a passage from the *romance* (no.440) that describes fulfilment in a dream:
Dime una hartazga de cielo
en tan altas maravillas;
maté la hambre al deseo,
y enriquecí la codicia. (ll.41-4)

33 *Sonetos completos*, ed. Biruté Ciplijauskaité (Madrid, 1976), 125.

34 Art. cit., 39.

35 For example, nos.313, 429, 431, 443, 449, 501. The incidence is more significant if it is borne in mind that the Midas myth is not one of the more popular ones for poets of the time. It is not included in Cossío's encyclopaedic survey as a consequence.

36 Notably 'A una mina' (no.136), 'Exhortación a una nave nueva al entrar en el agua' (no.138), and 'El escarmiento' (no.12). I shall refer to the last-named in some detail in Chapter 5.

37 In his sonnet, 'A Tántalo', Juan de Arguijo also likens Tantalus' punishment to the condition of a miser. The final tercet has a clear lexical affinity with Quevedo's sonnet:
¿Cómo de muchos Tántalos no miras
ejemplo igual? Y si cudicias uno,
mira al avaro en sus riquezas pobre.
See *Obra poética*, ed. Stanko B. Vranich (Madrid, 1971), 61.

38 Both the 1603 and the revised versions are printed and discussed by Crosby, *Poesía varia*, 87-93.

39 Compare his *Cartas del Caballero de la Tenaza, Obras satíricas*, 72-90, especially, 81-4; and the sonnet in dialogue form between a *galán* and his lady (no.586) where the latter deflates the Petrarchist compliments of her suitor: 'el oro en bolsa, y no en cabellos rojos'..

40 See Valentín de Pedro, 'América en la genial diversidad de Quevedo', *América en las letras españolas del Siglo de Oro* (Buenos Aires, 1954), 169-84.

41 Ed. cit., 67.

42 *Conjunciones y disyunciones* (Mexico City, 1969), 27-40.

43 'Quevedo: la óbsesión excremental'.

44 The love poetry of Herrera offers evidence of a similar procedure when he relates the amatory experience to a patriotic or heroic level by the use of terminology that belongs to both. See Oreste Macrí, op. cit., 475.

45 *Courtly Love in Quevedo*, 3. On the basis of his analysis of another Quevedo sonnet (no.358), Olivares also refers to a 'change in the conception of the woman in the literature of that period' (op. cit., 77). It has to be admitted, though, that there is much evidence to the contrary, notably in the sonnets of Villamediana, whose idealism and sparse manner recall the works of Boscán and the *cancionero* poets.

CHAPTER IV
The Greatest Love: Lisi

Efforts to discover the identity of the various *amadas* named in Quevedo's love poetry constitute perhaps the most unsatisfactory part of critical approaches to his work. The aim is a misguided one; the outcome is, at best speculative, at worst fanciful, and, in any case, muddled. This approach relates to critical misconceptions concerning a poet's sincerity and a consequent desire to interpret poetry in terms of biography: to see it as a reflection rather than as a transformation of experience. The errors arising from this simplistic approach are compounded in the case of Quevedo by a dearth of information on his relationships with women. What may be true for Lope and half-true for Garcilaso cannot be tested with Quevedo. But what condemns this approach more than anything is the rationale on which it is founded. One need neither appeal to the Renaissance understanding of the function of a poem nor point to the anachronistic nature of terminology such as sincerity, artificiality and originality.[1] To read any poem primarily as a biographical statement and to analyse it accordingly as a *roman à clef* is to misunderstand crucially its role.[2]

As an illustration of the pitfalls that can occur in a biographical analysis, I refer to Green's observations on the *amada*, Floris, who, he claims, represents La Ledesma, Quevedo's mistress.[3] Apart from the flimsy biographical evidence, the poems themselves, both to Floris and in the larger *Flor*-group provide little joy to the *roman à clef* analyst. On the contrary, one can extrapolate a strikingly conflicting datum: that the poems allegedly addressed to Quevedo's mistress and mother of his children are not among the small number of poems that refer to the fulfilment of love;[4] but two of Quevedo's 'dream' poems are to Floralba and Floris respectively (nos. 337, 440) while a third such poem has no named addressee (no. 365). Floralba or Floris is thus the name chosen for poems that speak of a frustrated desire that finds an outlet only in a world of dreams — a contradiction that cannot be easily explained in a biographically centred exegesis.

Roger Moore is rightly sceptical about Green's identification of Floris as La Ledesma.[5] Interesting in the light of some of my previous observations is Moore's suggestion that the poems in the *Flor*-group have a tendency to a 'certain vulgarity' and to make use of 'double-edged compliments' (p. 14). These are features that I have argued might be termed characteristically Quevedian, though they are by no means confined to this group where there is, besides, a larger number of conventional utterances than Moore implies.[6] In the case of the poems to Lisi, however, Moore himself falls into the biographical trap, particularly in his attempts to discover real dates to match the twenty-two years of the relationship, mentioned in one poem (no. 491).[7] His suggestion that Quevedo loved Lisi from 1623 to 1645 departs from the generally accepted view of Astrana Marín, who suggests an earlier period.[8] Neither case has much to recommend it and, as I stated above, such an approach, in any case, begs the question. More attention has been focussed on the identity of Lisi. Astrana Marín's claim that she is Luisa de la Cerda of the Medinaceli family has been regarded with suspicion,[9] though a surprisingly large number of commentators have accepted and even developed this hypothesis. In his whimsical study of Quevedo, Ramón Gómez de la Serna takes this view to an extreme in a fictional reconstruction of Quevedo's courtship of Doña Luisa: 'Sólo se sabe que aquella amada se llamó Luisa de la Cerda, de la Casa de Medinaceli — casa de su asiduidad y predilección — , y se le ve rondarla, verla asomada a las ventanas del gran palacio de la Carrera de San Jerónimo, acercarse a ella en sus salones, quejoso y alabancioso a un tiempo, aunque durante veintidós años estuvo calabaceado y la muerte vino a hacer irreparable tan largo "no"' ('All that is known is that that lady was called Luisa de la Cerda of the House of Medinaceli — a house that attracted his close attention and interest — and he can be seen frequenting it, to see her appear at the windows of the great palace on the Carrera de San Jerónimo, or approaching her in her salons, both complaining and boastful, but for twenty-two years he was cold-shouldered and death came to make the consequences of such a long refusal irredeemable.').[10] Another critic has suggested that Lisi was the French Queen, Isabel de Borbón, daughter of Henry IV and wife of Philip IV.[11] Moore's appeal that 'due to the lack of evidence, the discussion should be discontinued' (p.16) should not fall on deaf ears; speculations about Lisi's identity have been irrelevant and distracting.

I turn to the more fruitful matter of defining the nature of the emotions conveyed in the poems themselves. One question that suggests itself is whether the approach to the amatory experience and to the beloved is notably different in this part of Quevedo's output. Is Lisi conceived in such a way as to distinguish her as poetic creation from, say, Aminta, Tirsi or Floralba?

A number of commentators, among them Dámaso Alonso and Manuel Durán,[12] are of the opinion that the emotions expressed in the Lisi cycle are of a Platonic nature. The former compares the poems to Lisi with those to Flora and sees in both groups 'una ascensión platónica desde la belleza particular hacia lo bello absoluto y eterno' ('a platonic ascent from a particular beauty towards absolute and eternal beauty');[13] while 'la pasión por Lisi fue platónica no cabe dudarlo' ('there can be no doubt that the passion for Lisi was platonic') (p.514). It was 'una muestra de galante vasallaje a una gran dama, a la que la respetuosa pasión que los versos expresaban nunca podía ofender, sí siempre halagar' ('the display of gallantry by a vassal to a great lady, who could never be offended, but, on the contrary, always flattered by the respectful passion expressed in his poetry') (p.514). It is true, admittedly, that there is a greater proportion of what could be termed Neoplatonic utterances in this section than in the love poetry as a whole, but, as my previous observations will have implied, there are many points of contact between the Lisi cycle and other love poems in the matter of ethos. Poems to Lisi figured prominently in my analysis of the lover's approach to love and the beloved. I drew attention on several occasions to the veiled but intense physical aspiration expressed in the sonnet, 'Si mis párpados, Lisi, labios fueran' (no. 448). Robert ter Horst in an analysis of the next poem in *El parnaso español*, 'En crespa tempestad del oro undoso' (no.449), suggests that it has a far greater sexual significance than hitherto considered.[14]

One could also point to the way in which Quevedo invests an occasional sonnet, in which he describes the lover envying a child asleep in Lisi's lap, with a boldness that the source, a sonnet by Luigi Groto, lacks.[15] Groto's sonnet contrasts the child's weeping with that of the lover, in the latter instance, a conventional allusion to the disappointment of unrequited love. The lover envies the child, who is the recipient of his mistress's kisses:

> Invidiato fanciullo, a cui concessi
> Sono i baci di quella, ch'amo tanto.

> Envied child, to whom are granted the kisses of her whom I love so much.

Quevedo's sonnet similarly makes use of a jealousy conceit, but expresses a more overt carnal yearning than does its model:

> Descansa en sueño, ¡oh tierno y dulce pecho!,
> seguro (¡ay cielo!) de mi enojo ardiente,
> mostrándote dichoso y inocente,
> pues duermes, y no velas, en tal lecho.
>   Bien has a tu cansancio satisfecho,
> si menor sol, en más hermoso Oriente,
> en tanto que mi espíritu doliente
> de invidia de mirarte está deshecho.
>   Sueña que gozas del mayor consuelo
> que la Fortuna pródiga derrama;
> que el precio tocas que enriquece al suelo;

que habitas fénix más gloriosa llama;
que tú eres ángel, que tu cama es cielo,
y nada será sueño en esa cama. (no.477)

Rest in sleep, oh sweet and gentle breast!, certain (oh Heaven!) of my ardent anger, as you show yourself to be happy and innocent, since you sleep and do not stay awake in a bed such as this. You have truly satisfied your weariness, though a lesser sun in a more beautiful Orient, while my grieving spirit is shattered as it enviously looks at you. Dream that you enjoy the greatest recompense that bountiful fate can bestow; for you touch the prize that enriches the earth; for you, a phoenix, dwell in the most glorious flame; for you are an angel, for your bed is Heaven, and nothing will be a dream in that bed.

Rather than focus on the lady comforting the child with kisses, Quevedo repeatedly refers to the idea of her lap providing the child with a bed. Were this to be the lover's bed, however, it would not be a place for sleep or dreams. The obviousness of his aspiration can also be seen in the allusion to touching (l.11), where the metaphor of wealth is yet again to be found; and in euphemisms such as 'mayor consuelo' and 'cielo' whose sexual connotation is beyond doubt; while the rhyme words pointedly and ironically contrast the child, privileged but innocent ('pecho', 'lecho', 'satisfecho'), with the aspiring but thwarted lover ('deshecho'). In all, the sonnet has that urgent note of frustrated longing so characteristic of Quevedo.

It has already been shown how, both in a sonnet to Flor (no.344) and in one to Lisi, 'Con la comparación de dos toros celosos, pide a Lisi no se admire del sentimiento de sus celos' ('With the comparison of two jealous bulls, he asks Lisi not to wonder at his feelings of jealousy') (no.497), the poet had used bulls as a means of expressing passion and outrage. Dámaso Alonso's observation concerning the lover's vassal-like respect to Lisi and his wish never to offend has to be qualified if this sonnet is borne in mind. Similar reservations are caused by a 'Carpe diem' sonnet to Lisi in which Carlo Consiglio detected 'una suerte de maliciosa intención':[16]

En una vida de tan larga pena,
y en una muerte, Lísida, tan grave,
bien sé lo que es amar, Amor lo sabe;
no sé lo que es amor, y Amor lo ordena.
　　Esa serena frente, esa sirena
para mayor peligro, más süave,
¿siempre escarmientos cantará a mi nave?
¿Nunca propicia aplaudirá a su entena?
　　¿No ves que si halagüeñas tiranías
me consumen, que, mustio, cada instante
roba tu primavera en horas frías,

> y al ya rugado y cárdeno semblante,
> que mancillan los pasos de los días,
> no volverá a su flor ni amor ni amante? (no.469)

In a life of such prolonged suffering, and in such a grievious death, Lisi, I know full well what it is to be in love, and Love knows it; I do not know what love is, and Love ordains it to be so. Will that serene brow, that siren, sweeter to imperil me the more, always sing its warnings to my ship? Will it never propitiously applaud my mast? Do you not see that if alluring tyrannies consume me, that each withered moment steals your Spring in cold hours, and neither love nor the lover will return to flower the now wrinkled and livid face, tarnished by the steps of time.

The poem is implicitly reproachful. There is no exhortation to the beloved to enjoy the pleasures of love as in the carefree *canción*, 'Llama a Aminta al campo en amoroso desafío' (no.389), which I considered in an earlier chapter. The first quatrain, stark and straightforward in expression, makes it clear that any invitation to love would be pointless. The second quatrain confirms this impression; in particular, the pun 'serena'-'sirena' hints at the poet's failure and dissatisfaction. The former epithet suggests radiance and tranquility, but this is offset by the word, 'sirena', with its associations of peril and doom — a characteristic effect of deflation as we have seen above. The tercets are gloomy; the diction and phraseology is reminiscent of some of Quevedo's most pessimistic utterances on the passing of time in his moral and metaphysical poetry. Compare the first part of a sonnet entitled 'Arrepentimiento y lágrimas debidas al engaño de la vida' ('Repentance and Tears due to Life's Deceit'):

> Huye sin percibirse, lento, el día,
> y la hora secreta y recatada
> con silencio se acerca, y, despreciada,
> lleva tras sí la edad lozana mía.
>   La vida nueva, que en niñez ardía,
> la juventud robusta y engañada,
> en el postrer invierno sepultada,
> yace entre negra sombra y nieve fría.
>   No sentí resbalar, mudos, los años . . . (no.6)

The day slowly, imperceptibly, flees and the secret, hidden hour approaches in silence, and takes away with it my vigorous life that it scorns. The new life, which burnt in childhood, the sturdy and deceived youth, lie buried in the final winter between dark shadows and cold snow. I did not perceive the years slip silently away . . .

The sonnet to Lisi, then, has something of the bitterness of the 'Carpe diem' poems considered in the previous chapter.

Frustration and exasperation come to the fore in this sonnet from the cycle:

Alimenté tu saña con la vida
que en eterno dolor calificaste,
¡oh Lisi!, tanto amé como olvidaste:
yo tu idólatra fui, tú mi homicida.
    ¿Cómo guarecerá fe tan perdida
y el corazón que, ardiente, despreciaste?
Siendo su gloria tú, le condenaste,
y ni de ti blasfema ni se olvida.
    Mas para ti fabricará un infierno
y pagarán tus ansias mis enojos,
pues negaste piedad al llanto tierno.
    Arderán tu victoria y tus despojos;
y ansí, fuego el Amor nos dará eterno:
a ti en mi corazón, a mí en tus ojos. (no.467)

I nourished your anger with a life that you placed in eternal pain, oh Lisi!, my love was as great as your neglect. I was your worshipper, you, my killer. How can a faith that is so doomed be preserved, and the burning heart that you so despised? Although you were its glory, you condemned it, and it neither curses nor forgets you. But it will manufacture a hell for you and your anguish will pay for my vexations, since you refused pity to my tender weeping. Your victory and your spoils will burn; and thus Love will grant us eternal fire: for you in my heart, for me in your eyes.

The emotional argument is broadly similar to that in the 'Carpe diem' sonnet. The rejected lover reproaches his lady for her neglect and indifference, contrasts this hostility with his devotion and, somewhat indignantly, questions her behaviour towards him. The upshot is a desire for revenge. Unwilling, as so often, to accept his suffering, the lover meditates on the prospect of the beloved's death when she will burn in hell. This is a hell of the poet's making, seemingly, as the subject of 'fabricará' is 'corazón' and she is punished for being the agent of the lover's death in life. The spirit of these tercets looks forward to the bitter mood of Bécquer's *rima* XXXVII ('Antes que tú me moriré'), where the jilted lover anticipates a confrontation with the beloved after death. I quote the last three stanzas:

Entonces que tu culpa y tus despojos
la tierra guardará,
lavándote en las ondas de la muerte
como en otro Jordán;

allí donde el murmullo de la vida
temblando a morir va,
como la ola que a la playa viene
silenciosa a expirar;

allí donde el sepulcro que se cierra
abre una eternidad . . .
¡Todo lo que los dos hemos callado
lo tenemos que hablar![17]

Then the earth will preserve your guilt and your spoils, washing you in the waves of death like in another Jordan; there, where the murmur of life goes trembling to its death, like the wave which comes in silently to expire on the shore; there, where the closing sepulchre opens an eternity . . . All that we both have left unsaid, we shall have to discuss!

Worth recalling also in connection with an examination of the variety of the lover's response to Lisi are the sonnets that detail her beauty (nos.443, 445, 501), in which a certain ambivalence of approach was discernible.

It is in the cycle to Lisi that we find the most anguished questioning of the value of human love in the whole of Quevedo's amatory verse. In two sonnets, the lover speaks of the suffering, futility and error of his life or, to preserve the metaphor employed in these poems, his journey through love. The governing emotion is disillusionment and regret:

¡Qué perezosos pies, qué entretenidos
pasos lleva la muerte por mis daños!
El camino me alargan los engaños
y en mí se escandalizan los perdidos.
　　Mis ojos no se dan por entendidos;
y por descaminar mis desengaños,
me disimulan la verdad los años
y les guardan el sueño a los sentidos.
　　Del vientre a la prisión vine en naciendo;
de la prisión iré al sepulcro amando,
y siempre en el sepulcro estaré ardiendo.
　　Cuantos plazos la muerte me va dando,
prolijidades son, que va creciendo,
porque no acabe de morir penando. (no.475)

What weary feet, what lingering steps does death bear for my misfortunes! The deceits prolong my path and even the damned are scandalized by me. My eyes pretend not to catch on; and in order to misdirect my disillusionments, the years conceal the truth from me and keep my senses in slumber. With birth I came from the belly to the prison; from the prison I shall go to the tomb loving, and I shall be burning in the tomb for ever. All the postponements that death is granting me are prolixities that it increases so that I may not finish dying of grief.

Cargado voy de mí: veo delante
muerte que me amenaza la jornada;
ir porfiando por la senda errada
más de necio será que de constante.

Si por su mal me sigue ciego amante
(que nunca es sola suerte desdichada),
¡ay!, vuelva en sí y atrás: no dé pisada
donde la dio tan ciego caminante.
　　Ved cuán errado mi camino ha sido;
cuán solo y triste, y cuán desordenado,
que nunca ansí le anduvo pie perdido;
　　pues, por no desandar lo caminado,
viendo delante y cerca fin temido,
con pasos que otros huyen le he buscado. (no.478)

I am weighed down with myself: ahead I see death that threatens my journey; to continue persistently along the wrong road will be folly rather than constancy. If, to his detriment, a blind lover should follow me (for misfortune is never unaccompanied), ah!, let him come to his senses: let him not step where such a blind traveller placed his feet. See how wayward my path has been; how lonely and sad, and how disordered, for a lost foot never trod it like this; so, in order not to retrace the steps I have taken, and as I see the feared end directly ahead, I seek it with steps from which others have fled.

The poet concludes both sonnets by stating that he will continue to love, but this is not the voice of a lover defiantly or triumphantly asserting itself over the moralist but rather one of bleak helplessness and resignation to fate. The spirit of 'escarmiento' is evident in both these sonnets (no.475, l.4; no.478, ll.3-8), as it is in the first tercet of a sonnet that marks the sixth anniversary of the poet's first sight of Lisi:

Atrás se queda, Lisi, el sexto año
de mi suspiro: yo, para escarmiento
de los que han de venir, paso adelante. (no.461)

The sixth year of my lament remains behind, Lisi: I carry on, as a warning to those who are to come.

This notion of the lover's unhappy and futile, not to say foolish (see no. 478, ll.3-4), experience serving as a deterrent to others is not one that we find outside the Lisi cycle. As a point of comparison, a sonnet from *Las tres Musas* begins in such a way as to suggest that it could develop into an expression of regret at the folly of love:

Por la cumbre de un monte levantado,
mis temorosos pasos, triste, guío;
por norte llevo sólo mi albedrío,
y por mantenimiento, mi cuidado.
　　Llega la noche, y hállome engañado,
y sólo en la esperanza me confío;
llego al corriente mar de un hondo río:
ni hallo barca ni puente, ni hallo vado.

> Por la ribera arriba el paso arrojo;
> dame contento el agua con su ruido;
> mas en verme perdido me congojo.
> Hallo pisadas de otro que ha subido;
> párome a verlas; pienso con enojo
> si son de otro, como yo, perdido. (no.363)

Along the peak of a lofty mountain, I sadly lead my fearful steps; as a lodestar I only have my free-will, and for nourishment, my love. Night arrives and I find myself deceived, and I trust in hope alone; I reach the flowing tide of a deep river: I find neither boat nor bridge, nor do I find a ford. I cast my steps up along the shore; the noise of the water is pleasing; but I am distressed at being lost. I discover the steps of someone else who has climbed; I stop to see them; I wonder angrily if they are of another who is as lost as I am.

The situation described in this sonnet has a clear affinity with the two sonnets to Lisi: the lover is a weary traveller through a hostile terrain. However, in the eighth line, a change of emphasis is seen. It clearly hints at the lover's frustration, his inability to proceed further or to any effect, on his journey through love. The sound of the flowing water is pleasing initially in that it reminds him of love, or even promises it, but the realization that he has lost his way — that he cannot cross the water (a significant symbol!) — provokes feelings of evident exasperation ('me congojo', 'pienso con enojo'). It is thus the failure, not the folly, of love that the lover bemoans.[18] If Lisi inspires the greatest love in the lover-persona in Quevedo's poetry, which by dint of the number of poems and by the duration of the relationship she would seem to do, she is also a cause of greater questioning about the value of the amatory experience and a motive for more searching self-examination than any of the other *amadas*.

Of the portrayal of Lisi little need be said: nothing in Quevedo's conception of her distinguishes her from the other ladies. Rather than representing a single woman, she is an amalgam of women or an ideal of woman. She is the conventional 'belle dame sans merci' of the courtly-Petrarchist tradition, both as regards her physical appearance and her attitude towards the lover. There is no attempt to create a character; there is none of the psychological probing of behaviour and motive that we sometimes glimpse in Petrarch. In this sense, she is less interesting and less human than Laura. The poems that describe Lisi's activities contain a number of imitations, including two of Groto.[19] The anecdotal element is conventional, not specifically personal, and the principal function is that it should provide a basis for witty argument and analogy. It scarcely bears repeating that the extrapolation of biographical facts from the Lisi cycle would be a sterile exercise.

It is clear, then, that in the Lisi poems the concepts of love and the beloved are neither superficially nor radically distinctive, with the exception of one theme to which I shall address myself below. This is best done after an examination of the structure of the cycle, to which it bears some relation. It is to the structure rather than to the substance of the cycle that we must look to discover the distinguishing features and the fuller significance of this passion.

In his introduction to the poems to Lisi in the fourth section (*Musa Erato*) of *El Parnaso español*, González de Salas states that Quevedo intended imitating Petrarch: 'Confieso, pues, ahora, que advirtiendo el discurso enamorado que se colige del contexto de esta sección, que yo reduje a la forma que hoy tiene, vine a persuadirme que mucho quiso nuestro poeta este su amor semejase al que habemos insinuado del Petrarcha. El ocioso que con particularidad fuese confiriendo los sonetos aquí contenidos, con los que en las rimas se leen del poeta toscano, grande paridad hallaría sin duda, que quiso Don Francisco imitar en esta expresión de sus afectos' ('I acknowledge then, by observing the story of love which can be inferred from the text of this section [the poems to Lisi] which I converted into its present form, that I was persuaded that our poet wished very much that this love of his should resemble the one that we have glimpsed in Petrarch. If one were to compare in close detail the sonnets contained therein with those to be read in the verses of the Tuscan poet, one would doubtless find much similarity: that don Francisco sought to imitate in this expression of his emotions').[20] But as Consiglio has shown, [21] this is not a pronounced feature as regards direct imitation of the *Canzoniere*; Quevedo found poets as diverse as Groto, Boscán, Camões and Marino more fruitful in this respect. But the Petrarchan influence is evident in the overall concept of the cycle. This was the work of González de Salas, although it is not unlikely that he was acting in accordance with the poet's advice and instructions. The poems are arranged in such a way as to reflect and commemorate a devoted passion, sustained over many years, to a single addressee.

Sara Sturm-Maddox has shown how the explicit narrative element that appears as the connecting prose commentaries in Dante's *Vita Nuova* is skilfully incorporated into an exclusively poetic narrative in the *Canzoniere* through 'the careful sequential arrangement of the poems' which 'provokes the reader's identification of a temporal continuity of events in the life of a single protagonist throughout the collection, in a first-person "story" whose coherence depends not on its possible and occasional correspondence to events in the life of the historical Petrarch but rather on its function in the *Canzoniere* as literary text'.[22] From this there arises a 'story-line' because 'the experience recorded emerges as meaningful' (p.133).

Such collections of poems were common throughout the sixteenth century, albeit to a lesser extent in Spain than in other countries, possibly because Spanish poets of the Golden Age were generally indifferent about publishing their own work. Thus there is a dearth of carefully planned cycles of poems to a single addressee; the love poetry of Garcilaso and Herrera does not bear comparison as ordered units with such collections as Sannazaro's *Rime* (1530), Scève's *Délie* (1544), Ronsard's *Sonnets pour Hélène* (1578-84) and Sir Philip Sidney's *Astrophel and Stella* (1591). In varying degrees, these collections have a narrative thread, a pseudo-biographical fabric and a sense of development and continuity.

The question of arrangement and sequence is complicated in the case of Quevedo's poems to Lisi not only because they were published posthumously but also because not all the surviving poems appeared in González de Salas' 1648 edition. A further fourteen poems were to appear in Pedro Aldrete's complementary edition, *Las tres Musas*, in 1670. In his edition, González de Salas had arranged the sonnets in such a way as to suggest a chronology: for example, the only poem that alludes to Lisi *in morte* comes at the end, while further decisions regarding arrangement clearly relate to a desire to provide a kind of story-line, as we shall see. A major problem, which has yet to be satisfactorily resolved, concerns the location of the fourteen sonnets from the 1670 edition. In his editions, Blecua places all these after those from *El Parnaso español*, thereby destroying the narrative element, in that none of the sonnets from *Las tres Musas* have to do with Lisi's death and thus cannot form a sequel to those from the earlier edition. In fairness, however, it should be stated that it was not Blecua's intention to create a Petrarchist *canzoniere*. Astrana Marín's solution is more practical in this regard, as he retains the order of *El Parnaso español* and inserts the fourteen sonnets from Aldrete's edition *en masse* at a point roughly half-way through the cycle. By this arrangement, the sonnet alluding to Lisi's death remains at the end of the series and the ones so obsessed with old age and death immediately precede it. But even this distribution is not altogether satisfactory as poetic narrative or pseudo-biography. A number of the sonnets from the latter (1670) edition have thematic affinities more with the early poems of the cycle which describe the *persona* as a young man or at an early stage of his relationship than with the central section of the series, which is where Astrana Marín has located them.

In view of the inconsistency between modern editions in the matter of the order of the poems, a future editor of the Lisi cycle who does not opt for

Blecua's method, which ignores the story-line element, would of necessity have to involve himself in a further rearrangement of the cycle, including some modification of González de Salas' ordering in the light of the additional poems from the 1670 edition. What every edition of the Lisi cycle suggests, even if it does not fully realize it, is that there was an intention to create a unified series on the lines of the *Canzoniere* and Renaissance sonnet sequences. In an appendix I suggest an arrangement that seems to me to correspond best to this aim, and which departs neither in principle nor in general outline from González de Salas' original scheme.[23]

The sonnet placed first in both the original and modern editions can be interpreted as the experience of the persona when he sees Lisi for the first time and immediately falls in love with her. This is a poem, considered in the previous chapter, which contains violent contrasts between freedom and servitude, suggestive of the revolution that has occurred in the poet-protagonist's life:

> ¿Qué importa blasonar del albedrío,
> alma, de eterna y libre, tan preciada,
> si va en prisión de un ceño, y, conquistada,
> padece en un cabello señorío? (no. 442)

Of what use is it to boast of free-will, of a soul that is eternal, free and so valued, if it goes in the prison of a frown and, defeated, suffers in an imperious strand of hair?

There is here something of the breathless wonder experienced by Petrarch on first seeing Laura[24] and by Dante when he fell in love with Beatrice. A quotation from the *Vita Nuova* could serve as an epigraph to the first sonnet to Lisi: 'Ecce Deus fortior me qui veniens dominabitur mihi' ('Behold a God stronger than me who has come and will dominate me').[25]

The final sonnet of the 1648 edition and that of Astrana Marín contains the only reference to Lisi's death. This marks a substantial divergence from Petrarch's *Canzoniere*, where more than a quarter of the poems are to Laura *in morte*. In this sonnet (LXX), Quevedo refers to Lisi's death as 'fin' ('end') rather than 'muerte' ('death'), not so much as an euphemism as in order to avoid ambiguity, since the latter term is repeatedly used in the final part of the cycle as a metaphor for the lover's emotional condition, as in the tercets of the final sonnet:

> ¿Cuándo aquel fin a mí vendrá forzoso,
> pues por todas las vidas se pasea,
> que tanto el desdichado le desea
> y que tanto le teme el venturoso?

> La condición del hado desdeñoso
> quiere que le codicie y no le vea:
> el descanso le invidia a mi tarea
> parasismo y sepulcro perezoso.
>   Quiere el Tiempo engañarme lisonjero,
> llamando vida dilatar la muerte,
> siendo morir el tiempo que le espero.
>   Celosa debo de tener la suerte,
> pues viendo, ¡oh, Lisi!, que por verte muero,
> con la vida me estorba el poder verte. (no. 492)

When will that necessary end come to me, since it strolls through every life, an end that is as desired by the unfortunate as it is feared by the lucky? The nature of scornful fate wants me to covet it and not to see it: rest begrudges my labours a paroxysm and a lazy tomb. Flattering Time wishes to deceive me by labelling as life the delaying of death. I must have a jealous fate, since as it sees, oh Lisi!, that I die to see you, with life it hinders me from seeing you.

The penultimate sonnet (LXIX) celebrates the twenty-second anniversary of the meeting:

> Hoy cumple amor en mis ardientes venas
> veinte y dos años, Lisi, y no parece
> que pasa día por él; y siempre crece
> el fuego contra mí, y en mí las penas. (no.491)

Today love fulfills twenty-two years in my burning veins, Lisi, and yet it seems that not a day has passed on his account; and the fire always grows against me and the punishment within me.

It might not be entirely frivolous to note that Petrarch loved Laura in life for twenty-one years and that perhaps Quevedo wanted to go one better, literally, than his illustrious predecessor. As in the case of the *Canzoniere*, Quevedo included sonnets in which there are references to the length of the relationship. In addition to the penultimate sonnet, there are another two poems containing such allusions. One mentions the sixth anniversary: 'Atrás se queda, Lisi, el sexto año/de mi suspiro' ('The sixth year of my lament remains behind, Lisi') (XXXIII; no. 461); while another speaks with pride of the ten years during which the poet has sustained his passion:

> Diez años de mi vida se ha llevado
> en veloz fuga y sorda el sol ardiente,
> después que en tus dos ojos vi el Oriente,
> Lísida, en hermosura duplicado. (XLIV; no.471)

Ten years of my life have been borne away in rapid and noiseless flight by the burning sun, since I saw the Orient in your two eyes, Lisi, in doubled beauty.

These are the only sonnets that refer directly to the passage of time, but others afford evidence of sequence and progression even while adhering to González de Salas' arrangement. After the opening sonnet describing the overwhelming experience of the protagonist, what could be more fitting than to provide a picture of the woman who could inspire such passion? The second sonnet (II; no.443) is the first of a number of what could be termed portrait sonnets, where the beloved is described in conventionally idealized and fanciful, though occasionally ambivalent, terms. The fourth sonnet of the 1648 edition (VI; no.445) is a portrait sonnet in which the poet compares the lady's beauty to the riches sought by the avaricious merchant. It is appropriate that these sonnets should appear among the early poems of the cycle. Like a story-teller, the poet introduces and describes the object of his affection at an early stage. It would thus be justifiable to juxtapose with the second sonnet from the 1648 edition one from the 1670 edition, which is a tribute to Lisi's beauty and which likewise opens with an allusion to her golden hair: 'Rizas en ondas ricas del rey Midas' ('You curl in rich waves of King Midas') (III; no.501). These two portrait sonnets are companion pieces and for this reason too might well appear alongside each other, as I shall explain below.

Another feature is that some mention is made in the early sonnets of the series to the youth and vigour of the poet-persona, just as in the later part of the cycle it is clear that the poet is referring to someone older. Although there are expressions of suffering among the early sonnets, there are also present images that convey a sense of vitality, the hopes and desires of a young man, of one new to love. In this section there is the sonnet 'Si mis párpados, Lisi, labios fueran' ('If my eyelids, Lisi, were lips') (XI; no.448), an intense expression of longing for physical contact, and following it the sensual, if not sexual implication of 'En crespa tempestad del oro undoso' ('In a curly storm of wavy gold') (XII; no.449). The central myth-symbol of this sonnet is that of the Phoenix, which hints at the continual hope for fulfilment, suggestive of the optimism of youth. The next sonnet (XIII; no. 450) begins with the same myth. Its positive connotations are enhanced by the succeeding phrases that emphasize the vigour, indeed the potency, of the youthful persona:

> Hago verdad la fénix en la ardiente
> llama, en que renaciendo me renuevo;
> y la virilidad del fuego pruebo,
> y que es padre, y que tiene descendiente.[26]

I give credence to the Phoenix in the burning flame in which I renew myself as I am reborn; and I prove the virility of the flame, that it is a father and that it has an offspring.

In another of the early sonnets, the myth of Hercules is used as a point of comparison (XV; no.452); while the next poem (XVII; no.453) alludes to Jupiter:

¿Temes, ¡oh Lisi!, a Júpiter Tonante,
y pálido tu sol sus llamas mira,
cuando Jove, del ceño de tu ira,
tiembla vencido y se querella amante?

Do you fear Jove the Thunderer, Lisi, as your pale sun looks at his flames, when it is he who trembles, vanquished by your angry frown, and utters complaints like a lover.

It is one of the lighter compositions in the cycle, where Lisi's fear of storms is the basis for the poet's praise as he imagines Jupiter himself, the bringer of storms, more fearful of Lisi's disdain. There is an implicit identification here between the lover and Jupiter, and when we read the final tercet there is more than a hint of carnal aspiration and virility:

Al robre baja en rayo y a ti en oro;
y si renueva Amor la antigua traza,
en lugar de tronar, bramará toro.

He comes down in a ray of lightning to the oak-tree and to you in gold; and if Love renews the old design, instead of thundering, he will bellow as a bull.

The next sonnet (XIX; no.454) has as its image a storm at sea that correlates the passions and perils of the lover. It has a violence of imagery that is not to be found in the later part of the cycle:

Molesta el Ponto Bóreas con tumultos
cerúleos y espumosos; la llanura
del pacífico mar se desfigura,
despedazada en formidables bultos.

The North Wind disturbs the ocean with foaming blue tumults; the plain of the tranquil sea is disfigured and broken into massive shapes.

The persona is a 'náufrago amante y peregrino' ('shipwrecked, wandering lover'), while the description of his emotions as 'borrasca de amor' suggests the turbulence and perhaps the impetuosity of his passion.

In the first part of the cycle, then, the poet-narrator describes his infatuation, introduces the beloved, and suggests the youthful intensity of his passion. The last sonnets provide a stark contrast as they hint at the approach of old age, accompanied by a degree of disillusionment and an ever-increasing awareness of death. The final part could be seen to be ushered in by sonnets that speak of the lover's experience in terms of a journey. It is here, for the first time, that it is suggested that the persona is growing old. In one sonnet (LVII; no.474), the phrase 'largo camino' makes it clear that much time has elapsed:

> ¿Qué buscas, porfiado pensamiento,
> ministro sin piedad de mi locura,
> invisible martirio, sombra obscura,
> fatal persecución del sufrimiento?
>   Si del largo camino estás sediento,
> mi vista bebe, su corriente apura;
> si te promete albricias la hermosura
> de Lisi, por mi fin, vuelve contento.

What do you seek, stubborn thought, merciless minister of my madness, invisible martyrdom, dark shadow, lethal persecutor of my suffering? If you are thirsty of the long path, drink my eyes, drain their flow; if the beauty of Lisi promises you a reward, on account of my end, return happy.

while in the tercets play is made on the contrast of literal and metaphorical death — an idea that is to become increasingly dominant in the final section:

> Yo muero, Lisi, preso y desterrado;
> pero si fue mi muerte la partida,
> de puro muerto estoy de mí olvidado.
>   Aquí para morir me falta vida,
> allá para vivir sobró cuidado:
> fantasma soy en penas detenido.

I am dying, Lisi, imprisoned and exiled; but if my death was the departure, sheer death has made me forget myself. Here I lack life in order to die, there in order to live, there was an excess of anxiety: I am a ghost detained in suffering.

It occurs too in the next sonnet (LVIII; no.475), one of the 'escarmiento' poems, where the lover examines the value of his experience. In the 1648 edition, two sonnets intervene before the second 'escarmiento' poem that describes the weary lover ('Cargado voy de mí') nearing his journey's end (LIX; no.478).

A concern with death is prominent in the following sonnet (LX; no.479). The poet regrets his coming death:

> Siento haber de dejar deshabitado
> cuerpo que amante espíritu ha ceñido;
> desierto un corazón siempre encendido,
> donde todo el Amor reinó hospedado.

I regret having to leave a body that has contained a loving spirit unoccupied; and a constantly burning heart, where love reigned supreme, deserted.

This is offset by the hope that his love may be eternal ('Señas me da mi ardor de fuego eterno') ('My ardour gives indications of eternal fire') — one of the key ideas of the series, as we shall see. Again there is a reference to the length of the relationship: 'tan larga y congojosa historia' ('such a long and distressful tale').

The next sonnet is a gloomy one (LXI; no.480). Its images of darkness and perdition suggest the waning strength of the persona and the last flickers of his passion:

> Por yerta frente de alto escollo, osado,
> con pie dudoso, ciegos pasos guío;
> sigo la escasa luz del fuego mío,
> que avara alumbra, habiéndome abrasado.

Along the hard face of a high rock, boldly and with uncertain step, I lead my unseeing feet; I follow the scanty light of my fire which gives a miserly glow now that it has burnt me.

After this, in *El Parnaso español*, there comes a sonnet that (see page 44) contrasts the joyous arrival of spring with the bleakness of the lover's experience (LVI; no.481). Not for him now the renewal of passion and the hope for fulfilment, such as was implied in the early section of the cycle through the image of the Phoenix. For reasons of grouping (to be discussed below), this sonnet could be placed at a slightly earlier position in the cycle.

The three sonnets that follow in the 1648 edition do not pursue the idea of old age and approaching death and might well be located elsewhere (XXVII-XXIX; nos.482-4). The antepenultimate sonnet, which deals with the lover's absence from the beloved, could similarly appear earlier in the cycle (L; no.490). The five remaining sonnets of the final section that precede the penultimate one — the poem that marks the twenty-second anniversary of the meeting (LXIX; no.491) — form an appropriate close (LXIV-LXVIII; nos.485-9). In the first of these (LXIV; no.485), the lover alludes to his physical weariness and decay, notably in the second quatrain:

> Bebe el ardor, hidrópica, mi vida,
> que ya, ceniza amante y macilenta,
> cadáver del incendio hermoso, ostenta
> su luz en humo y noche fallecida.

My dropsical life drinks the ardour, for now, a gaunt and loving cinder, a corpse of that beautiful fire, it displays its deceased light as smoke and darkness.

The persona is only a shadow of the virile figure encountered in the early sonnets; the images of brilliance and light present, for example, in the sonnet on Lisi's hair ('En crespa tempestad del oro undoso') have yielded to those of darkness and desolation. This mood persists in the next poem (LXV; no.486); the first tercet provides a concise and emotive expression of the persona's decline:

> Todo soy ruinas, todo soy destrozos,
> escándalo funesto a los amantes,
> que fabrican de lástimas sus gozos.

I am all ruins, all ravages, a baneful scandal for the lovers who manufacture their pleasures from complaints.

The next sonnet refers to the poet-lover's old age explicitly, as he confesses to Love that he is too weary to pursue what is required of him as a correct lover. He longs for the rest of death:

> Ya que pasó mi verde primavera,
> Amor, en tu obediencia l'alma mía;
> ya que sintió mudada en nieve fría
> los robos de la edad mi cabellera;
>   pues la vejez no puede, aunque yo quiera,
> tarda, seguir tu leve fantasía,
> permite que mi cuerpo, en algún día,
> cuando lástima no, desprecio adquiera.
>   Si te he servido bien, cuando cansado
> ya no puedo, ¡oh Amor!, por lo servido,
> dame descanso, y quedaré premiado. (LXVI; no.487)

Now that my green spring has gone, Love, and my soul is obedient to you; and now that my hair, changed into cold snow, has perceived the thefts of age; since old age cannot, even if I should wish it, follow slowly your fickle fancies, allow my body, at some time, to acquire scorn, if not pity. If I have served you well, now that I am weary and cannot, oh Love!, for the sake of the service I have rendered you, grant me rest and I will be rewarded.

In the first quatrain, the poet contrasts youth and age by the familiar symbols of the seasons: 'verde primavera' and 'nieve fría', the latter referring to his white hair.

The next two sonnets (LXVII, LXVIII; nos.488, 489) play on the idea of the poet's physical death succeeding his metaphorical death, the death-in-life of the unhappy lover. In both these sonnets, the persona refers to himself as 'ceniza' ('cinder'). This term is used with increasing frequency in the later sonnets and corresponds to a decrease in more positive signifiers of amatory experience such as 'fuego' ('fire') or 'llama' ('flame') and also to the appearance of these images in negative contexts or with negative qualifiers.[27] This is another indication of the waning powers of the poet-protagonist; his emotion is only a remnant of the passion he had displayed as a young man.

What could be termed the central section of the cycle contains, for the most part, some of the more conventional topics of the love poetry of the period, including a group of Neoplatonic poems (XXIV-XXIX;nos. 456-8, 482-4) that has been mistakenly considered to be characteristic of the whole series, as I have mentioned above. References to the passing of time or more indirect allusions to the poet's age are limited to two anniversary sonnets (XXIII, XLIV; nos.461, 471), and this part of the cycle provides more problems in rearranging the poems, especially as regards the position of the poems from the 1670 edition yet to be accounted for.

In this connection another criterion might with justification be employed for the purposes of constructing a cycle. From González de Salas' 1648 edition there is evidence that sonnets that have similar themes or images or which treat similar events tend to be grouped together, in pairs or larger groups, or to appear in close proximity to each other. Examples can be found in every part of the cycle. In the early section, the two sonnets containing the important myth of the Phoenix were placed together; in the central section, there is a grouping of Neoplatonic sonnets; in the final section, sonnets that use the image of the journey to describe the lover's experience appear in close proximity to each other; while, at the very end, two sonnets that make much of the contrast of literal and metaphorical death are placed together.

This kind of presentation is not a matter of mere coincidence, nor is it confined to the cycle to Lisi, as such juxtaposition and groupings occur among the other love poems.[28] In Petrarch's *Canzoniere*, which González de Salas cites as Quevedo's model, and perhaps his own also in his capacity as editor, there are many examples of poems concerned with the same idea or event being grouped together.[29] It is not unlikely that this had an influence on Quevedo or González de Salas or both. Indeed, in a series of poems designed to form a single work, such a procedure lends a greater sense of continuity and of logical and apparently spontaneous development. At times an impression is created whereby it is as if an idea or image overflowed from one sonnet into the next, and there seems to be no dividing-line between the two. This can be seen to good effect in the case of the sonnet that describes the tenth anniversary of the meeting (XLIV; no.471) and the following one, 'Cerrar podrá mis ojos la postrera' (XLV; no.472). The idea of the poet's love surviving death, that is so eloquently expressed in the latter, is anticipated in the final tercet of the former. This had begun, however, purely as an anniversary sonnet, and in a sense its final tercet is more closely related to the succeeding poem than to the preceding quatrains.[30] To quote another instance of this process: the image of the Phoenix that had appeared in a sonnet inspired by the beauty of Lisi's hair

(XII; no.449) is the starting-point for the following poem (XIII; no.450): 'Hago verdad la fénix'.

Such a criterion, then, is a valuable aid in reconstructing the series. It serves to make slight but justifiable modifications to González de Salas' original order and to find appropriate locations for the sonnets from Aldrete's 1670 edition. The result is consistent with González de Salas' intention, and follows the example of the *Canzoniere* and Renaissance sonnet sequences.

An awareness of a narrative thread, of sequence and chronology, adds a further dimension to our understanding of the cycle. Sara Sturm-Maddox's observations on the *Vita Nuova* and the *Canzoniere* refer to the richness achieved by the careful sequential arrangement of the poems, as a result of which, perspective becomes a complex factor. Her comments can also be applied to the Lisi cycle. In the case of the *Vita Nuova*, 'while the poems express immediate intimate experience, the meaning of that experience is revealed only retrospectively and repeatedly qualified. In the *Canzoniere* the implicit or occasionally explicit commentary of the protagonist on the record of his past experience invests the sequential arrangement of the lyrics with further significance: with the passing of time and the accretion of additional moments of experience, both the larger pattern of his experience and its meaning are gradually disclosed'.[31]

Read after a group of sonnets which focus obsessively on the poet-persona's acute awareness of old age and death, the sonnet that refers to Lisi's death (LXX; no.492) comes as a surprise and an irony. The poet, prey to the passing of time and afflicted by emotional and physical weariness, survives, while Lisi, the unchanging ideal, seemingly unaffected by such processes, dies. The lack of more poems to Lisi *in morte*— whether by accident, if there are missing poems, or by design, as seems more likely[32] — enhances this sense of shock. It makes for an abrupt and bitter conclusion to the cycle.

The passing of time and the consciousness of death are at the root of perhaps the profoundest and most elusive theme in Quevedo's love poetry, which has been variously defined as the 'ceniza enamorada'[33] and 'amor constante'[34] theme. It revolves around an assertion that the body, like the soul and its faculties, is eternal and as such retains its amatory significance even after death. This finds its supreme expression in one of the greatest sonnets in the Spanish language:

> Cerrar podrá mis ojos la postrera
> sombra que me llevare el blanco día,
> y podrá desatar esta alma mía
> hora a su afán ansioso lisonjera;

> mas no, de esotra parte, en la ribera,
> dejará la memoria, en donde ardía:
> nadar sabe mi llama la agua fría,
> y perder el respeto a ley severa.
>   Alma a quien todo un dios prisión ha sido,
> venas que humor a tanto fuego han dado,
> medulas que han gloriosamente ardido,
>   su cuerpo dejará, no su cuidado;
> serán ceniza, mas tendrá sentido;
> polvo serán, mas polvo enamorado. (XLV; no.472)

The last shadow that takes white day from me will be able to close my eyes, and there will arrive an hour that, indulgent to the anxious yearning of this soul of mine, will release it; but it will not leave the memory of where it burnt on the other shore; my flame can swim across the cold water, and lose its respect for the harsh law. A soul which has been a prison to a whole god, veins that have given humour to so much fire, marrows that have gloriously burnt: it will abandon its body, but not its love; they will be ashes, but it will still have its feeling; they will be dust, but dust in love.

This poem has attracted so much critical attention that a detailed analysis of its meaning and structure, in particular, would be largely superfluous.[35] I wish, however, to examine its significance in the context of the cycle. As Carlos Blanco Aguinaga has shown, this sonnet comes after a number of premonitions in the form of tentative enunciations ('aproximaciones') of the great idea.[36] In one of the Neoplatonic sonnets we read: 'No verán de mi amor el fin los días' ('The days will not see the end of my love') (XXV; no.457); and of more weight in this regard is a sonnet which, like several, begins with a hypothesis but which, as Price has indicated, changes dramatically in the tercets into assertion.[37] The supposition is taken as fact:

> Si hija de mi amor mi muerte fuese,
> ¡qué parto tan dichoso que sería
> el de mi amor contra la vida mía!
> ¡Qué gloria, que el morir de amar naciese!
>   Llevara yo en el alma adonde fuese
> el fuego en que me abraso, y guardaría
> su llama fiel con la ceniza fría
> en el mismo sepulcro en que durmiese.
>   De esotra parte de la muerte dura,
> vivirán en mi sombra mis cuidados,
> y más allá del Lethe mi memoria.
>   Triunfará del olvido tu hermosura;
> mi pura fe y ardiente, de los hados;
> y el no ser, por amar, será mi gloria. (XXXII; no.460)

If my death were daughter of my love, what a happy birth would be that of my love against my life! What glory, that dying should be born of loving! I would carry in my soul, wherever I would go, the fire in which I am consumed, and I would keep its loyal flame with the cold cinder in the same tomb in which I slept. On the far side of harsh death, my love will live in my shadow, and my memory, beyond the Lethe. Your beauty will triumph over oblivion; my pure and burning faith over the fates; and not being through loving will be my glory.

The poet underlines the surprise produced by the change of tense by inducing the reader into a false expectation, through his playing on the idea of death. The juxtaposition of love and death at the opening of the sonnet leads us to think immediately in terms of death as a metaphor of unhappy love, a consequence of thwarted aspiration — the daughter image could be seen as correlating the notion of outcome: love gives rise to death (i.e., extreme suffering). But in the course of the sonnet, particularly after the first quatrain, our understanding of the concept of death changes, and this transformation parallels the switch in the tense. Words and phrases like 'sepulcro', 'esotra parte', 'Lethe' and 'el no ser' gradually effect this change in our understanding, and at the end we are left with a glimpse of the eternal potentiality of love. This is not love seen in purely spiritual terms, related to Neoplatonic philosophy, as was the case in the earlier sonnet (XXV; no. 457) or, for example, the sonnet to Flora where the poet proclaims: 'eterno amante soy de eterna amada' ('I am the eternal lover of an eternal beloved') (no.331). Here something more drastic is proposed, that clearly looks forward to 'Cerrar podrá mis ojos': the survival of emotion. Allusions to 'hermosura' and to 'pura fe' might suggest a Neoplatonic striving, but 'cuidados' and the epithet 'ardiente' hint at the idea of the imperishability of human love.

As I have already mentioned, the sonnet that immediately precedes 'Cerrar podrá mis ojos' provides an undoubted thematic anticipation. It celebrates the tenth anniversary of the meeting and at first sight seems an unclouded and assertive utterance. The poet-protagonist repeats the phrase 'diez años' as though it were magical, something to be cherished:

> Diez años de mi vida se ha llevado
> en veloz fuga y sorda el sol ardiente,
> después que en tus dos ojos vi el Oriente,
> Lísida, en hermosura duplicado.
>   Diez años en mis venas he guardado
> el dulce fuego que alimento, ausente,
> de mi sangre. Diez años en mi mente
> con imperio tus luces han reinado.
>   Basta ver una vez grande hermosura;
> que, una vez vista, eternamente enciende,
> y en l'alma impresa eternamente dura.
>   Llama que a la inmortal vida trasciende,
> ni teme con el cuerpo sepultura,
> ni el tiempo la marchita ni la ofende. (XLIV; no.471)

> Ten years of my life have been borne away in rapid and noiseless flight by the burning sun, since I saw the Orient, in your two eyes, Lisi, in doubled beauty. For ten years I have kept the sweet fire that, in my absence, I nourish on my blood. For ten years your lights have reigned imperiously over my mind. It is enough to see great beauty once; for, once seen, it burns eternally and lasts forever, imprinted in the soul. The flame that extends to immortal life neither fears the tomb with the body, nor does time wither or harm it.

As I have shown elsewhere, however, the triumphant appearance masks a troubled contradiction.[38] The last line of the sonnet — a line arrived at after much heart-searching, as Quevedo's autograph manuscript reveals[39] — speaks of time as a threat, not as a source of celebration as had been the case in the quatrains. Though he was referring specifically to Quevedo's moral verse, Manuel Durán's perceptive view on the psychology of time is appropriate to this anniversary sonnet: 'nuestra vida está hecha de tiempo, pero este tiempo es precisamente lo que nos acaba y destruye' ('our life is made of time, but this selfsame time is what finishes and destroys us').[40] The lover's celebratory mood is prompted by the realization that he can point to the certainty of an experience in which he has participated. His constancy as a lover for ten years cannot be doubted, but were this to be all, he would be subject to the laws of time and death. The transition to the intuition of eternal love is achieved via the common notion that a single glimpse of the beloved is all that is needed to engender and to sustain a passion.[41] From this Quevedo creates an insight that is complex and moving.

It is also only a step away from the emotional atmosphere of the succeeding sonnet, 'Cerrar podrá mis ojos'. Here the poet seems to have freed himself from that awareness of the limitations of mortal striving that lent the anniversary sonnet its haunting uneasiness. The poem is a monumentally defiant utterance, not only because of the immediate appeal of its rhetorical garb, but also because of the seemingly logical nature of its development.[42] As Arthur Terry has shown, though, the sonnet's majestic conclusion incorporates a syllogism that betrays errors of logic: 'the soul is immortal; the soul of the poet is in love; therefore his love will be immortal. But Quevedo says more than this: such love involves the body while it is still alive (ll.9-11); the body is destroyed by death, but what remains ("ceniza . . . polvo") will still bear the signs of love ("tendrá sentido"); therefore, in a sense, this will be immortal too. In logical terms, there is an example of the fallacy of *secundum quid*: the second term (immortal) is related, first to a field in which it is probably true (that of the spirit), then to another (the poet's love) where the equation is not necessarily true, since human love moves on the physical plane'.[43] This blurring of the distinction between the body and the spirit — an antithesis that Terry sees as the central truth of the poem — was evident too, as we have seen, in the tercets of one of the sonnets that anticipate 'Cerrar podrá mis ojos', the one that begins with a hypothesis (XXXII; no.460): 'hermosura', 'pura fe', on the one hand; 'cuidados', 'ardiente', on the other.

Terry suggests that the 'errors in logic' (p.220) do not detract from the central truth of the poem; indeed I believe that they contribute positively towards its fundamental experience. In this connection, Terry's reference to S.L. Bethell's article on Gracián and Tesauro is illuminating.[44] A clear distinction can be made between dialectic and rhetoric: the former strives after truth, the latter seeks to persuade and in this connection, it may employ fallacious dialectic. Wit has an aesthetic function: it is 'not primarily concerned with truth but with beauty addressed to the understanding, yet it is only *more* concerned with beauty than with truth; and as the beauty aimed at is that of order as found in nature, this is, in any event, only another aspect of truth. Wit expresses truth by way of fiction and fallacy'.[45] The truth of 'Cerrar podrá mis ojos' includes an awareness by the poet that what he has been asserting has a hollowness which neither the rhetorical resonance nor the impression of logic can conceal. Quevedo did not seek to conceal this hollowness; he strove to create it, and the rhetorical and quasi-logical processes are part of his intent.[46] As with the preceding sonnet, there is a contradiction. The gesture of defiance is no less real for its futility but once more a celebratory, indeed incantatory, mood coexists with a deep insecurity. What these two sonnets imply is an ultimately tragic view of the experience of amatory striving; the grandiose expectation is impossible, confronted by time and death.

The emotional reality of 'Cerrar podrá mis ojos' is in my opinion best summarized by Lázaro Carreter as 'un ansia de sobrevivir, típicamente agónica, pertinazmente quevedesca' ('a longing for survival, typically agonized, obstinately Quevedian').[47] This understanding of the sonnet's ulterior significance is confirmed if we consider its position in the cycle, not only as it appears in my suggested reconstruction but also in the editions of González de Salas and Astrana Marín. It is, in a sense, the high point of the series — a peak towards which the poet-narrator has been climbing, as witness the various premonitions or anticipations. The poems that follow it (XLVI to the end of the cycle) provide an impression of desolation and almost unrelieved despair, not only or not so much as a result of purely amatory sorrow, but as a consequence of an insidious awareness of death, decay and old age. In the context of the cycle, then, the sonnet 'Cerrar podrá mis ojos' both represents the climax of one perception of experience and, through the deliberate fragility of its assertion, heralds the descent to the persona's despair and decay and finally to Lisi's death.

Carlos Blanco Aguinaga believes that the poems to Lisi lack variety as compared with those of Petrarch and Shakespeare as regards what could be termed the raw materials of poetry: themes, images and conceits.[48] But even if this is true, there is adequate compensation in Quevedo's creation of a poet-persona whose response to experience reveals great diversity. By turns spiritual and carnal, respectful and reproachful, doubting and accepting, triumphant and despairing, and contradictory on occasions even within the confines of a single poem, the lover displays not only variety of approach but a sense of integrity. In the Lisi poems, more than in any other collection of love poetry from the Spanish Golden Age, we have a poetic document of the fullness and complexity of human love.

1 Cautionary observations in this regard are provided by A.J. Krailsheimer in his introduction to *The Continental Renaissance* (Harmondsworth, 1971), 15; and by Arthur Terry, *An Anthology of Spanish Poetry. Part One*, xvii-xxii.

2 See Wellek and Warren, op.cit., 75-80. The hazards of the biographical approach to the works of Garcilaso have been convincingly outlined by David H. Darst, 'Garcilaso's Love for Isabel Freire: The Creation of a Myth', *Journal of Hispanic Philology*, III (1978-9), 261-8.

3 *Courtly Love in Quevedo*, 21-3.

4. These total only nine poems, two of which (nos. 412, 413) may well not be by Quevedo, as my article, 'Concerning the Authenticity of Two Madrigals', argues. Another of the poems (no.342) is more in the nature of a moralistic appraisal of love fulfilled, while three more (nos.337,365,440) describe fulfilment in a dream.

5 *Towards a Chronology of Quevedo's Poetry* (Fredericton, New Brunswick, 1977), 15.

6 Beside the ambivalence and 'vulgarity' of nos. 328, 332 and 340, could be set two sonnets of Neoplatonic inspiration (nos.321,324) and the light-hearted conventionality of some madrigals (nos. 405, 408 and 409).

7. Op.cit., 16-21.

8 *La vida turbulenta*, 518; and see Bleznick, op.cit.,36.

9 *La vida turbulenta*, 516.

10 Op.cit., 186.

11 Fernando Valera, 'Reinvención de D. Francisco de Quevedo: cuatro cartas literarias a Luis Capdevila', *Cuadernos del Congreso por la Libertad de la Cultura*, VII, no.34 (1959), 65-74.

12 Op.cit., 39

13 *Poesía española*, 517.

14 Compare his analysis (art.cit.) with those of A.A. Parker, 'La "agudeza" en algunos sonetos de Quevedo', *Estudios dedicados a Menéndez Pidal*, III, Madrid, 1952, 351-3; and Arthur Terry, 'Quevedo and the Metaphysical Conceit', *Bulletin of Hispanic Studies*, XXXV (1958), 215-17.

15 See Fucilla, *Estudios*, 208.

16 'El *Poema a Lisi* y su petrarquismo', *Mediterráneo*, IV, nos. 13-15 (1946), 89.

17 *Rimas*, ed. José Luis Cano (Madrid, 1975), 70.

18 The presence in the cycle to Lisi of a sonnet that speaks of the failure rather than the folly of love (LVIII; no.480) and which has a clear affinity with the one from *Las tres Musas* (no.363) does not invalidate my point regarding the greater variety of attitudes towards love in the cycle to Lisi.

19 See nos. 482 and 505.

20 Quoted in Francisco de Quevedo y Villegas, *Obras completas: obras en verso*, ed. Astrana Marín (Madrid, 1943), 909.

21 Art.cit., 76-83.

22 'Transformations of Courtly Love Poetry: *Vita Nuova* and *Canzoniere*', in *The Expansion and Transformations of Courtly Literature*, ed. Nathaniel B. Snow and Joseph T. Snow (Athens, Georgia, 1980), 132.

23 Subsequent references to the Lisi poems in this Chapter take the form of a Roman numeral to indicate their suggested new position, followed by an Arabic numeral referring to the Blecua editions.

24   Trovommi Amor del tutto disarmato,
               et aperta la via per gli occhi al core,
               che di lagrime son fatti uscio e varco.
                           (*Canzoniere*, no.3)
    (*Il Canzoniere*, ed. Dino Provenzal (Milan, 1954), 13)

25 *Opere*, ed. E. Moore (Oxford, 1923), 205.

26 Compare Paterson's comments on the sonnet 'Alma es del mundo Amor' (no.332) where he focusses on the significance of phrases like 'varonil virtud' and 'paterna actividad' (art.cit., 139).

27 For example, 'siglo la escasa luz del fuego mío' (LXI; no.480), and 'nada dejó por consumir el fuego' (LXVIII; no.489).

28 See nos. 318 and 319 (rivers), 329 and 330 (philosophy of love), 331 and 332 (Neoplatonic and carnal love), 333 and 334 (beauty as a mystery), 350 and 351 (fountains).

29 For example: nos. 31-4 (Laura's illness), 71-3 (her eyes), 77-8 (her portrait), 176-7 (the poet's journey through a forest), 199-201 (Laura's glove), 251-2 (the vision of Laura dead).

30 See my article, 'Conflicting Views of Time in a Quevedo Sonnet: An Analysis of "Diez años de mi vida se ha llevado"', *Journal of Hispanic Philology*, IV (1979-80), 143-56.

31 Art.cit., 133.

32 In the next chapter I consider the reasons for the lack of poems to Lisi after her death.

33 Pedro Laín Entralgo, 'La vida del hombre en la poesía de Quevedo', *Cuadernos Hispanoamericanos*, I, no.1 (1948), 95.

34 Moore, op.cit., 16-18.

35 See J.O. Crosby, *Guía bibliográfica para el estudio crítico de Quevedo* (London, 1976), 127, where the reader is referred to no fewer than eleven studies on the poem.

36 '"Cerrar podrá mis ojos": tradición y originalidad', *Filología*, VIII (1962), 57-78; rpt. in Sobejano, op.cit., 300-18.

37 Ed.cit., 101. An examination of the principal conceit of the sonnet, the one based on the commonplace that love causes death, is to be found in Olivares, op.cit., 122-7.

38 'Conflicting Views of Time', especially 152-5.

39 See J.O. Crosby, 'La creación poética en ocho poemas autógrafos', in *En torno a la poesía de Quevedo* (Madrid, 1967), 20; 29-31.

40 Op.cit., 101.

41 Compare *El alcalde de Zalamea*, Act II, ll. 101-16.

42 Compare the emotional and rhetorical character of Donne's sonnet, 'Death be not proud', which similarly combines defiance with wit and logic.

43 'Quevedo and the Metaphysical Conceit', 220.

44 'Gracián, Tesauro and the Nature of Metaphysical Wit', *The Northern Miscellany of Literary Criticism*, I (1953), 19-40.

45 Terry, 'Quevedo and the Metaphysical Conceit', 221.

46 In an article on the impact of Quevedo on modern Spanish poets ('Resonancias de Quevedo en la poesía española del siglo veinte', *Kentucky Foreign Language Quarterly*, IX (1962), 105-13), Douglas C. Sheppard quotes a sonnet by Luis Jiménez Martos which refers scathingly to Quevedo's penchant for the grand gesture and in which he (Jiménez Martos) distances himself from such a tendency: 'yo me ahorro/de acercarme a la lírica ensalada'. I quote the final tercet:

    Me prohibo bajar a los infiernos
    retórico-mortales. No resisto
    el ayayay marcial que a tango suena.

Whether the poet had 'Cerrar podrá mis ojos' in mind when he penned these lines is not certain, but Quevedo's sonnet seems to correspond to the kind of rhetoric to which he takes exception. Unwittingly, however, he has detected an important emotional element of 'Cerrar podrá mis ojos', as my observations reveal.

47 'Quevedo, entre el amor y la muerte', *Papeles de Son Armadans*, I, no. 2 (1956), 145-60; rpt. in Sobejano, op.cit., 291-9 (on p.299).

48 Art.cit., 309.

CHAPTER V

The Renunciation of Love: the Heráclito cristiano

There is evidence that Quevedo suffered a crisis of some significance in, and perhaps immediately before, 1613, the year in which he left for Sicily as secretary to the Duke of Osuna.[1] Letters from this period certainly create the impression; in one to Don Tomás Tamayo de Vargas, dated 12 November, 1612, he refers to himself as 'malo y lascivo' ('wicked and lewd') and fears that this bad reputation might detract from the value of his works.[2] There is a new note of sobriety in much of Quevedo's output in the years leading up to 1613 that in two cases, at least, provides clear indications of a personal crisis. His early works are predominantly burlesque in character. Apart from the obviously jocose if biting mood of the *premáticas (Proclamations)* and prose sketches of life at court in the first decade of the seventeenth century and the light-hearted *romances* the young Quevedo was so adept at composing,[3] more ambitious projects such as the early *Sueños* also reveal this same tendency. Even the third of the series, *El sueño del infierno (The Vision of Hell)* (1608) has a pronounced jocular streak, albeit interspersed with greater moralizing traits than hitherto.[4]

Between the appearance of the third and fourth *Sueños*, a period of four years elapsed during which time Quevedo had begun to translate and paraphrase Greek and Latin writers. From this period also date the bleak pages of the *Doctrina moral del conocimiento propio y del desengaño de las cosas ajenas (Moral Doctrine of Self Knowledge and of Disillusionment with Things Alien to Oneself)*, a treatise inspired by Stoic philosophy that years later Quevedo was to convert into *La cuna y la sepultura (The Cradle and the Tomb)*,[5] and a translation of the prophet Jeremiah.[6] The fourth *Sueño, El mundo por de dentro (The World from Within)*, completed in 1612, is not only a more restrained and carefully structured work than its predecessors but a far more sombre production. Quevedo presents a limited number of scenes, exploited to the full by the cutting edge of his satire and seemingly by the bitterness of his own experience.

The experience expressed in prose in *El mundo por de dentro* is to be found also in what might be considered a companion-piece in verse, the *Heráclito cristiano (Christian Heraclitus)*, written in 1613. Both these intense utterances are key works for a knowledge of Quevedo and important for a fuller understanding of his approach to love in the amatory verse, for, as I shall show, in the *Heráclito cristiano* in particular, the voice of the lover vies on occasion with that of the moralist.

In *El mundo por de dentro*, unlike the earlier *Sueños*, the narrator (the 'yo') is also a protagonist, not merely an observer. There is a greater personal involvement: self-examination has been added to social criticism so that the perspective is more complex. The persona's confusion is conveyed by the symbol of the labyrinth as he wanders through the world of pleasure and self-indulgence:

> me hallé todo en poder de la confusión, poseído de la vanidad de tal manera, que en la gran población del mundo, perdido, ya corría donde tras la hermosura me llevaban los ojos, ya donde, tras la conversación, los amigos; de una calle en otra, hecho fábula de todos.[7]

> I found myself totally in the grip of confusion, possessed by vanity to such an extent that, lost in the vast city of the world, at one moment I ran where my eyes bore me in pursuit of beauty, at the next where my friends led me in search of conversation; from one street to the next, I had become a source of scandal to everyone.

The nightmarish experience is intensified:

> Al fin, de una calle en otra andaba, siendo infinitas, de tal manera confuso, que la admiración aún no dejaba sentido para el cansancio . . . (p.164)

> Finally, I wandered from one street to another, an infinity of them, in such a fashion bewildered that my wonder did not leave scope for tiredness . . .

But then:

> llamado de voces descompuestas y tirado porfiadamente del manteo, volví la cabeza. (p164)

> summoned by chaotic voices, and feeling an insistent tug on my cloak, I turned my head.

Amid the turmoil the protagonist is confronted by Desengaño:

> un viejo venerable en sus canas, maltratado, roto por mil partes el vestido y pisado. No por eso ridículo: antes severo y digno de respeto (p.164)

> a venerable old man with white hair, ill-treated, whose clothes were torn in a thousand places, and trampled upon. Not that this made him ridiculous: on the contrary, he was grim and inspired respect.

The whole scene recreates in vivid terms the drama of the soul's waywardness, its surrender to sin and the sudden prospect of disillusion. But at first, the old man is not heeded. The youthful protagonist's response is one of scorn and rejection. He has thought only of the pleasures of life and Desengaño can have no place in his world:

Déjame, que siempre los ancianos aborrecéis en los mozos los placeres y deleites, no que dejáis de vuestra voluntad, sino que por fuerza os quita el tiempo. Tú vas, yo vengo. Déjame gozar y ver el mundo. (p.164)

Leave me alone, for you old people always loathe young men to have pleasures and delight, not because you relinquish them willingly but because time, of necessity, takes them away from you. You are going out, I'm on my way in. Let me enjoy myself and see the world.

Worldliness is not easily relinquished, but the old man prevails and the *Sueño* is to be constructed from the lessons he will provide, drawing on his own mature apprehension of life. The work expresses overall a powerful conflict between attachment to and release from the worldly, the unifying element being hypocrisy. There is no resolution of this conflict, for at the end, when the persona is advised to rest by Desengaño, the process of disillusionment is still not complete:

— Forzoso es que descanses. Que el choque de tantas admiraciones y de tantos desengaños fatigan el seso, y temo se te desconcierte la imaginación. Reposa un poco para que lo que resta te enseñe y no te atormente. (p.184)

You must rest. For the shock of so many marvels and such disillusionment tires the mind, and I fear your imagination may be disturbed. Rest awhile so that what is left to be seen may instruct and not torment you.

The full title of the collection of poems written in 1613 — *Heráclito cristiano y segunda arpa a imitación de David (Christian Heraclitus and a Second Harp in Imitation of David)* — acknowledges two influences: the Greek philosopher Heraclitus and the Book of Psalms. The former was known in antiquity as the 'Dark Philosopher' and as the 'Weeping Philosopher'; pessimism and contempt for mankind are features of his thought. The influence of the Book of Psalms is reflected superficially in Quevedo's labelling each poem a *salmo (psalm)* and, more profoundly, in the work's penitential aspect and the way in which the poet often addresses God to express a variety of emotions: praise, wonder, guilt, inadequacy and fear. The *Heráclito cristiano* may have been influenced by Petrarch's seven Penitential Psalms. The Psalms of David were Petrarch's favourite poems and his own Penitential Psalms were popular in their day; they were widely translated, and paraphrased by the Elizabethan poet, Chapman.[8] The penitential poem was not the favoured form of literary religious expression in Spain in the Golden Age; worthy of note, though, are Jorge de Montemayor, whose interest in the Psalms is reflected in the poetry of his *Segundo cancionero espiritual* (1558),[9] and Lope de Vega, whose *Rimas sacras* appeared in 1614 and are thus almost exactly contemporary with the *Heráclito cristiano*.

The *Heráclito cristiano* is prefaced by two dedications. In the general dedication to the reader, Quevedo describes the work as 'el sentimiento verdadero y arrepentimiento de todo lo demás que he hecho' ('the true feeling and penitence for all the other things that I have done'), while in a letter to his aunt, Doña Margarita de Espinosa, dated 3 June, 1613, he is appropriately more personal: 'Esta confesión, que por ser tan tarde hago no sin vergüenza, envío a Vm. para que se divierta algunos ratos, bien que empleándolos todos, en su viudez y retiramiento, con Dios, antes será hurtárseles. Sólo pretendo, ya que la voz de mis mocedades ha sido molesta a Vm. y escandalosa a todos, conocer por este papel diferentes propósitos' ('I send you this confession which, because of its belatedness I make not without shame, so that you may be amused for a few moments, though if you could use them in your widowed and withdrawn condition with God, it would, rather, be to steal them from you. All I seek, since the voice of my youth has been vexatious to you and a cause of scandal to everybody, is to acknowledge with this document different intentions.').[10] At the start of the latter dedication, he suggests the difficulty of his struggle and the protracted nature of the conflict between sin and repentance as he refers to the belatedness of his 'confesión'. He alludes to his scandalous life as a young man and this brings to mind the opening of *El mundo por de dentro* and the developed symbol of the labyrinth. In the letter to his aunt, however, there is at least a resolution to seek a new mode of living.

As with the poems to Lisi, the *Heráclito cristiano* presents problems of arrangement. A revised version entitled *Lágrimas de un penitente (Tears of a Penitent)* was published in Aldrete's 1670 edition. Twelve of the original poems were suppressed while three more were added. The most reliable manuscript is one owned by Don Eugenio Asensio Barbarín and it is from this that Blecua has made his reconstruction.[11] Blecua's edition is not only the most comprehensive but, with one or two exceptions, also provides evidence of a carefully organized sequence of poems with a chronological pattern rather on the lines of the cycle of poems to Lisi.

The collection contains some of Quevedo's best-known poems, the sonnets on time and death: 'Miré los muros de la patria mía' ('I looked at the walls of my native place') (no.29), 'Todo tras sí lo lleva el año breve' ('The brief year bears all away with it') (no.30) and '¡Cómo de entre mis manos te resbalas!' ('How you slip from between my hands!') (no.31). These poems, however, are concerned with only part of the complex experience that Quevedo attempts to convey in the *Heráclito cristiano*. In terms of the spiritual awakening described in the collection, they form only a stage towards the eventual goal of redemption. This is the spiritual state towards which the poet strives throughout, from the impassioned plea at the start of the first poem:

Un nuevo corazón, un hombre nuevo
ha menester, Señor, la ánima mía;
desnúdame de mí, que ser podría
que a tu piedad pagase lo que debo. (no.13)

My soul needs a new heart, a new man, Lord; strip me of myself, so it could be that I pay what I owe to your mercy.

A similar sentiment is to be found in *salmo* XXII, which alludes to the Sacrament of Holy Communion and which, though not the final poem in Blecua's edition, might be repositioned at the end of the collection, thus marking the successful outcome of the poet's struggle:

Pues hoy pretendo ser tu monumento,
porque me resucites del pecado,
habítame de gracia, renovado
el hombre antiguo en ciego perdimiento. (no.34)

Because, today, I seek to be your monument so that you restore me from sin, inhabit me with grace, now that the old man in his blind perdition has been made new.

But this process is by no means a straightforward progression. There are frequent lapses into the old way of life since the allurements of pleasure at times prove too much for the poet. In the sixth *salmo*, the clash between the attraction of sin and the prospect of disillusionment is particularly intense. The sinner recognizes his sin but cannot relinquish it:

tan ciego estoy en mi mortal enredo,
que no te oso llamar, Señor, de miedo
de que quieras sacarme de pecado.
¡Oh baja servidumbre:
que quiero que me queme y no me alumbre
la Luz que la da a todos!
¡Gran cautiverio es éste en que me veo!
¡Peligrosa batalla
mi voluntad me ofrece de mil modos!
No tengo libertad, ni la deseo,
de miedo de alcanzalla.
¿Cual infierno, Señor, mi alma espera
mayor que aquesta sujeción tan fiera? (no.18)

I am so blind in my mortal entanglement that I dare not call upon you, Lord, for fear that you may wish to remove me from sin. Oh base servitude: for I wish the light that is given to everyone to burn and not to illuminate me! This is a great bondage in which I see myself! My will provides me with a perilous battle in a thousand ways! I have no freedom, nor do I desire it for fear of attaining it. What hell, Lord, can my soul expect that is greater than this frightful subjection?

In *El mundo por de dentro*, too, Desengaño speaks of the difficulty in achieving true disillusionment. It is an unattractive proposition; man may be willing but the intent soon fades:

> Yo soy el Desengaño. Estos rasgones de la ropa son de los tirones que dan de mí los que dicen en el mundo que me quieren, y estos cardenales del rostro, estos golpes y coces me dan, en llegando, porque vine y porque me vaya. Que en el mundo todos decís que queréis desengaño, y, en teniéndole, unos os desesperáis, otros maldecís a quien os le dio, y los más corteses no le creéis. (p.165)

> I am Disillusionment. These rents in my clothing are from the tugs given me by those who say in the world that they want me, and these weals on my face, these blows and kicks they give when they attain me, because I came and in order that I should go away. For in the world you all say that you wish disillusionment, and once you have it, some of you despair, others of you curse him who gave it to you, and the more restrained among you do not believe it.

The eighth *salmo* is concerned with the deceiving facade of sin:

> Dejadme un rato, bárbaros contentos,
> que al sol de la verdad tenéis por sombra
> los arrepentimientos;
> que la memoria misma se me asombra
> de que pudiesen tanto mis deseos,
> que unos gustos tan feos
> hiciesen parecer hermosos tanto. (no.20)

> Leave me a moment, cruel pleasures, for in the sun of truth you have repentance as a shadow; for my memory itself is frightened that my desires could do so much that they made such ugly pleasures appear so beautiful.

The poet is again very conscious of the overwhelming lure of sin, and in the opening imperative ('Dejadme'), he expresses a frantic effort to rid himself of it. Man's inordinate desire blinds him to the reality that surrounds him — one of the main points of *El mundo por de dentro*. The discrepancy between appearance and reality is illustrated throughout the *Sueño*: the hypocrisy of the widower and widow, the feigned zeal of the *alguacil*, and the beauty of the woman that the protagonist desires so much.

The tenth *salmo* refers to the beguiling nature of the sin that the poet seeks to eschew. This is no longer seen in terms of 'bárbaros contentos', but more insidiously and perilously in the following way:

> Trabajos dulces, dulces penas mías;
> pasadas alegrías
> que atormentáis ahora mi memoria,
> dulce en un tiempo, sí, mas breve gloria . . . (no.22)

Sweet hardships, sweet punishments of mine; past joys that now torment my memory, once so sweet indeed, but a brief glory.

The third line is nicely ambiguous. Is it torment because of past sins or because the sins are past? The latter seems more likely if the wistful regret implicit in the repeated allusions to the sweetness of the experience are borne in mind.

The fourteenth *salmo* represents a halt, if not a step backwards, on the journey towards repentance, especially as it immediately follows one of the more hopeful utterances thus far where the poet speaks positively of his relationship with God (no.25). What follows is a poem of doubt concerned with 'la escuridad del corazón del hombre', not only as a past condition:

> Nególe a la razón el apetito
> el debido respeto,
> y es lo peor que piensa que un delito
> tan grave puede a Dios estar secreto,
> cuya sabiduría
> la escuridad del corazón del hombre,
> desde el cielo mayor, la lee más claro. (no.26)

Appetite denied reason a proper respect, and what is worse, it thinks that such a serious crime can be hidden from God, Who, in His wisdom, can read with utmost clarity the darkness in the heart of man from the height of Heaven.

but as a present reality:

> Yace esclava del cuerpo el alma mía,
> tan olvidada ya del primer nombre,
> que no teme otra cosa
> sino perder aqueste estado infame,
> que debiera temer tan solamente . . .

My soul lies enslaved by the body, so oblivious now of the first name that it fears nothing other than the loss of that vile state which it should only fear . . .

This is perhaps the most tortuous poem in the collection. The sentences are long and rambling and reflect the torment of moral or spiritual crisis; it is the product of much heart-searching.

In his journey towards spiritual rehabilitation, the poet undergoes a process that could be described as one of purgation. In the first poem (no.13) he pleads to be stripped of the trappings of the sinful self and in other poems in the early part of the collection, he speaks of his utter desolation (e.g. the 'yermo' ('wilderness') image in the third *salmo*). Later, there is a conscious effort to renounce the worldly and the material. In two *salmos* (nos.23, 27), the poet condemns wealth and praises the frugal life. The well-known sonnets on time and death also belong to this pattern of renunciation of the worldly. The consideration of time passing is expressed by Desengaño in *El mundo por de dentro* soon after his confrontation with the young protagonist. The old man asks:

> ¿Tú, por ventura, sabes lo que vale un día? ¿Entiendes de cuánto precio es una hora? ¿Has examinado el valor del tiempo? Cierto es que no, pues así, alegre, le dejas pasar, hurtado de la hora que, fugitiva y secreta, te lleva, preciosísimo robo. ¿Quién te ha dicho que lo que ya fue volverá, cuando lo hayas menester, si lo llamares? Dime: ¿has visto algunas pisadas de los días? No, por cierto, que ellos sólo vuelven la cabeza a reírse y burlarse de los que así los dejaron pasar. (p.164)

> Do you, by chance, know what a day is worth? Do you understand how much an hour costs? Have you examined the value of time? Obviously not, since blithe as you are, you let it pass away, stolen by the hour that fleetingly and secretly takes you away, the most precious of thefts. Who has told you that, if you were to call it, what once was will return when you have need of it? Tell me: have you seen any footprints of the days? No obviously not, since they only turn their heads to mock and laugh at those who let them pass in such a fashion.

The point about the poems on time in the *Heráclito cristiano*, in the context of the struggle, is that the poet *does* examine the value of time. There is now a full and painfully achieved awareness of mortality; and if in other poems the persona is striving towards a detachment from the material and the worldly, here he moves towards emotional detachment and resignation. The acute awareness of mortality that emerges in the sonnets on time is the dark night of the poet's soul, the void through which he must pass on his path to spiritual health. It is in this context that the mood of these bleak poems should be assessed. The Stoic sentiments of *salmo* XVI:

> Esta lágrima ardiente con que miro
> el negro cerco que rodea a mis ojos,
> naturaleza es, no sentimiento. (no.28)

> This ardent tear with which I look at the black circle that surrounds my eyes is nature not feeling.

and the better-known *salmo* XVIII:

> Breve suspiro, y último, y amargo,
> es la muerte, forzosa y heredada:
> mas si es ley, y no pena, ¿qué me aflijo? (no.30)

> Death, necessary and inherited, is a brief and final and bitter sigh: but if it is a law and not a punishment, why do I complain?

could be read as the necessity of death to the 'old' man (the 'hombre antiguo' of *salmo* XXII) before the 'new' man can emerge (the 'nuevo

corazón' and 'hombre nuevo' referred to at the very start of the collection).
The anguish and veiled protest of the above lines have been interpreted as
an effort by the poet to come to terms with the inevitability of death. [12] In the
context of the *Heráclito cristiano*, it could be read as another instance of the
clash caused by the protagonist clinging to the mode of life he knows he has
to reject and yet which constantly beckons him. The metaphorical
interpretation of death within life as a necessary condition prior to
redemption needs to be borne in mind for an understanding of the
celebrated, and occasionally misinterpreted, sonnet 'Miré los muros de la
patria mía' (no.29). It is a poem about decay and ruin, which correlate the
old way of life the persona is striving to renounce:

> Miré los muros de la patria mía,
> si un tiempo fuertes, ya desmoronados,
> de la carrera de la edad cansados,
> por quien caduca ya su valentía.
>   Salíme al campo, vi que el sol bebía
> los arroyos del yelo desatados,
> y del monte quejosos los ganados,
> que con sombras hurtó su luz al día.
>   Entré en mi casa; vi que, amancillada,
> de anciana habitación era despojos;
> mi báculo, más corvo y menos fuerte;
>   vencida de la edad sentí mi espada.
> Y no hallé cosa en que poner los ojos
> que no fuese recuerdo de la muerte. [13]

I looked at the walls of my native place, once strong and now dilapidated,
weary with the passing of time, as a result of which their strength is now
sapped. I went out into the countryside, I saw that the sun drank the streams
released from ice, and the cattle complaining that the mountain stole their
daylight with its shadows. I went into my house; I saw that it was the rubble of
an old, tarnished habitation; my walking-stick, more curved and less strong; I
felt my sword overcome by age. And I found nothing on which to set my eyes
that was not a reminder of death.

The opening line has been popularly interpreted as a reference to the
decline of Spain. But such a view is incompatible with the rest of the sonnet,
in which objects of personal, rather than national, significance are
described, and even more so with the collection as a whole, where there is
no concern with a national theme. [14] The image of walls is used negatively in
other poems in the collection: in the twelfth poem (no.24) where the poet,
meditating on the destruction of past civilizations, refers to the walls of
Carthage; and in the nineteenth poem where the wall is a symbol of youth
and life, powerless before the rapid onset of death:

> Feroz, de tierra el débil muro escalas,
> en quien lozana juventud se fía . . . (no.31)

Fiercely, you scale the fragile wall of earth that vigorous youth relies upon . . .

As the poet contemplates the countryside, his house and his possessions, he sees in these things a reflection of his own spiritual state. The first quatrain expresses a pervasive awareness of mortality and of the transience of things; the epithet 'cansados' suggests the weariness of the 'old' man. The second quatrain has an air of observed reality that Quevedo's descriptions of the natural world in his love poetry lack. The poet points to the speed with which the processes of time occur: no sooner, apparently, are the streams freed from winter ice than they evaporate in the sun's heat. The shadow overhanging the fields has an obvious symbolic value. Through the various images of the tercets, the poet conveys the experience of a man dissatisfied with his world ('patria').[15] There is an understanding of the futility and the fragility of the material world; and overall, it is a poem about one who needs to cast off the mantle of sin and, in view of its retrospective character, one who may be about to achieve this goal. It is a bleak poem, but a less tormented utterance than, say, *salmo* XIV (no.26) with its doubts and unease.

Salmos XXIII-XXV (nos.35-7) are meditations on religious subjects that correspond in structural importance within the cycle to the poems on time and death. In these three poems, the poet muses on incidents from the life of Christ in the manner prescribed in the Ignatian scheme of meditation.[16] In the last two *salmos* he imagines himself kneeling before the Cross:

> viendo al Señor que adoro
> teñido en sangre y anegado en llanto . . . (no.36)

seeing the Lord I adore, stained with blood and drowned in weeping . . .

> Mas veros en un leño mal pulido,
> de vuestra sangre, por limpiar, manchado,
> sirviendo de martirio a vuestra Madre . . . (no.37)

But seeing You on an unpolished timber, stained by the blood that has not been wiped, acting as a martyrdom to Your Mother . . .

The quality of these poems does not approach that of the sonnets on time and death. They are conventional religious utterances. The second, by far the longest poem in the collection, is a rambling composition that, by itself, seems too mellifluous. In the context of a spiritual struggle, however, it emerges as a significant stage in the poet-sinner's progress towards the goal of redemption.

Before the final poem (no.40) in Blecua's edition, comes a poem (no.39) which seems out of place, as it refers to a continuing state of sin: 'Yo, dormido, en mis daños persevero' ('I, asleep, persevere in my ills'). This seems inappropriate at this point in the collection, especially as it immediately follows a sonnet that ends with a clear expression of a hard-won disillusionment:

> Y vengo a conocer que, en el contento
> del mundo, compra el alma en tales días,
> con gran trabajo, su arrepentimiento. (no.38)

And I come to recognize that, in the joy of the world, on such days, the soul buys its repentance with a great deal of hardship.

The poet has now relinquished sin — a sentiment repeated in the final poem: 'Ya del error pasado me arrepiento' (no.40) ('Now I repent of my past error'). As I stated previously, the collection would ideally conclude with *salmo* XXII (no.34) with its clear allusions to Holy Communion.[17] But even without this amendment, the cycle ends with the poet reconciled with his Creator after having taken the reader on a journey through complex and profound experiences.

It now remains to determine the nature of the sin or sins with which the poet has been struggling. At the start of *El mundo por de dentro*, the youthful protagonist was depicted as being engaged in various activities; in the labyrinthine world of indulgence were streets which bore the names of some of the deadly sins:

> Ya por la calle de la ira, descompuesto, seguía las pendencias pisando sangre y heridas; ya por la de la gula veía responder a los brindis turbados. (pp.163-4)

One minute, I brazenly followed the fights, treading on blood and wounds, along the street of anger; the next moment, along the street of gluttony I saw chaotic toasts being answered.

In the *Heráclito cristiano*, however, the references to sin, both direct and implicit, make it clear that it is of an erotic nature. In the final poem, there is an unequivocal statement to that effect:

> Amor me tuvo alegre el pensamiento,
> y en el tormento, lleno de esperanza,
> cargándome con vana confianza
> los ojos claros del entendimiento. (no.40)

Love held my thought in happiness and full of hope in its torment, filling my bright eyes of understanding with vain trust.

It is love, then, that has been the cause of his torment; it is his 'error pasado', 'daños' and 'culpa' (no.40) ('past error, ills and blame'). But when we turn to the preface to the collection, there is a reference to past misdemeanours as 'el apetito, la pasión o la naturaleza' ('appetite, passion or nature'). This contradiction in defining the experience is not confined to the example I have chosen. There are several instances of this dual view, that is to say whether the experience is to be described in terms of love or lust. The word 'apetito', used in the dedication to the reader, is repeated in two poems. In the one that alludes to Holy Communion, the poet asks to be invested with grace lest he return to his old ways:

> Pues hoy pretendo ser tu monumento,
> porque me resucites del pecado,
> habítame de gracia, renovado
> el hombre antiguo en ciego perdimiento.
>   Si no, retratarás tu nacimiento
> en la nieve de un ánimo obstinado
> y en corazón pesebre, acompañado
> de brutos apetitos que en mí siento. (no.34)

Because today I seek to be your monument so that you restore me from sin, inhabit me with grace, now that the old man in his blind perdition has been made new. For, otherwise, you will depict your birth in the snow of a stubborn soul and in a manger heart, accompanied by brute appetites that I feel within me.

At the start of the fourteenth *salmo*, the poet contrasts reason and appetite: 'Nególe a la razón el apetito/el debido respeto' ('Appetite denied reason a proper respect') (no.26) — a variation of the contrast of love and reason, commonly encountered in medieval and Renaissance love poetry. In the same poem, the poet-sinner refers to the subordination of the soul to the body: 'Yace esclava del cuerpo el alma mía' ('My soul lies enslaved by the body'). This has a parallel with the first sonnet to Lisi (no.442) where the persona's noble faculties of reason and free-will are overthrown by the apparently insignificant physical traits of the beloved.

In the eighth *salmo*, the poet speaks of past pleasure with scorn and revulsion:

> Dejadme un rato, bárbaros contentos,
> que al sol de la verdad tenéis por sombra
> los arrepentimientos;
> que la memoria misma se me asombra
> de que pudiesen tanto mis deseos,
> que unos gustos tan feos
> hiciesen parecer hermosos tanto. (no.20)

> Leave me a moment, cruel pleasures, for in the sun of truth you have repentance as a shadow; for my memory itself is frightened that my desires could do so much that they made such ugly pleasures appear so beautiful.

What the poet had considered to be the beauty of love was in reality or, more correctly, from a retrospective, viewpoint, no more than disguised lust. This is a case of appearances being deceptive, one of the keynotes of *El mundo por de dentro*, to which I shall return below. The concluding phrase of the eighth *salmo* — 'las aguas del abismo/donde me enamoraba de mí mismo' ('the waters of the abyss where I fell in love with myself') — expresses powerfully a sense of indulgence and depravity which is how the poet-sinner considers his conduct at this juncture.

The fifth poem of the collection (no.17) provides an interesting comparison with a passage from the *Buscón*:

> Mas, ¡ay!, que si he dejado
> de ofenderte, Señor, temo que ha sido
> más de puro cansado
> que no de arrepentido.

> But, ah!, for if I have stopped offending You, Lord, I fear that it has been more from sheer tiredness rather than repentance.

Pablos expresses an identical sentiment at the end of the novel when he speaks of his intention to leave for the Indies in the company of a prostitute with whom he has fallen in love:

> Yo, que vi que duraba mucho este negocio, y más la fortuna en perseguirme — no de escarmentado, que no soy tan cuerdo, sino de cansado, como obstinado pecador — , determiné, consultándolo lo primero con la Grajal, de pasarme a las Indias con ella, por ver si mudando mundo y tierras, mejoraría mi suerte.[18]

> Now seeing that this affair was dragging out and, moreover, as fortune was pursuing me — not because I had learnt my lesson, for I am not so wise, but out of weariness like the persistent sinner that I am — after talking it over first with Grajal, I resolved to leave for the Indies with her, to see if I could improve my lot by changing world and lands.

The context of this quotation is significant, too, for comparative purposes. It appears after a scene of sacrilege and carnality when Pablos and his companions make love to prostitutes in the sanctuary of a church in which they have taken refuge from the law. Like the poet of the *Heráclito cristiano*, Pablos realizes his life has been sinful and resolves, though not from the soundest of motives, to reform. Pablos hopes this may be achieved by leaving for the Indies, an idea that may be compared to the poet's search for a new and better life in the *Heráclito cristiano*. The outcome is different, however: Pablos fails in his intention ('pues nunca mejora de estado quien muda solamente de lugar, y no de vida y costumbres') ('for he who only changes the place he lives and not the manner of his life never improves his condition'), while the poet is successful. As a footnote, it is perhaps significant that shortly after completing the *Heráclito cristiano* — the culmination of a period of personal crisis — Quevedo himself was to leave for a new kind of life as Osuna's secretary in Sicily.

In the second *salmo* (no.14), though the poet's view of his sin is again condemnatory, the references to the erotic experience are more oblique and the overall tone is less scathing than in the *salmos* previously considered. I quote the quatrains:

> ¡Cuán fuera voy, Señor, de tu rebaño,
> llevado del antojo y gusto mío!
> Llévame mi esperanza el tiempo frío,
> y a mí con ella un disfrazado engaño!
>   Un año se me va tras otro año,
> y yo más duro y pertinaz porfío,
> por mostrarme más verde mi albedrío
> la torcida raíz do está mi daño.

How far I stray, Lord, from Your flock, borne away by my whims and pleasures! Cold time takes away my hope, and a disguised illusion bears me off with it. A year escapes me and then another, while I carry on, more inured and stubborn than ever, so the twisted root wherein lies my ill can show my free-will to be even greener.

'Gusto' is not as extreme a term as 'apetito', and the epithets the persona applies to himself in the second quatrain ('duro y pertinaz') bring to mind the constancy and perseverance of the courtly lover.[19]

In other poems too, the view of the sinner's experience is more mellow. This tends to occur in those poems where the protagonist is torn between the old and the new and where consequently he regrets the passing of pleasure. This is seen to good effect at the opening of the tenth poem:

> Trabajos dulces, dulces penas mías;
> pasadas alegrías
> que atormentáis ahora mi memoria,
> dulce en un tiempo, sí, mas breve gloria,
> que llevaron tras sí mis breves días . . . (no.22)

Sweet hardships, sweet punishments of mine; past joys that now torment my memory, once so sweet indeed, but a brief glory, that carried my brief days off with them . . .

I have already commented on the repetition of the adjective 'dulce(s)', and the amatory association of these lines is enhanced by the allusion to a well-known love sonnet. They are clearly reminiscent of Garcilaso's tenth sonnet:

¡Oh dulces prendas por mi mal halladas,
dulces y alegres cuando Dios quería,
juntas estáis en la memoria mía
y con ella en mi muerte conjuradas![20]

Oh sweet gifts, encountered for my misfortune, sweet and joyous while God willed, you are together in my memory and conspire with it to kill me!

This affinity is not confined to lexical similarity, for Garcilaso writes nostalgically of an experience that has now gone while Quevedo muses wistfully on past pleasure. Both poets speak of the torment of recollection, and the idea of transience is allied to a nostalgic mood rather in the way Dante's Francesca da Rimini refers to her experience:

E quella a me: 'Nessun maggior dolore
che ricordarsi del tempo felice
ne la miseria; e ciò sa 'l tuo dottore. (V, ll.121-3)[21]

And she said to me: 'There is no greater grief than to recall happy times in misery; and this your doctor knows.'

As Quevedo's poem progresses, however, the lover's regret vies with the voice, albeit muted, of the moralist who finds compensation in the gain of self-knowledge:

mal derramados llantos,
si sois castigo de los cielos santos,
con vosotros me alegro y me enriquezco,
porque sé de mí mismo que os merezco,
y me consuelo más que me lastimo;
mas si regalos sois, más os estimo,
mirando que en el suelo,
sin merecerlo, me regala el cielo.

badly shed tears, if you are a punishment from the holy heavens, I rejoice in you and I am enriched, because I know, for my own part, that I deserve you, and I console rather than pity myself; but if you are gifts, I esteem you more, seeing that Heaven rewards me on the earth without my having deserved it.

The opening of the preceding poem, *salmo* IX, also alludes to a Garcilaso sonnet and would almost certainly convey the idea of an amatory experience to a reader of Quevedo's day:

Cuando me vuelvo atrás a ver los años
que han nevado la edad florida mía;
cuando miro las redes, los engaños

> donde me vi algún día,
> más me alegro de verme fuera dellos,
> que un tiempo me pesó de padecellos. (no.21)

> When I turn around to see the years that have snowed on my florid life; when I
> look at the nets, the deceits where I found myself once, the happiness I
> experience at seeing myself away from them is greater than the grief I felt
> when I suffered them.

The first line is particularly rich in association. Although the reader would probably be reminded of Garcilaso's first sonnet ('Cuando me paro a contemplar mi 'stado') ('When I stop to consider my condition'), the original source, the first line of which Quevedo translates literally, is Petrarch's sonnet 'Quand'io mi volgo in dietro a mirar gli anni' ('When I turn around to look at the years') (*Canzoniere*, no.298). It was a line imitated also by Lope and Argensola, though they appear to have had the secondary source of Garcilaso's *soneto* I in mind. Like both these poets, Quevedo develops a moral rather than amatory vein.[22] The 'redes' of the third line suggests the snares of love, but thereafter the poem is primarily a meditation on time. The idea of the poet's eventual redemption is rather summarily expressed, however, and the poem is overall less anguished than most in the collection. Indeed, despite the poet's awareness of the vanity of his past experience and of the brevity of life, the notion of the pleasure of love lingers after the haunting and allusive opening.

Amatory and moral terminology coincide in words like 'redes' and 'enredo', which bring to mind both the emblematic idea of the lover being trapped by the lady's beauty and disdain and the notion of moral or spiritual bewilderment, such as was correlated by the labyrinth symbol in *El mundo por de dentro*. A line from the first *salmo* similarly relates to the two perspectives:

> Dudosos pies por ciega noche llevo . . . (no.13)

> I bear my uncertain steps through a dark night . . .

Here two images are juxtaposed: the poet proceeding tentatively and darkness. They represent the poet's confused progress through life as a result of his sin. The same juxtaposition occurs in a late sonnet to Lisi, describing the fate of the lover who is lost and confused on love's journey:

> Por yerta frente de alto escollo, osado,
> con pie dudoso, ciegos pasos guío;
> sigo la escasa luz del fuego mío,
> que avara alumbra, habiéndome abrasado. (no.480)

Along the hard face of a high rock, boldly and with uncertain step, I lead my unseeing feet; I follow the scanty light of my fire which gives a miserly glow now that it has burnt me.

Another love sonnet provides a more explicit connection between the perilous journey in darkness and the idea of spiritual inadequacy or moral blindness:

> Por la cumbre de un monte levantado,
> mis temerosos pasos, triste, guío;
> por norte llevo sólo mi albedrío,
> y por mantenimiento, mi cuidado.
> Llega la noche, y hállome engañado,
> y sólo en la esperanza me confío ... (no.363)

Along the peak of a lofty mountain, I sadly lead my fearful steps; as a lodestar I only have my free-will, and for nourishment, my love. Night arrives and I find myself deceived, and I trust in hope alone ...

Just as images of bewilderment and aimlessness are present in *El mundo por de dentro*, so too is that of blindness as a metaphor for the youthful protagonist's inability to make sound judgements. In the passage where he is rebuked by Desengaño for his carnal impulses, his rational deficiency is analysed via the image of blindness:

Triste fue tu vida; no naciste sino para admirado. Hasta ahora te juzgaba por ciego, y ahora veo que también eres loco, y echo de ver que hasta ahora no sabes para lo que Dios te dio los ojos ni cuál es su oficio: ellos han de ver, y la razón ha de juzgar y elegir; al revés lo haces, o nada haces, que es peor. Si te andas a creerlos, padecerás mil confusiones, tendrás las sierras por azules, y lo grande por pequeño, que la longitud y la proximidad engañan la vista. (p.179)

Sad indeed was your life; you were born only to wonder at things. Until now I took you for blind, and now I see that you are also mad, and I notice that until now you do not know for what reason God gave you eyes nor what their function is: they are for seeing, and reason is for judging and choosing; you do it in the opposite way or you do nothing at all, which is worse. If you keep on believing them, you will suffer a thousand bewilderments; you will take the mountain-ranges to be blue, and what is large to be small, for distance and proximity both deceive the sight.

In two poems in the collection (nos.23, 27), the poet speaks of the need to renounce wealth and to lead a simple life. This conventional topic may have a more personal significance, however, if the connection between gold and the beloved and avarice and desire, ubiquitous in the love poetry, as we have seen, is borne in mind. The second of these poems, a sonnet, opens in a way that is reminiscent of the description of the lady in the love poetry:

Pise, no por desprecio, por grandeza,
minas el avariento fatigado;
viva amando, medroso y desvelado,
en precioso dolor, pobre riqueza. (no.27)

Let the weary miser tread on mines not out of scorn but from a desire for
greatness; let him live fearfully and sleeplessly, loving the poverty of riches in
his precious anguish.

'Minas' was a term used on several occasions as a means of witty allusion to
golden hair; the verb 'viva amando' requires no comment; and the last line
of the quatrain offers a clear parallel with the close of the sonnet, 'En crespa
tempestad del oro undoso' (no.449): 'Avaro y rico y pobre, en el tesoro, /
el castigo y la hambre imita a Midas, / Tántalo en fugitiva fuente de oro'
(Greedy and rich and poor, in the treasure, the punishment and hunger, it
imitates Midas, Tantalus in a fleeing fountain of gold).

In Chapter Three, I drew attention to the significance of gold as a
metaphor for beauty and as a source and symbol of greed. I also described
Quevedo's repeated comparison of the lover and the gold-seeker, as a
result of which, gold and the beloved were seen as objects of inordinate
desire. The dual perspective on love in the *Heráclito cristiano* — the
constant changes of attitude whereby the lover and the moralist vie for
power — serves, I believe, to confirm the ambivalence of the lover's
approach and descriptions in a number of love poems. The way in which
Quevedo interrelates the moral and the amatory through his distinctive use
of terminology so that it might refer to either experience or approach is
paralleled by the ambiguity and contradiction inherent in the experience
described in the *Heráclito cristiano*.

Conflicting attitudes towards the erotic experience are thus a marked
feature of the collection. The same contrast is to be found in one of the most
striking passages of *El mundo por de dentro*. After the initial allegorical
description of the persona wandering through the labyrinth of sin and
indulgence, his role had been essentially that of pupil-observer as his
venerable mentor, Desengaño, had instructed him as to the discrepancy
between appearance and reality. When the persona sees a beautiful and
seductive woman pass by, however, he attempts to join the throng of
admirers who follow in her wake, only to stumble over Desengaño's long
beard. The description of the woman contains Petrarchan metaphors for
aspects of her beauty, while the antithesis 'nevaban . . . abrasaban' in the
following quotation clearly belongs to the courtly-Petrarchist tradition:

Venía una mujer hermosa trayéndose de paso los ojos que la miraban y
dejando los corazones llenos de deseos. Iba ella con artificioso descuido
escondiendo el rostro a los que ya le habían visto y descubriéndole a los que

estaban divertidos. Tal vez se mostraba por velo, tal vez por tejadillo. Ya daba un relámpago de cara con un bamboleo de manto, ya se hacía brújula mostrando un ojo solo, ya tapada de medio lado, descubría un tarazón de mejilla. Los cabellos martirizados hacían sortijas a las sienes. El rostro era nieve y grana y rosas que se conservaban en amistad, esparcidas por labios, cuello y mejillas. Los dientes transparentes y las manos, que de rato en rato nevaban el manto, abrasaban los corazones. El talle y paso, ocasionando pensamientos lascivos. Tan rica y galana como cargada de joyas recibidas y no compradas. Vila, y arrebatado de la naturaleza, quise seguirla entre los demás, y, a no tropezar en las canas del viejo, lo hiciera. (p.178)

There approached a beautiful woman bearing in her wake eyes that looked at her and leaving hearts full of desire. She moved with an artful nonchalance, hiding her face from those who had already seen it and revealing it to those who were distracted. One moment she revealed herself through the veil, the next moment pulling it aside. One moment she gave a flash of lightning with her face by swaying her robe, the next, she made herself a peephole, showing just the one eye, and afterwards, muffled on one side of her face, she uncovered a slice of her cheek. Her martyred hair formed ringlets on her temple. The face was snow, scarlet and roses, preserved in friendship, and scattered on her lips, neck and cheeks. The transparent teeth and the hands, which from time to time covered her robe with snow, inflamed hearts. Her figure and her movements inspired lewd thoughts. She was so rich and elegant for she was laden with jewels that nature had bestowed upon her and which had not been bought. I saw her and, carried away by my desires, I started to follow her along with the others, and if I hadn't tripped over the white hair of the old man, I would have done so.

The passage blends the courtly-Petrarchist elements I have already mentioned with allusions to the persona's response in terms of lust ('pensamientos lascivos', 'arrebatado de la naturaleza'). This duality in defining the erotic experience is a characteristic of the *Heráclito cristiano*.

The protagonist reacts angrily to Desengaño's intervention. It marks the point in the work where the process of disillusioning meets its strongest challenge; it can be compared to the occasional lapses of the poet-protagonist in the *Heráclito cristiano*. The young man launches into an impassioned defence of sensual love, concluding with a rebellious justification of the desires aroused in him:

— Quien no ama con todos sus cinco sentidos una mujer hermosa, no estima a la naturaleza su mayor cuidado y su mayor obra. Dichoso es el que halla tal ocasión, y sabio el que la goza. ¡Qué sentido no descansa en la belleza de una mujer, que nació para amada del hombre! . . . ¡Qué ojos tan hermosos honestamente! ¡Qué mirar tan cauteloso y prevenido en los descuidos de una alma libre! ¡Qué cejas tan negras, esforzando recíprocamente la blancura de la frente! ¡Qué mejillas, donde la sangre mezclada con la leche engendra lo rosado que admira! ¡Qué labios encarnados, guardando perlas, que la risa muestra con recato! ¡Qué cuello! ¡Qué manos! ¡Qué talle! Todos son causa de perdición, y juntamente disculpa del que se pierde por ella. (pp.178-9)

— He who does not love a beautiful woman with all his five senses does not esteem the most carefully created product of nature. Happy is the man who finds such an opportunity and wise the one who enjoys it. What sense does not rest in the beauty of a woman who was born to be loved by man! . . . What chastely beautiful eyes! What a cunning and premeditated glance at the negligence of a soul that is free! What dark eyebrows, that reciprocally enhance the whiteness of the forehead! What cheeks, where the blood mingled with milk creates an admirable pinkness! What dark red lips, that contain pearls which her laughter shyly reveals! What a neck! What hands! What a figure! All these are a source of perdition and at the same time an excuse for him who is doomed because of her.

Desengaño rebukes him for his lustful inclination and then embarks on an extensive and bitter attack on woman and love, contrasting appearance and reality as he had done in the earlier illustrations. It is in the same vein as a passage from the eighth poem of the *Heráclito cristiano*:

> que la memoria misma se me asombra
> de que pudiesen tanto mis deseos,
> que unos gustos tan feos
> hiciesen parecer hermosos tanto. (no.20)

for my memory itself is frightened that my desires could do so much that they made such ugly pleasures appear beautiful.

The attack on woman in *El mundo por de dentro*, however, has a Swiftian intensity and, although it corresponds to the moralistic appraisals of the erotic experience in the *Heráclito cristiano*, it is far more venomous. I quote the opening of the diatribe:

> ¿Viste esa visión, que, acostándose fea, se hizo esta mañana hermosa ella misma y hace extremos grandes? Pues sábete que las mujeres lo primero que se visten, en despertándose, es una cara, una garganta y unas manos, y luego las sayas. Todo cuanto ves en ella es tienda y no natural. ¿Ves el cabello? Pues comprado es y no criado. Las cejas tienen más de ahumadas que de negras; y si como se hacen cejas se hicieran las narices, no las tuvieran. Los dientes que ves y la boca era, de puro negra, un tintero, y a puros polvos se ha hecho salvadera. La cera de los oídos se ha pasado a los labios, y cada uno es una candelilla. ¿Las manos? Pues lo que parece blanco es untado. (p.179)

Did you see that vision that, though ugly on going to bed, made itself beautiful and makes a lot of fuss about it. Well, you should know that the first thing that women put on when they wake up is a face, a throat and hands, and then their skirts. All you see in her is display, it is not natural. Do you see the hair? Well, it's bought and not grown. The eyebrows are smoked black rather than being naturally so; and if nostrils were made like eyebrows, then she wouldn't have any. Those teeth you see and that mouth were so utterly black that they were an inkwell, and with all the powders she has used it has become a pounce-box. The wax from her ears has gone to her lips and both are a small candle. As for the hands, well, what seems so white is nothing but grease.

In the *princeps* edition, this savage passage formed the conclusion of the *Sueño*, and there is no doubting the heat engendered by the exchange. That this may represent something close to the author's heart is suggested by the sudden transformation of the persona-observer into an active protagonist; while, as we have seen, the debate, unresolved in the *Sueño*, was to continue in the *Heráclito cristiano* in the following year.

In his merciless and bleak condemnation of love and woman, Desengaño stressed not only their deceptive nature but also the ugliness that lay beneath the surface. This process may have a parallel in the *Heráclito cristiano* when the poet fixes almost obsessively on the fragility of life. This is seen, for example, in the sombre irony of a phrase like 'Antes que sepa andar el pie, se mueve/camino de la muerte' ('Before the foot knows how to walk, it moves on death's road.') (no.30), in the denial of youth and strength, and particularly in the imagery of ruin and decay that permeates much of the collection and which symbolizes the necessary destruction prior to rehabilitation. In one of the later *salmos*, the poet describes a state of emptiness after relinquishment. Knowledge comes after the removal of the old way of life:

> sólo se queda entre las manos mías
> de un engaño tan vil conocimiento,
> acompañado de esperanzas frías. (no.38)

> there only remains in my hands the knowledge of such a base deceit, accompanied by cold hopes.

Images of decay and ruin also occur frequently towards the end of the Lisi cycle, as do ideas of physical decline and old age. In successive sonnets from *El Parnaso español* we read:

> Bebe el ardor, hidrópica, mi vida,
> que ya, ceniza amante y macilenta,
> cadáver del incendio hermoso, ostenta
> su luz en humo y noche fallecida. (no.485)

> My dropsical life drinks the ardour, for now, a gaunt and loving cinder, a corpse of that beautiful fire, it displays its deceased light as smoke and darkness.

> Todo soy ruinas, todo soy destrozos,
> escándalo funesto a los amantes . . . (no.486)

> I am all ruins, all ravages, a baneful scandal for the lovers . . .

> Ya que pasó mi verde primavera,
> Amor, en tu obediencia l'alma mía;
> ya que sintió mudada en nieve fría
> los robos de la edad mi cabellera;
>   pues la vejez no puede, aunque yo quiera,
> tarda, seguir tu leve fantasía . . . (no.487)

Now that my green Spring has gone, Love, and my soul is obedient to you; and now that my hair, changed into cold snow, has perceived the thefts of age; since old age cannot, even if I should wish it, follow slowly your fickle fancies . . .

> El cuerpo, que de l'alma está desierto
> (ansí lo quiso Amor de alta belleza),
> de dolor se despueble y de tristeza:
> descanse, pues, de mármoles cubierto. (no.488)

Let the body, which is devoid of the soul (thus Love wished it for the sake of a lofty beauty), be emptied of pain and sadness: let it find rest, then, covered in marble.

> Yo soy ceniza que sobró a la llama;
> nada dejó por consumir el fuego
> que en amoroso incendio se derrama. (no.489)

I am a cinder that remained after the flame; the fire, that flows into a conflagration of love, left nothing to be consumed.

The old age and decay mentioned in these poems refers, as we have seen, to the poet-lover after a lengthy period of sustained devotion and aware of his coming death. But if the use of similar imagery in the *Heráclito cristiano*, notably 'Miré los muros de la patria mía' (no.29), is borne in mind, then one can discern in these late sonnets a certain regret at love and a wish for renunciation. In one of the sonnets on decay and old age, the persona referred to himself as an 'escándalo funesto a los amantes' (no.486) while earlier sonnets had also revealed the spirit of 'escarmiento', of warning to others (nos.461,473,478). It might thus not be unreasonable to ascribe to the idea of decay in the last part of the Lisi cycle a metaphorical as well as literal intent given the background of muted disillusionment.

In Petrarch's *Canzoniere*, the palinodic aspect is a sizeable feature, but one that neither structurally nor substantially had much, if any, effect on the cycle of poems to Lisi. The lack of a palinode for the poems to Lisi — for the isolated expressions of regret quoted above do not amount to a palinode to be compared to the last quarter of the *Canzoniere* — cannot be a matter of chance. As I have argued throughout this study, the poetry of

Quevedo tends far less to the spiritual than that of his contemporaries and predecessors, including Petrarch. The lack of the palinode explicitly attached to part or the whole of the love poetry is consistent with the picture and the behaviour of the love poet that has emerged in the preceding chapters.

Nonetheless, a future editor of Quevedo's work might be tempted to place the *Heráclito cristiano* after the cycle of poems to Lisi, thereby inviting us to read it as a palinode for the poet's passion for Lisi.[23] The idea of disillusionment and the imagery of ruin and decay that characterize the later poems of the cycle could then be seen as an anticipation of the terms in which the poet-moralist describes his struggle, renunciation and eventual victory in the *Heráclito cristiano*. But it is questionable whether this can be considered a true or convincing palinode; it is not, for the most part, a clear and definitive renunciation but rather a perilous and anguished quest for it. In the collection, the lover figures as an antagonist to and mirror-image of the moralist. What the latter sees as base instincts, the former considers to be the sweetness of love — an experience that is expressed in terms of the courtly-Petrarchist tradition, as in the Garcilaso reminiscences, and thus at a far remove from the moralist's rationalization. There is consequently a polarization of attitudes in the *Heráclito cristiano* even allowing for the moralist's ultimate victory; the focus is by no means stable and there is not that certainty of voice that distinguishes the true palinode.

A specific point of contact between the *Heráclito cristiano* and the poems to Lisi is provided by the sonnet placed last in Blecua's edition of the former collection, in which the poet declares that love has been the source of his waywardness (no.40). This poem is, as I have shown elsewhere,[24] a close imitation of an anniversary sonnet by Petrarch to Laura *in morte* which refers to the twenty-one years that he loved her while she was alive: 'Tennemi Amor anni vent 'uno ardendo' ('Love held me burning for twenty-one years') (no.364). Quevedo's first line ('Amor me tuvo alegre el pensamiento') ('Love held my thought in happiness') omits the reference to the duration of his love while retaining the subject, verb and object of the original. There are another two *salmos* in the *Heráclito cristiano*, which are freer imitations of the *Canzoniere*, and which, like the sonnet mentioned previously, have as their source, anniversary sonnets. The anniversary element is suppressed in the *Heráclito cristiano* where it would have no significance, though Quevedo makes much of it in the cycle to Lisi, as has already been shown. Indeed, the opening of the sonnet that commemorates the twenty-second anniversary of the meeting may well derive from the same Petrarch sonnet as had the *salmo*, 'Amor me tuvo alegre el pensamiento' (no.40): 'Hoy cumple amor en mis ardientes venas/veinte y

dos años, Lisi . . . ' (no.491) ('Today love completes twenty-two years in
my burning veins, Lisi . . .'). Petrarch's anniversary sonnets are penitential
utterances as the poet draws attention to the fact that his first sight of Laura
occurred on Good Friday; the sonnet that marks the eleventh anniversary
refers to the sacred significance of the anniversary:

> Or volge, Signor mio, l'undecimo anno
> ch'i' fui sommesso al dispietato giogo
> che sopra i più soggetti è più feroce:
>   miserere del mio non degno affanno:
> redùci i pensier vaghi a miglior luogo:
> rammenta lor come oggi fusti in croce. (no.62)

Now I have reached, Lord, the eleventh year since I was subjected to the
merciless yoke which is crueller to the most abject: have pity on my unworthy
anguish: bring my wandering thoughts back to a better place: remind them
how today you were on the Cross.

Quevedo's imitation of the anniversary sonnets from the *Canzoniere* thus
reveals two motives: in the Lisi cycle, his own 'canzoniere', they mark the
passage of time and provide a skeletal chronology; in the *Heráclito
cristiano*, the imitations reveal the same concern with repentance as the
source poems. But it must be emphasized that Quevedo separates these two
functions carefully: while he celebrates the constancy and duration of his
passion, he has not the misgivings and doubt that Petrarch has on such
occasions about the value of his amatory experience. To interpret the
Heráclito cristiano as a palinode for the Lisi poems thus seems unwise on
two counts. Firstly, there is the character of the *Heráclito cristiano* itself —
tormented, occasionally ambivalent — which militates against such an
interpretation. Secondly, there is no evidence that Quevedo wished the
cycle to Lisi to contain a palinodic section; indeed in the light of significant
divergences from Petrarch in the case of the anniversary sonnets from the
Canzoniere, he seems to be consciously disassociating himself from a move
in that direction.

I have chosen to argue the case against seeing the *Heráclito cristiano* as a
palinode to the poems to Lisi by an examination of the texts rather than on a
biographical basis because, as we have already seen, as far as Quevedo is
concerned, the latter is a factor that is fraught with uncertainty. But on this
occasion, what biographical evidence there is tends to corroborate my
conclusions. It is probable, though not certain, that Quevedo wrote most of
the Lisi poems after 1613,[25] the year in which he wrote the *Heráclito
cristiano*. On the basis of Quevedo's poetry and letters, Green supposes
that for years after, indeed for the rest of his life, Quevedo oscillated
between the way of the flesh and the spirit.[26] A later, more classic, example

of a palinode is provided by 'El escarmiento' ('The Warning') (no.12), a poem Quevedo wrote or, more probably, revised in the last year of his life.[27]

It covers the same emotional and lexical territory as the *Heráclito cristiano*, though it is a far less tormented utterance, having none of the rebellion that we find in the earlier work and in *El mundo por de dentro*. There are a number of allusions both to an amatory experience and, consciously or otherwise, to the poet's own work. I quote the second stanza as illustration:

> En la que escura ves, cueva espantosa,
> sepulcro de los tiempos que han pasado,
> mi espíritu reposa,
> dentro en mi propio cuerpo sepultado,
> pues mis bienes perdidos
> sólo han dejado en mí fuego y gemidos,
> vitorias de aquel ceño,
> que, con la muerte, me libró del sueño
> de bienes de la tierra,
> y gozo blanda paz tras dura guerra,
> hurtado para siempre a la grandeza,
> al envidioso polvo cortesano,
> al inicuo poder de la riqueza,
> al lisonjero adulador tirano.
> ¡Dichoso yo, que fuera de este abismo,
> vivo, me soy sepulcro de mí mismo!

In the fearful dark cave that you see, a tomb of the time that has gone, my spirit rests, buried in my own body, since my lost joys have left only fire and sobbing in me, the victories of that frown which, with death, freed me from the dream of happiness on earth, and I enjoy sweet peace after a hard war, separated for ever from what is grand, the envious, courtly dust, the iniquitous power of wealth, the flattering, fawning tyrant. How happy am I who, out of this abyss, am, in life, my own tomb!

The phrase 'bienes perdidos', referring to lost pleasure, recalls the 'bien perdido' of the tenth poem of the *Heráclito cristiano* (no.22), while the ideas and images that follow are strongly suggestive of an erotic experience. 'Fuego' and 'gemidos' represent two keynotes of the lover's emotions: passion and suffering. The phrase 'victorias de aquel ceño' brings to mind a specific and significant love poem — the first sonnet of the Lisi cycle:

> ¿Qué importa blasonar del albedrío,
> alma, de eterna y libre, tan preciada,
> si va en prisión de un ceño ... (no.442)

Of what use is it to boast of free-will, of a soul that is eternal, free and so valued, if it goes in the prison of a frown ...

The juxtaposition of 'gemidos' and 'vitorias' is paralleled in the final tercet of the same sonnet:

> y no tienen consuelo mis gemidos;
> pues ni de su vitoria están ufanos,
> ni de mi perdición compadecidos.

And my moans are inconsolable; for those attributes of hers are neither proud of their victory nor compassionate with my defeat.

The image of the 'dura guerra' recalls the 'peligrosa batalla' ('perilous battle') of the sixth *salmo* of the *Heráclito cristiano* (no.18), while that of the abyss is used in a similar way at the end of the eighth poem to correlate sin and self-indulgence: 'las aguas del abismo/donde me enamoraba de mí mismo' ('the waters of the abyss where I fell in love with myself') (no.20).

The third stanza also contains a number of amatory allusions. I quote the first part:

> Estas mojadas, nunca enjutas, ropas,
> estas no escarmentadas y deshechas
> velas, proas y popas,
> estos hierros molestos, estas flechas,
> estos lazos y redes
> que me visten de miedo las paredes . . .

These soaked clothes that are never dry, these shattered sails, prows and sterns that have not learnt their lesson, these annoying irons, these arrows, these bows and nets that clothe my walls with fear . . .

The nautical imagery, the shipwreck and the wet clothing recall the sonnet in which the lover complains unavailingly of his loss of freedom (no.300). The following images — 'hierros', 'flechas', 'lazos' and 'redes' — are common amatory terms suggesting a lover wounded by the arrows of love, enslaved by his lady and trapped by the snares of her hair. As in the *Heráclito cristiano*, the reformed sinner speaks of his renunciation of ambition and wealth: the fatal lure of the riches of the Indies — often a metaphor for the beloved — attracts him no more:

> ni a Fortuna me entrego,
> con la codicia y la esperanza ciego,
> por cavar, diligente,
> los peligros preciosos del Oriente . . .

nor do I hand myself over to fortune, blind with greed and hope, busily to dig the precious dangers of the Indies . . .

As in the later poems of the *Heráclito cristiano*, so towards the end of 'El escarmiento' there is an emphasis on greater awareness, of disillusionment after sin and of wisdom after folly, though the religious aspect is not as explicit in the later poem. The poet's hope for liberation from the shackles of life is couched in terms that are reminiscent of the lover's voice:

> aguardo que desate de mis venas
> la muerte prevenida
> la alma, que anudada está en la vida,
> disimulando horrores
> a esta prisión de miedos y dolores,
> a este polvo soberbio y presumido,
> ambiciosa ceniza, sepultura
> portátil, que conmigo la he traído . . .

I wait for anticipated death to release from my veins my soul that is tied up in life, as I conceal my horror of this prison of fears and griefs, of this conceited and haughty dust, this ambitious cinder, a portable tomb, that I have carried along with me . . .

Words like 'venas', 'polvo' and 'ceniza' are distinctive fingerprints of Quevedo's style, especially in the case of the poems to Lisi, where they are often invested with profound and elevated emotional overtones. Their appearance here serves perhaps to underline the extent of the poet's victory, by suggesting that even the noblest and most lofty amatory experience and aspiration has now been renounced. At the very end, images of wealth are presented as a source of greed and, from what can be understood from other places, of desire — 'codicia':

> Cánsate ya, ¡oh mortal!, de fatigarte
> en adquirir riquezas y tesoro;
> que últimamente el tiempo ha de heredarte,
> y al fin te dejarán la plata y oro.

Get weary, oh mortal one!, of exhausting yourself by the acquisition of wealth and treasures; for ultimately time will have your inheritance, and in the end silver and gold will leave you.

This is perhaps Quevedo's last word on love. What remains to be asked is whether it should be the abiding impression: the last word on Quevedo, love poet.

1 Henry Ettinghausen (*Francisco de Quevedo and the Neostoic Movement* (Oxford, 1972)) suggests that this period was decisive for Quevedo's development as a Neostoic and that it was 'marked by what seems to have been an acute and prolonged crisis of conscience' (p.15), dating from 1609 until the departure for Sicily in 1613. Blecua (*Poesía original*,xxv) also refers to a 'crisis' but implies that it was shorter-lived though still very intense: 'El año de 1613 es decisivo para la poesía metafísica española, puesto que en el retiro de la aldea, al cumplir los treinta y tres años, pasa por una tremenda crisis que se traduce en el *Heráclito cristiano*'.

2 *Epistolario*, 15.

3 For example, the ones included in Espinosa's anthology, *Flores de poetas ilustres de España*, (Madrid, 1603). See Crosby, *Poesía varia*, 45-93.

4 There are startling juxtapositions of the solemn and the frivolous in this *Sueño*. For example: the humorous description of the 'putos', 'viejas' and 'cornudos' is immediately followed by a sombre meditation on mortality; a description of a man tormented, not by the lurid punishments of a Boschian hell, but by his own conscience, is abruptly succeeded by the narrator's mirth at the sight of the innkeepers who, according to one demon, are 'tan diablos como nosotros'; the amusing account of a poet who suffers as a result of the dire consequences of the dictates of rhyme is followed by a solemn passage on those consigned to hell because they were unable to pray.

5 The relationship of these two works is discussed by Ettinghausen, *Francisco de Quevedo and the Neostoic Movement*, 73-91.

6 *Lágrimas de Hieremias Castellanas*. This work has been edited by J.M. Blecua and E.M. Wilson (Madrid, 1953).

7 *Sueños y discursos*, ed. Felipe C.R. Maldonado (Madrid, 1972), 163.

8 See Morris Bishop, *Petrarch and His World* (London, 1964), 190.

9 There is no modern edition of this work, but see Terry, *An Anthology of Spanish Poetry 1500-1700. Part One*, 77-80.

10 Blecua, *Poesía original*, 19.

11 'En la reconstrucción del *Heráclito cristiano* . . . sigo el orden en que figuran los poemas en cierto manuscrito de don Eugenio Asensio Barbarín, que contiene 26 de los poemas, siendo así el códice que más salmos copia'. *Poesía original*,cxxxi.

12 See for example, Laín Entralgo, art. cit., 77.

13 I quote the revised version. Both this and the original are printed by Crosby in *Poesía varia*, 114-16, and the merits of the two versions are discussed by R.M. Price, 'A Note on the Sources and Structure of "Miré los muros de la patria mía"', *Modern Language Notes*, LXXVIII (1963), 194-9.

14 This is clearly demonstrated by J.M. Blecua, 'Sobre un célebre soneto de Quevedo', *Ínsula*, III, no.31 (July, 1948), 3.

15 'Patria' implies the spatial limits of the poet's experience: wherever he lives, there is his homeland. In a moral sonnet (no.70), Quevedo refers to the world as 'patria de tu cuerpo', while in his *De los remedios de cualquier fortuna*,a translation of a work attributed to Seneca, in a section which offers consolation for those who are exiled, he writes: 'Dejaré mi casa por otra, y por otro lugar el mío; mas nunca podrán hacer que deje mi tierra . . . Dejaré una parte de mi patria por otra'. *Obras completas: obras en prosa*, ed. Felicidad Buendía (6th ed.) (Madrid, 1974), 1076.

16 For a summary of the Ignatian scheme of meditation, see Louis L. Martz, *The Poetry of Meditation* (New Haven, 1954), 25-39.

17 See Price, ed. cit., 99-100.

18 Ed. cit., 269-70.

19 Compare Sempronio's remarks to Calisto: 'La perseuerancia en el mal no es constancia; mas dureza ó pertinacia la llaman en mi tierra. Vosotros los filósofos de Cupido llamalda como quisiérdes'. Fernando de Rojas, *La Celestina*, ed. J. Cejador y Frauca, 2 vols. (Madrid, 1968), I, 43.

20 Ed. cit., 46.

21 *La Divina Commedia I. Inferno*, ed. Carlo Grabher (Milan, 1965), 70.

22 See my article, 'Three Examples of Petrarchism in Quevedo's *Heráclito cristiano*', *Bulletin of Hispanic Studies*, LVIII (1981), 22-5.

23 See Green, *Courtly Love in Quevedo*, 74.

24 'Three Examples of Petrarchism', 27-9. I draw on this article for my following observations.

25 The stylistic maturity of the Lisi sonnets argues against regarding them as products of Quevedo's youth, though Moore's suggestion (op. cit., 52) that the date of the Lisi poems corresponds to the hypothetical period of the relationship (1623-45) is, I feel hazardous and misguided. Even Moore himself admits that the dates are 'highly speculative'.

26 *Courtly Love in Quevedo*, 72-6.

27 See Henry Ettinghausen, 'Un nuevo manuscrito autógrafo de Quevedo', *Boletin de la Real Academia Española*, LII (1972), 218.

CONCLUSION
From the Work to the Man

No one who works his way through the *Heráclito cristiano* can fail to be moved by the struggle depicted therein, even if he is not altogether in sympathy with the terms in which the conflict is conceived and presented. It is a work that has an immediacy created by the strong awareness of self. But, whether it is, as Green claims, one of those works that present the fullest or truest picture of Quevedo is another issue.[1] It is something of a truism to conclude that the 'genuine' Quevedo is the one who speaks of a 'yo' that can be related with some confidence to Quevedo, the man. But it does scant justice to other facets of his creative personality. To support his claim, Green points to the recurrence of such penitential expressions over a long period of Quevedo's life (pp.78-9). But this view can be challenged on two counts at least. Firstly, there is, as we have seen, the very character of a work like the *Heráclito cristiano* with its doubts and backsliding. Secondly, one has to reckon with the prominence in Quevedo's literary output of a burlesque and irreverent vein which spans, if anything, a longer period than that covered by the penitential manner. I refer not to the social satirist in pursuit of vice and folly such as we find, for instance, in most of the *Sueños*, and who complements the tormented critic of self, but to the writer — both in verse and in prose — whose aim is humour and ridicule, and whose imaginative fecundity and élan leads him paradoxically, and unlike the satirico-moralist, almost to celebrate the deficiencies and ugliness of mankind. Revulsion leads and gives way to sheer creative pleasure.[2] Here Quevedo delights, he does not bemoan. The laughter is cruel and sardonic, but it is laughter no less. We are a long way from a poet inspired by the Weeping Philosopher and by the noble humanity of the Psalms.

Another image of Quevedo, another contender for the role of the true voice, is presented by the figure that has been the subject of this study. Much more caution is needed in this regard, however, than in the case of the *Heráclito cristiano* for a 'works to man' approach, in view of the variety of possibilities offered to the Renaissance poet by the interaction of the real and the fictional, convention and individuality, the creator and his persona. What picture of Quevedo, the man, can be gleaned from his love poetry? Is the love poet, such as I have defined him, less true than the penitent or the satirist or the humourist? These are questions that cannot produce clear answers, in view of the lack of information on certain key aspects of Quevedo's emotional life, but there are, I believe, some significant pointers that contribute to a fuller understanding of the complex and elusive figure of Quevedo.

Attempts to discover Quevedo's definitive view of love and woman, and thereby to attain a significant insight into his character, present a bewildering picture. The most simplistic appraisal is, not surprisingly, Astrana Marín's:

> Era proverbial su galantería con las damas, y el gran ascendiente que sobre ellas ejercía, por sus dichos y agudezas. Don Francisco no tuvo aquí rival ni posible competidor. Desde muy joven repartió en él tan liberalmente la sal y la gracia Naturaleza, que dijérase no haberle quedado ninguna para otros.[3]

> His chivalry with ladies was proverbial, as was the great power he exercised over them by his sayings and wit. In this, Don Francisco had neither a rival nor a likely competitor. From a very young age, nature bestowed upon him charm and grace so liberally that one would have said that nothing had been left for anyone else.

And:

> No es extraño en consecuencia, que por sus chistes, burlas, chanzas y donaires, gustara tanto de oirle el bello sexo, y que él, muy enamoradizo de suyo, procurara excederse ante las damas en su gracia natural. (p.529)

> It is not strange, consequently, that by his tales, jokes, banter and charm, the fair sex should like to listen to him so much, and that he, for his part, should, with his amorous disposition, try to excell in natural grace in the company of ladies.

These are startling statements if we think of the lame, myopic misanthrope, and it is symptomatic of Astrana Marín's whole approach to Quevedo, which smacks of idealization and hero-worship. Most crucially perhaps, he ignores the complex relationship between creator and artefact.

Dámaso Alonso comes to a different conclusion:

> Del turbio revoltijo de aparentes contradicciones que forman a este ser, desde su fachada exterior hasta su ambiente moral, podrían salir muchas imágenes distintas; la que no sale, la que no nos podemos representar, es la de un Quevedo galanteador de damiselas. Hay hombres que, por demasiado hombres, no tienen mucho éxito con las mujeres, y de este tipo me parece que era Quevedo. Les falta en su persona moral y física un plano que resbale hacia lo feminino y que sirva para la unión de esos dos hemisferios siempre en guerra que forman el mundo humano.[4]

> Many different images could arise from the confused mess of apparent contradictions that constitute this being, from its outward aspect to its moral essence; the one that does not emerge, the one that we cannot accept, is that of a Quevedo who is a courter of damsels. There are men who, because they are

too manly, have little success with women, and I think that Quevedo was of this type. They lack in their moral and physical presence a level that slides into the feminine, and that serves for the union of those two constantly warring hemispheres shaped by the world of human relationships.

Amédée Mas arrives at a definition from an opposite direction. In the abundant examples of misogynism in Quevedo's work, Mas discerns a powerful attraction for women:

> La misogynie de Quevedo, disions-nous au début de cette étude, s'édifie sur le goût des femmes. On a trop affirmé sa misogynie, on l'a trop niée aussi. La vérité est sans doute qu'il déteste les femmes parce qu'il les aime trop. Trop pour la tranquillité de sa conscience chrétienne.[5]

This view is consistent with the struggle outlined in the *Heráclito cristiano* and the debate on love in *El mundo por de dentro*, but it is not one that takes the love poet primarily into account. Manuel Durán, as has already been seen, contends that Quevedo was drawn to courtly love ideas because they offered a refuge for his reserve and timidity.[6] Like Mas, he is attracted to the notion of a misogynistic paradox, but he departs from the French critic to put forward a thesis that owes something to Ayala's character-study of Quevedo:[7]

> Yo creo, por mi parte, que el odio a la mujer es para Quevedo una manifestación secundaria del temor a enamorarse, porque en el amor — no en un amor platónico, como el que se manifiesta en los sonetos a Lisi; sí en un amor vivido, auténtico — Quevedo se hubiera visto obligado a contemplar, para ofrecerse íntegro a su amada, su personalidad total, su cuerpo y su alma. (p.39)

> For my own part, I think that the hatred of women is for Quevedo a secondary symptom of the fear of falling in love, because in love — not in a platonic relationship like that revealed in the sonnets to Lisi but, on the contrary, in a lived, authentic love-affair — Quevedo would have been obliged to contemplate his entire personality, body and soul, in order to offer himself completely to his beloved.

The attractive courtier, the epitome of masculinity, the misogynist *malgré lui*, the timid lover — such are the definitions that confront us. It would not be difficult to find evidence for all of these views in Quevedo's poetry, but can it be claimed that any one of them represents the true, or even the dominant, voice of the love poet? I believe that conclusions based on my foregoing survey lend support to some of these views and also help to explain the contradictions.

Critics have spoken of Quevedo's sincerity as a love poet.[8] This is a quality that is difficult to assess, and it is not a term that I myself would choose, though perhaps it corresponds to what I have characterized and labelled as individuality in the course of this study. But it should again be emphasized that it has not been my aim to represent the love poetry of Quevedo as conspicuously or consistently at odds with the ethos that Pozuelo Yvancos terms the courtly-Petrarchist-Neoplatonic synthesis. The nature of my study has led me to focus on the unusual and the apparently exceptional, but I do not believe this to be a distortion. A keynote of Quevedo's love poetry is a directness that goes beyond the conventional in such matters as approach, request, description and complaint; the accepted boundaries of formula and expression are transgressed on a significant number of occasions. There is an impatience and exasperation in his view of the amatory experience that is both indecorous and urgent; most strikingly, notions of suffering as a welcome indicator of amatory identity and of love as an ennobling power leave him cold. The experience is envisaged far more in terms of carnal aspiration, striving and expectation than is the case with his contemporaries and predecessors. In short, convention is not flouted, but it is on various occasions modified, ignored or challenged.

Two ways in which this individuality and independence assert themselves can be succinctly summarized. There is, as has been seen in a number of places in my study, a favoured semantic field which clearly connotes the directness and boldness to which I have referred. One could, for example, extract a series of key terms that are related by association and punning: *fuente — beber — comer — comercio — oro — minas — Midas — Tántalo — fuente* (fountain — drinking — eating — commerce — gold — mines — Midas — Tantalus — fountain). Here are references to two myths, and this is another area where Quevedo's distinctiveness as love poet can be seen. Popular myths such as those of Orpheus and Icarus and the whole range of association they provoke do not appeal to Quevedo. Indeed, in the former instance he reveals an unusually negative response in those few love poems where the myth is developed in any detail (nos.297, 299). Tantalus, Midas and Vulcan are favoured myths and sometimes closely identified with the poet. But, as Cossío's study implies,[9] these are not the myths most commonly encountered in the work of Golden Age writers. The first two are clearly and distinctively associated with the extremes of desire and frustration, while Quevedo's treatment of the myth of Vulcan is especially significant, as my observations in Chapter Two will have suggested. Through this mythological figure, punningly related to Venus, Quevedo expresses a sense of hurt and vulnerability; and by its peculiar presentation he hints at reserve and concealment. In this, we are not so far from Durán's suggestion regarding Quevedo's timidity and Ayala's concerning his sensitivity. This is an issue which I now wish to explore in more detail.

Quevedo's satire of love and woman is, as Mas has illustrated, as comprehensive as it is scathing — little escapes his merciless humour. But for all its linguistic brilliance, the attack is, in the main, conventional, owing much to Latin satirists such as Juvenal, while in spirit, it is an inheritance of medieval anti-feminist writing.[10] But what is of particular interest is the fact that Quevedo ridicules not only the conventions of love, but also aspects of the amatory experience that are distinctively his. On the one hand, the anti-Petrarchist sentiment of the following sonnet from *El Parnaso español* is but one of many examples in Quevedo's work,[11] and such as may be found in that of his contemporaries, notably in Lope's *Rimas de Tomé de Burguillos*:

> Sol os llamó mi lengua pecadora,
> y desmintióme a boca llena el cielo;
> luz os dije que dábades al suelo,
> y opúsose un candil, que alumbra y llora.
>   Tan creído tuvistes ser aurora,
> que amanecer quisistes con desvelo;
> en vos llamé rubí lo que mi abuelo
> llamara labio y jeta comedora.
>   Codicia os puse de vender los dientes,
> diciendo que eran perlas; por ser bellos,
> llamé los rizos minas de oro ardientes.
>   Pero si fueran oro los cabellos,
> calvo su casco fuera, y diligentes,
> mis dedos los pelaran por vendellos. (no. 559)

My sinful tongue called you sun, and the sky glaringly gave the lie to it; I told you that you gave light to the earth, and a lamp that gives but a dribbling light contradicted this. With you I called a ruby what my grandfather would have called a plain lip and a greedy gob. I made you greedy to sell your teeth, by saying that they were pearls; because they were pretty, I called your curls burning mines of gold. But if the hair were gold, the head would be bald, as my busy hands would fleece it in order to sell it.

But the comparison of the lady's hair to 'minas de oro ardientes' provides a more personal touch: it parallels the conceit found in a sonnet to Lisi: 'Minas ardientes, al jardín unidas' ('Burning mines, joined to the garden') (no.501). As we saw with the closing passage of 'El escarmiento', Quevedo is disposed to recall and echo phrases and key images from his own work in an entirely different context.

In a number of places in his burlesque and satirical works, Quevedo ridicules the long-suffering courtly lover. Even within his love poetry, he shows no inclination for endless patience and perseverance, as my comments in Chapters One and Two have implied. In more comical vein is the 'galán de monjas' ('nuns' suitor') episode in the penultimate chapter of the *Buscon.*[12] A similar equation of the courtly lover with the nun's suitor is to be found in the *Memorial . . . pidiendo plaza en una academia (Petition . . . Applying for a Place in an Academy).* I quote from the passage where Quevedo parodies the granting of indulgences:

> Primeramente, todos aquellos que, descuidados de sí mismos, pusieren sus sentidos en la monja devota que aman, y trayendo consigo la medalla o insignias, hicieren exclamaciones solitarias, coplas o sonetos en su alabanza, y las escribieren cartas contemplativas, — se les concede quince años de bobería y otras tantas cuarentenas de tiempo perdido.
>
> Item, a cualquier devoto que, llevado de su afición, diere dineros, piezas de oro, plata u otra cosa de valor, a su devota, — se le conceden veinte años de arrepentimiento y otros tantos de bolsa vacía.[13]

> Firstly, all those who, careless about themselves, should direct their senses towards the devout nun that they love, and bringing with them the medal or insignias, should utter solitary exclamations, verses or sonnets in her praise, and who write contemplative letters — to these is granted fifteen years of nonsense and a similar period of quarantine for lost time.
>
> Moreover, to any devotee who, carried away by his emotion, should give money, gold pieces, silver or any other object of value to his beloved — to him is granted twenty years of repentance and as many of an empty wallet.

The concessions granted to the suitors of nuns are here defined in units of years, corresponding to what the writer considers to be the extent of the lovers' folly. The passage provides perhaps a grotesque parallel to the persona's allusions to the duration of his love in the anniversary sonnets to Lisi. In this connection, too, in a sonnet entitled 'A un hombre casado y pobre' ('To a poor married man') — an attack on marriage — there is a line that recalls the key phrase ('diez años') from one of the most lofty sonnets to Lisi, the one that alludes to the tenth anniversary of the meeting (no.471). I quote the second quatrain of the satirical sonnet, which refers to the unfortunate husband:

> Diez años en su suegra estuvo preso,
> a doncella, y sin sueldo, condenado;
> padeció so el poder de su cuñado;
> tuvo un hijo no más, tonto y travieso. (no.612)

> For ten years he was imprisoned in his mother-in-law, condemned to a maidservant and without wages; he suffered under the power of his brother-in-law; he had one son (no more), and he was a mischievous idiot.

This brings to mind the twice-repeated assertion of the anniversary in the love sonnet. It is not unlikely, in view of the cross-referencing or self-quotation to which I have drawn attention, that Quevedo had the sonnet to Lisi in mind, for in the love poem, the phrase 'diez años' is almost in the nature of a motto. If this is so, then Quevedo is parodying the idea of a period of sustained devotion, comparing the hapless husband's treatment to the persona's love for Lisi.

I am less tentative about the implications of the following sonnet:

> Ostentas, ¡oh felice!, en tus cenizas,
> el afecto inmortal del alma interno;
> que como es del amor el curso eterno,
> los días a tus ansias eternizas.
>
> Muerto del tiempo, el orden tiranizas,
> pues mides, derogando su gobierno,
> las horas al dolor del pecho tierno,
> los minutos al bien que inmortalizas.
>
> ¡Oh milagro! ¡Oh portento peregrino!,
> que de lo natural los estatutos
> rompes con eternar su movimiento.
>
> Tú mismo constituyes tu destino:
> pues por días, por horas, por minutos,
> eternizas tu propio sentimiento. (no.380)

> You reveal, oh happy one!, in your ashes, the immortal emotions within your soul; for, as the course of love is eternal, you immortalize the days to your anguish. Dead in time, you tyrannize the order of events, since, having repealed its legislation, you measure the hours by the grief of the tender heart, the minutes by the joy you immortalize. Oh miracle! oh rare portent! for you break the laws of nature when you eternalize its movement. You, by yourself, constitute your destiny: since in days, hours, minutes, you perpetuate your own feelings.

This sonnet was not published in either *El Parnaso español* or *Las tres Musas*. It appears in five manuscripts of the Biblioteca Nacional, Madrid, some of which comprise works by various poets, others, works by Quevedo alone.[14] The sonnet is invariably located among Quevedo's satirical and burlesque verse, some of it apocryphal, but Blecua's inclusion of it in the love poetry seems, on the face of it, quite justified.

In this sonnet, the poet expresses admiration for a dead lover whose ashes have been placed in a sand-clock.[15] But it is very hard to take his repeated exclamations of surprise seriously. There is in the macabre circumstance, I believe, a strong element of black humour: the poet writes with his tongue in his cheek. What this sonnet represents is a flippant version, if not a parody, of the 'ceniza enamorada' ('loving cinder') idea, of the loftiest and most mysterious of poetic themes. But what was noble and transcendental in the poems to Lisi is here focussed upon in a literal and deflating manner: the body which once housed so much love, so many emotions, has been reduced to ashes, but in the manuscript sonnet, these are functional not metaphysical ashes. The body still has a meaning, but not one that is related to triumphant defiance, as in 'Cerrar podrá mis ojos' (no.472), but to mundane utilitarianism. When the compiler or compilers of the various manuscripts placed this sonnet among predominantly jocular and satirical verse, he or they recognized its true nature. As a flippant and mocking composition it cannot be considered a love poem proper, though it sheds light on the love poetry and on the character of Quevedo.

The same parody is also found in a poem from *Las tres Musas* entitled 'Al polvo de un amante que en un reloj de vidrio servía de arena a Floris, que le abrasó' ('To the dust of a lover who served as sand in a glass clock belonging to Floris, who inflamed him') (no.420). I quote the opening of the poem:

> Este polvo sin sosiego,
> a quien tal fatiga dan,
> vivo y muerto, amor y fuego,
> hoy derramado, ayer ciego,
> y siempre en eterno afán;
> éste fue Fabio algún día . . .

This dust without rest, that is wearied in life and death, in love and in fire, is spilt today, was blind yesterday, and will always be in eternal anxiety; this was Fabio once . . .

The resemblances between this poem and the sonnet are obvious and the former does not require detailed analysis. Its air of mocking is well illustrated by the opening of the second stanza where the matter-of-fact announcement ('éste fue Fabio algún día') represents a deliberate anti-climax after the rather portentous note struck by the preceding phrases. In addition to these frivolous and mocking versions of the 'ceniza enamorada' idea,[16] it is worth recalling again how at the end of 'El escarmiento' the emotive terms 'venas', 'polvo' and 'ceniza' figured prominently in the disillusioned poet's expression of his renunciation of love.

How are we to judge these trivializing and negative versions of the great theme of Quevedo's poems to Lisi? To dismiss them as insignificant trifles seems to me to sidestep a clear problem; these are parodies that require some explanation. To accept them as Quevedo's definitive or true view is consistent with only one side of his personality — that of the cynic — and it does scant justice to a body of amatory verse that has an impressive coherence and individuality. But can both sides be true? I believe that this is the case and that the ambivalence we have seen in a number of love poems as well as the conflicts in the *Heráclito cristiano* provide abundant precedents and parallels.[17] The key to the mocking and the parody resides in Quevedo's tendency to secrecy and reserve perspicaciously analyzed by Ayala.[18] In this respect, the myth of Vulcan and its peculiarly disguised presentation is significant. This form of hidden, punning, identification occurs in poems where the lover's sense of indignation and injustice is especially acute. There is the implication that these feelings derive from the lover's experience of being mocked, deceived and cheated as regards his emotional commitment. To an extent, it is explicable in terms of conventional role assignment: the *amada*'s negative response and the lover's consequent dejection. But the sonnets that refer obliquely to Vulcan have a particular vehemence that is more than a matter of stylistic individuality. Vulcan, whom Quevedo is careful not to name directly, represents for him the epitome of the mocked and deceived: lame like Quevedo, who was much ridiculed for this defect,[19] and also a cuckold. According to Ayala, Quevedo felt an aversion to marriage because of an intense fear of being deceived; he refers to his 'preocupación obsesiva con los cuernos' ('obsessive preoccupation with cuckoldry') (p.114). There is evidence, too, so Ayala believes, that Quevedo's physical defects were a source of acute resentment to him: the cruel jibes to which he was subjected left a deep impression. This can be seen in the way in which he refers to his defects, especially when he endeavours to make light of them: 'tanto más cuando pretende hacerlo burlesco' ('the more so when he seeks to make a joke out of it') (p.105). Quevedo is willing to overlook other insults, but 'burlarse de sus desgracias corporales era, en cambio, golpear en la llaga' ('to make fun of his physical misfortunes was, on the contrary, to rub salt in the wound').

Something of the same sensitivity is revealed in the hidden allusions to Vulcan when he refers to hurt and deception in his love poetry. Here there is the implication that he does not wish to declare too deep and too intimate an experience. Perhaps he is wary about providing too vulnerable a picture of himself, one that would be more personal and particular than that provided by the conventional complaints of the courtly-Petrarchist lover. Why supply his enemies and detractors with another easy target? Why admit such sensitivity, even to himself? No such reserve is necessary when he declares his amatory aspirations or chides the *amada* or questions the validity of spiritual love. These do not betray an image of assertion and masculinity that other parts of his output confirm in differing ways. But when it comes to the admission of hurt pride, of expectations that are cruelly crushed, he enters a far more sensitive area. There is something approaching recoil. Vulcan, epitome of cuckoldry — the ultimate deception for Quevedo — must not be named:

> Del volcán que en mis venas se derrama,
> diga su ardor el llanto que fulmino;
> mas no le sepa de *mi voz* la Fama. (no.322) (my italics)

Let the weeping I thunder express the ardour of the volcano that overflows in my veins; but may *my voice* be unknown to Fame.

I believe that Quevedo's parody of the 'ceniza enamorada' idea to be a reflection of the same sensitivity — another instance of the functioning of an emotional defence-mechanism. In the sweep and rhetoric of a sonnet like 'Cerrar podrá mis ojos' there is no holding back, no possibility of metamorphosing the self — there is nowhere to hide. But fearful of overcommitment to a transcendental emotional experience, one that is distinctively his, and of wearing his heart on his sleeve, Quevedo compensates by writing poems that deride this most impossible and most exposed of experiences. Unconsciously perhaps, he anticipates and forestalls ridicule by his own parody.

One of the images that posterity has conferred upon Quevedo is that of the heroic critic and satirist; like so much else about him, this is part truth, part exaggeration and part legend. Recent studies have tended to take a sceptical view of the picture of Quevedo received from biographers such as Astrana Marín. Ayala[20] has pointed to Quevedo's meek conformity; and Durán[21] has shrewdly analyzed the consequences of Elliott's discovery that treason is probably the cause of Quevedo's final imprisonment. In this connection, my observations on deception and secrecy in the love poetry offer a parallel if not a pointer. The bluster and irreverence that are such obvious traits of Quevedo's work and which, on occasion, lead him to crudity and obscenity have contributed undoubtedly to the image of a fearless, outspoken critic. The extremes of taste and ridicule do not belong to this image, however. It is to the sensitive and defensive Quevedo that they relate and from this pathologico-creative response his love poetry is not immune.

The outcome is the enrichment of a body of work that is, in any case, both a strikingly individual contribution to the poetry of his age and a distinctive part of his own output. We have encountered a voice and a figure that impress themselves powerfully. What has emerged is an amatory ethos that knows tradition but is not confined to it; that recognizes convention but is not bound to it. The experience of love to which Quevedo's amatory verse is witness is neither exclusively spiritual nor carnal; it does not readily lend itself to categorization, to division into parts. There is a double source of tension: between the individual and the conventional and, on occasion, within the poet himself, between reserve and declaration, secrecy and commitment. The various pressures that bear on the poetic act make for love poetry that has a profound integrity. Here, more than in any other part of his output, there is a sense of fulfilment: of both the realization and the loss of the self in art. It is the still centre of a restless mind; the haven for a suspicious and tormented human being.

1 'The palinodes in prose and verse, the renunciations of the attractions of the myth of courtly love with its cult of suffering and passion for their own sakes are not a mere bowing to a convention that demanded an *amende honorable*. They express the true Quevedo — the *penitente* — from his early thirties to the year of his death' (*Courtly Love in Quevedo*, 79).

2 According to one line of critical inquiry, best represented by Lázaro Carreter, the *Buscón* also fits into this category.

3 *La vida turbulenta*, 528.

4 *Poesía española*, 517-18.

5 Op. cit., 316.

6 Op. cit., 39.

7 Art. cit., 93-7.

8 Laín Entralgo, art. cit., 96-8; Ayala, art. cit., 110.

9 Neither Tantalus nor Midas figure in his survey; by contrast, consideration is given to no fewer than sixteen poets' treatment of the Orpheus myth.

10 See Price, ed. cit., 11-12.

11 See also nos 551 and 553; Desengaño's diatribe in *El mundo por de dentro*, quoted in the previous chapter (*Sueños y discursos*, 179-80); and the *Premática del desengaño contra los poetas güeros, chirles y hebenes*, quoted in the tenth chapter of the *Buscón* (ed. cit., 112-16).

12 Ibid, 246-56.

13 *Obras satíricas y festivas*, 121.

14 These are mss. 1952, 3919, 7370, 9636 and 18760. The following observations on the sonnet are drawn from my article, 'Concerning the Authenticity of Two Madrigals'.

15 Such a clock is the subject of the silva, 'El reloj de arena' (no.139). See also Crosby, *Poesía varia*, 507.

16 The wide range of the 'ceniza enamorada' motif is alluded to by Olivares, op. cit., 138.

17 In this connection, Alan Deyermond's comments on the function of parody in the *Libro de Buen Amor* are apposite: 'It can certainly not be assumed that Juan Ruiz's parodies of religious text and practices imply hostility to religion. Such parodies may, on the contrary, develop most freely within a secure framework of belief — thus we find that some of the most daring goliardic parodies are the work of eminent churchmen whose orthodoxy is unquestioned'. 'Some Aspects of Parody', *'Libro de Buen Amor' Studies*, ed. G.B. Gybbon-Monypenny (London, 1970), 76.

18 Art. cit., 94-5.

19 Ibid, 101-9.

20 Ibid, 114-16.

21 Op. cit., 29-35.

Appendix

A Suggested Rearrangement of the Poems to Lisi

The Roman numeral indicates the number of each poem in my redistribution. The first line of the poem is quoted, followed by the poem number as it appears in the Blecua editions (*Poesía original*, 2nd ed., and *Obra poética*). I provide a more detailed account of my changes in my article: 'Una nueva ordenación de los poemas a Lisi de Quevedo', *Criticón*, no.27 (1984), 55-70.

Selected Bibliography

For a fuller bibliography, the reader is advised to consult J.O. Crosby, *Guía bibliográfica para el estudio crítico de Quevedo* (London, 1976). Updated but less comprehensive bibliographies are to be found in *Francisco de Quevedo*, ed. Gonzalo Sobejano (Madrid, 1978), and in Crosby's recent anthology of Quevedo's poetry: *Poesía varia* (Madrid, 1981).

Editions of Quevedo's Works

Obras completas: obras en verso, ed. L. Astrana Marín (Madrid, 1943).

Epistolario completo de Don Francisco Quevedo-Villegas, ed. L. Astrana Marín (Madrid, 1945).

Lágrimas de Hieremías castellanas, ed. J.M. Blecua and E.M. Wilson (Madrid, 1953).

Obras satíricas y festivas, ed. J.M. Salaverría (Madrid, 1965).

El Buscón, ed. A. Castro (Madrid, 1967).

Obras completas I. Poesía original, ed. J.M. Blecua (2nd ed.) (Barcelona, 1968).

An Anthology of Quevedo's Poetry, ed. R.M. Price (Manchester, 1969).

Obra poética, 4 vols., ed. J.M. Blecua (Madrid, 1969-81).

Sueños y discursos, ed. Felipe C.R. Maldonado (Madrid, 1972).

Obras completas: obras en prosa, ed. Felicidad Buendía (6th ed.) (Madrid, 1974).

Poesía varia, ed. J.O. Crosby (Madrid, 1981).

Criticism and Works by Other Authors

Agrait, Gustavo. *El* Beatus Ille *en la poesía lírica del Siglo de Oro* (Río Piedras, 1971).

Aguirre, J.M. (ed.). Hernando del Castillo, *Cancionero general* (Salamanca, 1971).

Aldana, Francisco de. *Poesías*, ed. E.L. Rivers (Madrid, 1957).

Alighieri, Dante. *Opere*, ed. E. Moore (Oxford, 1923).
    La Divina Commedia I. Inferno, ed. Carlo Grabher (Milan, 1965).

Alonso, Dámaso. 'Sonetos atribuídos a Quevedo', *Ensayos sobre poesía española* (Madrid, 1944), 175-88.
    'El desgarrón afectivo en la poesía de Quevedo', *Poesía española* (5th ed.) (Madrid, 1971), 495-580.

Argensola, Lupercio Leonardo de. *Rimas*, ed. J.M. Blecua (Madrid, 1972).

Arguijo, Juan de. *Obra poética*, ed. Stanko B. Vranich (Madrid, 1971).

Astrana Marín, L. 'El gran poema de amor de Quevedo', *El cortejo de Minerva* (Madrid, 1930), 45-50.
    La vida turbulenta de Quevedo (Madrid, 1945).

Ayala, Francisco. 'Hacia una semblanza de Quevedo', *La Torre*, LVII (1967), 89-116.

Bécquer, Gustavo Adolfo. *Rimas*, ed. José Luis Cano (Madrid, 1975).

Bethell, S.L. 'Gracián, Tesauro and the Nature of Metaphysical Wit', *The Northern Miscellany of Literary Criticism*, I (1953), 19-40.

Bishop, Morris. *Petrarch and His World* (London, 1964).

Blanco Aguinaga, C. '"Cerrar podrá mis ojos": tradición y originalidad', *Filología*, VIII (1962), 57-78.

Blecua, J.M. 'Sobre un célebre soneto de Quevedo', *Ínsula*, III, no.31 (1948), 3.
   'Un ejemplo de dificultades: el *Memorial* "Católica, Sacra, Real Magestad"', *Nueva Revista de Filología Española*, VIII (1954), 156-73.

Bleznick, D.W. *Quevedo* (New York, 1972).

Boase, R. *The Origin and Meaning of Courtly Love. A Critical Study of European Scholarship* (Manchester, 1977).

Borges, J.L. 'Quevedo', *Otras inquisiciones* (Buenos Aires, 1960), 55-64.

Boscán, Juan. *Obras poéticas I*, ed. M. de Riquer, A. Comas and J. Molas (Barcelona, 1957).

Brown, Gary J. 'Rhetoric in the Sonnet of Praise', *Journal of Hispanic Philology*, I (1976-7), 31-50.

Cabañas, Pablo. *El mito de Orfeo en la literatura española*, (Madrid, 1948).

Calderón de la Barca, Pedro. *El alcalde de Zalamea*, ed. P.N. Dunn (Oxford, 1966).

Camões, Luís de. *Obras completas I*, ed. Hernâni Cidade (3rd ed.) (Lisbon, 1962).

Close, Lorna. 'Petrarchism and the Cancioneros in Quevedo's Love-Poetry: The Problem of Discrimination', *Modern Language Review*, LXXIV (1979), 836-55.

Consiglio, Carlo. 'El *Poema a Lisi* y su petrarquismo', *Mediterráneo*, IV, nos. 13-15 (1946), 76-93.

Cortázar, Celina S. de. *La poesía de Quevedo* (Buenos Aires, 1968).

Cossío, J.M. de. *Fábulas mitológicas en España* (Madrid, 1952).

Covarrubias Orozco, S de. *Tesoro de la lengua castellana* (Madrid, 1611); rpt. (Madrid, 1953).

Crosby, J.O. 'La huella de González de Salas en la poesía de Quevedo editada por Aldrete', *Homenaje a don A. Rodríguez-Moñino*, I (Madrid, 1966), 1·11-23.
   En torno a la poesía de Quevedo, Madrid, 1967.
   'Has Quevedo's Poetry Been Edited? A Review-Article', *Hispanic Review*, XLI (1973), 627-38.

Darst, David H. 'Garcilaso's Love for Isabel Freire: The Creation of a Myth', *Journal of Hispanic Philology*, III (1978-9), 261-8.

Donne, John. *The Elegies and the Songs and Sonnets*, ed. Helen Gardner (Oxford, 1965).

Durán, Manuel. *Francisco de Quevedo* (Madrid, 1978).

Elizalde, Ignacio. 'Quevedo, San Ignacio de Loyola y los Jesuitas', *Letras de Deusto*, X, no.20 (1980), 91-106.

Elliott, J.H. 'Nueva luz sobre la prisión de Quevedo y Adam de la Parra', *Boletín de la Real Academia de la Historia*, CLXIX (1972), 171-82.

Ettinghausen, Henry. *Francisco de Quevedo and the Neostoic Movement* (Oxford, 1972).
   'Un nuevo manuscrito autógrafo de Quevedo', *Boletín de la Real Academia Española*, LII (1972), 211-84.

Ferrante, Joan M. *Woman as Image in Medieval Literature* (New York, 1975).

Forster, Leonard. *The Icy Fire* (Cambridge, 1969).

Fucilla, J.G. 'Some Imitations of Quevedo and Some Poems Wrongly Attributed to Him', *Romanic Review*, XXI (1930), 222-35.
Estudios sobre el petrarquismo en España (Madrid, 1960).

Garcilaso de la Vega. *Poesías castellanas completas*, ed. E.L. Rivers (2nd ed.) (Madrid, 1972).

Gómez de la Serna, R. *Quevedo* (2nd ed.) (Madrid, 1962).

Góngora, Luis de. *Sonetos completos*, ed. Biruté Ciplijauskaité (Madrid, 1976).

González Palencia, A. *Del "Lazarillo" a Quevedo* (Madrid, 1946).

Goytisolo, Juan. 'Quevedo: la obsesión excremental', *Disidencias* (Barcelona, 1977).

Green, Otis H. 'Courtly Love in the Spanish *Cancioneros'*, *Publications of the Modern Language Association of America*, LXIV (1949), 247-301; rpt. in *The Literary Mind of Medieval and Renaissance Spain* (Lexington, 1970), 40-92.
Courtly Love in Quevedo (Boulder, Colorado, 1952).

Gybbon-Monypenny, G.B. (ed.). *'Libro de Buen Amor' Studies* (London, 1970).

Herrera, Fernando de. *Poesías*, ed. V. García de Diego (Madrid, 1970).

Horace. *The Works of Horace*, vol II, ed. E.C. Wickham (Oxford, 1891).
The Collected Works, translated by Lord Dunsany and Michael Oakley (London, 1961).

Huizinga, Johan. *The Waning of the Middle Ages* (London, 1924); rpt. (Harmondsworth, 1965).

Jones, R.O. *A Literary History of Spain. The Golden Age: Prose and Poetry* (London, 1971).

Kelley, Emilia N. *La poesía metafísica de Quevedo* (Madrid, 1973).

Krailsheimer, A.J. (ed.). *The Continental Renaissance* (Harmondsworth, 1971).

Laín Entralgo, Pedro. 'La vida del hombre en la poesía de Quevedo', *Cuadernos Hispanoamericanos*, I, no.1 (1948), 63-101.

Lázaro Carreter, F. 'Quevedo, entre el amor y la muerte', *Papeles de Son Armadans*, I, no.2 (1956), 145-60.

Lida, Raimundo. *Letras hispánicas* (Mexico City, 1958).

Macrí, Oreste. *Fernando de Herrera* (2nd ed.) (Madrid, 1972).

Martz, Louis L. *The Poetry of Meditation* (New Haven, 1954).

Mas, Amédée. *La caricature de la femme, du mariage et de l'amour dans l'oeuvre de Quevedo* (Paris, 1957).

Medrano, Francisco de. *Vida y obra de Medrano*, vol II, ed. Dámaso Alonso and Stephen Reckert (Madrid, 1958).

Mérimée, E. *Essai sur la vie et les oeuvres de Francisco de Quevedo* (Paris, 1886).

Moller, Herbert. 'The Meaning of Courtly Love', *Journal of American Folklore*, LXXIII (1960), 39-52.

Moore, Roger. *Towards a Chronology of Quevedo's Poetry*, (New Brunswick, 1977).

Olivares, Julián. *The Love Poetry of Francisco de Quevedo: An Aesthetic and Existential Study* (Cambridge, 1983).

Ortega y Gasset, J. *Estudios sobre el amor* (11th ed.) (Madrid, 1970).

Parker, A.A. 'La agudeza en algunos sonetos de Quevedo', *Estudios dedicados a Menéndez Pidal*, III (1952), 345-60.

Paterson, A.K.G. '"Sutileza del pensar" in a Quevedo Sonnet', *Modern Language Notes*, LXXXI (1966), 131-42.

Paz, Octavio. *Conjunciones y disyunciones* (Mexico City, 1969).

Pedro, Valentín de. 'América en la genial diversidad de Quevedo', *América en las letras españolas del Siglo de Oro* (Buenos Aires, 1954).

The Penguin Book of Elizabethan Verse, ed. Edward Lucie-Smith (Harmondsworth, 1965).

Pérez Bustamente, C. 'La supuesta traición del duque de Osuna', *Revista de la Universidad de Madrid*, I (1940), 61-74.
'Quevedo, diplomático', *Revista de Estudios Políticos*, XIII (1945), 159-83.

Petrarca, Francesco. *Il Canzoniere*, ed. Dino Provenzal (Milan, 1954).

Poe, Edgar Allan. *Works*, 8 vols. (Philadelphia, 1905).

Pozuelo Yvancos, J.M. *El lenguaje poético de la lírica amorosa de Quevedo* (Murcía, 1979).

Price, R.M. 'A Note on the Sources and Structure of "Miré los muros de la patria mía"' *Modern Language Notes*, LXXXVIII (1963), 194-9.

Rojas, Fernando de. *La Celestina*, ed. J. Cejador y Frauca, 2 vols. (Madrid, 1968).

Sheppard, Douglas C. 'Resonancias de Quevedo en la poesía española del siglo XX', *Kentucky Foreign Language Quarterly*, IX (1962), 105-13.

Sobejano, Gonzalo. (ed.) *Francisco de Quevedo* (Madrid, 1978).

Sturm-Maddox, Sara. 'Transformations of Courtly Love Poetry: *Vita Nuova* and *Canzoniere*', *The Expansion and Transformations of Courtly Literature*, ed. Nathaniel B. Snow and Joseph T Snow (Athens, Georgia, 1980), 128-42.

Ter Horst, Robert. 'Death and Resurrection in the Quevedo Sonnet: "En crespa tempestad"', *Journal of Hispanic Philology*, V (1980-1), 41-9.

Terry, Arthur. 'Quevedo and the Metaphysical Conceit', *Bulletin of Hispanic Studies*, XXXV (1958), 211-22.
(Ed.) *An Anthology of Spanish Poetry. 1500-1700*, 2 vols. (Oxford, 1965-8).
'Thought and Feeling in Three Golden-Age Sonnets', *Bulletin of Hispanic Studies*, LXIX (1982), 237-46.

Torre, Francisco de la. *Poesías*, ed. A. Zamora Vicente (Madrid, 1969).

Valera, Fernando. 'Reinvención de D. Francisco de Quevedo: cuatro cartas literarias a Luis Capdevila', *Cuadernos del Congreso por la Libertad de la Cultura*, VII, no.34 (1959), 65-74.

Vega Carpio, Lope Félix de. *Poesías líricas I*, ed. José F Montesinos (Madrid, 1960).

Villamediana, Conde de. *Obras*, ed. J.M. Rozas (Madrid, 1969).

Walters, D. Gareth. 'Conflicting Views of Time in a Quevedo Sonnet: An Analysis of "Diez años de mi vida se ha llevado"', *Journal of Hispanic Philology*, IV (1979-80), 143-56.

'Three Examples of Petrarchism in Quevedo's *Heráclito cristiano'*, *Bulletin of Hispanic Studies*, LXVIII (1981), 21-30.

'Camões and Quevedo: Some Instances of Similarity and Influence', *Bulletin of Hispanic Studies*, LXIX (1982), 106-19.

'Concerning the Authenticity of Two Madrigals Attributed to Quevedo', *Bulletin of Hispanic Studies*, LXI (1984), 483-90.

'Una nueva ordenación de los poemas a Lisi de Quevedo', *Criticón*, no.27 (1984), 55-70.

Wellek, R. and Warren, A. *Theory of Literature* (3rd ed.) (Harmondsworth, 1963).

West, David. *Reading Horace* (Edinburgh, 1967).

Whinnom, Keith. 'Hacia la interpretación y la valoración de las canciones del *Cancionero general* de 1511', *Filología*,XIII (1968-9), 361-81.

Williamson, E.H. 'The Conflict between Author and Protagonist in Quevedo's *Buscón'*, *Journal of Hispanic Philology*, II (1977-8), 45-60.

Wilson, E.M. 'Quevedo for the Masses', *Atlante*, III (1955), 151-66.

Index of Poems Cited

The first line of the poem is followed by the poem number in parenthesis. Poem numbers refer to the two Blecua editions as described in note 7 of the Introduction.

Index